China and Globalizatio

MW01093836

Series Editors

Huiyao Wang, Center for China and Globalization, Beijing, China

Lu Miao, Center for China and Globalization, Beijing, China

This series are designed to address the evolution of China's global orientation, challenges of globalization and global governance facing China and the rest of the world, actions and proposals for the future of sustainable development, prospects of China's further capital and market liberalization, and China's globalizing trajectories as experienced by the world.

This book series seek to create a balanced global perspective by gathering the views of highly influential policy scholars, practitioners, and opinion leaders from China and around the world.

More information about this series at https://link.springer.com/bookseries/16735

Kishore Mahbubani

The Asian 21st Century

 Springer

Kishore Mahbubani
Asia Research Institute
National University of Singapore
Singapore, Singapore

ISSN 2730-9983   ISSN 2730-9991 (electronic)
China and Globalization
ISBN 978-981-16-6813-5   ISBN 978-981-16-6811-1 (eBook)
https://doi.org/10.1007/978-981-16-6811-1

This Springer imprint is published by the registered company Springer Nature Singapore Pte Ltd.
The registered company address is: 152 Beach Road, #21-01/04 Gateway East, Singapore 189721, Singapore

Contents

Introduction

We live in hugely paradoxical times. We will see greater change in the twenty-first century than we have in any previous human century. Huge leaps in science and technology, accompanied by huge economic and social advances in many societies around the world, especially Asian societies, will mean that the texture and chemistry of the twenty-first century will be massively different from the nineteenth and twentieth centuries.

How will it be massively different? It will be different in three significant dimensions. First, we will see the end of the era of Western domination of world history. Second, we will see the return to the success of many Asian societies, especially the two most populous societies of China and India. Third, as a result of the rapid shrinkage of the world, through both technological leaps and growing interdependence, partly through global trade, humanity is no longer living on a vast planet. It is living in a small, densely interconnected global village. Indeed, when future historians look at the twenty-first century, they will marvel at how many big changes happened in the human condition in a small space of time.

In theory, the human species represents the most intelligent species on planet earth. One key test of intelligence is the ability to adapt to different circumstances. Sensible and intelligent adaptation and adjustment to changed circumstances explain how our human species has survived and thrived for thousands of years. Of course, some human tribes have performed better than other tribes in making these adaptations and adjustments.

Over the past 200 years, the best performing human tribe has been the Western tribe. Through their extraordinary performance, both in the fields of human organization and in science and technology, the Western societies outperformed the rest of the world. They didn't just outperform the world. They conquered the world.

It's not surprising that larger European societies like the British and French, were able to conquer territories around the world. Indeed, it was said in the nineteenth century that the sun never set on the British empire, as the British had conquered territories in all corners of the world. What was truly surprising was the ability of small European societies, like Portugal, to conquer territories all around the world.

© The Author(s) 2022
K. Mahbubani, *The Asian 21st Century*, China and Globalization,
https://doi.org/10.1007/978-981-16-6811-1_1

In the nineteenth century, the population of Portugal was only a few million. Yet, this small country, with a population of about the size of contemporary Singapore, was able to conquer territories in South America (like Brazil) and in Africa (like Angola and Mozambique). But what was truly astonishing was small Portugal's ability to conquer territories in the sixteenth century from India (population 115 million) and China (population 160 million) in Goa and Macau, respectively.

Given this extraordinary performance of the West for over 200 years, it would have been perfectly natural for the West to make intelligent and sensible adaptations and adjustments to the very different world of the twenty-first century. Instead, to my absolute shock and astonishment, the West has failed to make intelligent adaptations. The failure to make intelligent adaptations explain why many key Western populations, especially in the United States and Europe, feel very lost and pessimistic about the future.

As a friend of the West, I have been trying to explain to Western intellectuals why Western societies should adjust and adapt. This is why, for example, I published Beyond the Age of Innocence in 2005 in an effort to tell American intellectuals how the US should adapt to a different world. I learned a very important lesson when I published the book in 2005. In theory, the US is an open society, full of intellectuals open to listening to the views of the rest of the world. In practice, it is an open society with a closed mind. American intellectuals don't listen to the rest of the world. One small practical reason why this happened is because some American universities abolished "area studies" (for example, studying "Southeast Asian studies") because "area studies" were not considered "scientific" by American "social scientists", although some universities still do so. They include, for example, Asian Studies at Harvard University and Southeast Asian Studies at Yale.

What shocked me, even more, was to discover that the most "closed" minds in the American intellectual scene were the "liberal" minds. These "liberal" minds believed that on huge questions of how human societies should grow, develop and succeed, there could only be simple black and white answers. The "white" answer was that only the societies which copied the Western liberal ideal would succeed. The evidence for this strong claim is provided by the enormously enthusiastic response that all Western intellectuals gave to the essay published by Francis Fukuyama at the end of the Cold War. The essay was entitled *The End of History*. It made the preposterous claim that humanity had reached the "End" of History because it should now be clear to the rest of humanity, especially after the collapse of the Berlin Wall in 1989 and the collapse of the USSR in 1991, that the only way for all human societies to progress (no matter which culture or geography they belonged to) was to copy the Western liberal democratic model. Clearly, this was an absurd claim. Yet no major Western intellectuals disagreed with this thesis. Indeed, one of the most surprising things I have discovered about Western intellectuals is that they engage in "strategic groupthink". Fukuyama's essay gave a boost to this "groupthink" among Western minds.

This is why I have written in several places, including in my book *Has the West Lost it?* that this essay by Fukuyama did "brain damage" to Western minds. What was this brain damage? Since Western minds were convinced by Fukuyama's argument that the world had reached the "end of history" in the early 1990s, they didn't notice that instead of seeing the "end of history" at that time, humanity was instead experiencing the "return of history". What was this "return of history"? This was the "return" of the two most populous societies in the world, China and India. In the 1990s, both China and India made the strategically correct decision to open up their economies and integrate with the world around the same period. China began a little earlier in 1977 when Mr. Deng Xiaoping launched the "Four Modernizations" program. India started a decade later when the then Finance Minister, Manmohan Singh (who later became Prime Minister) launched the reforms that opened up India's economy in 1991.

Many of the problems faced by the West can therefore be explained by these two major strategic mistakes made by the West. The first is the failure to see that in the twenty-first century we have reached the end of Western domination of World History. The second is the failure to see that the world is now seeing the return of Asia, especially the most successful societies in East Asia, Southeast Asia and South Asia. These two major failures by the West explain why the first two sections of this book are devoted to these two big themes. In part one, we explain why the era of Western domination is over. In part two, we explain how and why Asia is reforming.

In part one, several essays try to explain why the West refuses to accept the painful reality that the West can no longer dominate the world. It may be useful to give one major concrete example of how the West is unable to see that it has developed some huge strategic weaknesses. For decades, especially after the end of World War II, the US outperformed the rest of the world because it provided "equality of opportunity" for even the poorest Americans to succeed and thrive. In short, American society created a level playing field. The rich could succeed. The poor could also succeed. All this explains why in the 1950s, 1960s, and 1970s, the American middle classes saw their incomes and standards of living improve. The US then probably had the happiest society on planet earth.

Now we know, both from the election of Donald Trump in 2016 and the storming of the US Capitol on 6 January 2021, that the US is today an unhappy society. Why has the US become unhappy? The simple answer is that American society no longer has a level playing field for the rich and poor. The rich can succeed. The poor cannot. Anyone who doubts this claim should read the essay entitled *Democracy or Plutocracy? America's existential question* in this volume.

This essay provides a vast amount of evidence to show that the US has become a plutocracy. What is a plutocracy? The simple answer is that a plutocracy is the opposite of a democracy. In a democracy, a society is structured to take care of the interests of a vast majority within a society, say 80 to 90 percent. In a plutocracy, a society is structured to take care of the interests of a small affluent minority, say the top 10 to 20 percent. Fortunately, I am not the only person to describe the US as a plutocracy. Many leading Western figures have described the US as a plutocracy. They include Mr. Paul Volker, the late Chairman of the US Federal Reserve, the Nobel Laureate Professor Joseph Stiglitz and Mr. Martin Wolf, the economics commentator from the Financial Times.

An even more significant Western philosopher, Plato, had warned the West about 2400 years ago about the dangers of having a society dominated by the rich and serving the interests of the rich. This is what he said, "…for what would happen if someone were to choose the captains of ships by their wealth, refusing to entrust the ship to a poor person even if he was a better captain? They would make a poor voyage of it." Yet, despite all these warnings, the US has effectively transformed itself into a plutocracy, allowing the wealthy to restructure American society to benefit the wealthy, not the poor.

In theory, since the US is the world's most open society, where there is a lot of freedom of speech, there should have been a healthy debate on how and why the US has become a plutocracy. It is therefore shocking that there is no such debate. This is therefore what makes this volume of essays truly special and unique. It provides unique insights into the failings of several Western societies that are not provided anywhere else.

It also provides insights that Western intellectuals refuse to confront honestly. For example, Western societies like to portray themselves as defenders of human rights. Yet, they refuse to acknowledge the instances when they have either violated human rights or aided or abetted the violation of human rights. In short, Western societies have been massively hypocritical. This is why the essay entitled *The Hypocrisy of the West* states categorically "In theory, the West condemns hypocrisy. In practice, sadly, it indulges in hypocrisy massively". This essay provides some examples of blatant hypocrisy.

Another issue that the West fails to confront honestly is that a healthy society requires more than just democratic elections. It needs to raise the living standards of its people. This means that the fruits of the economy must be shared across the entire population, and not just the top one percent, as in a plutocracy. However, the US is the only developed country in the world where the incomes of the bottom 50% declined in the three decades from 1980 to 2010. As I argue in the essay entitled *Trump, Macron and the Poverty of Liberalism*, many in the West believe that being able to vote freely in elections is enough for social stability, ignoring the critical insight from the American political philosopher John Rawls that social and economic inequalities are to be arranged so that they are to "everyone's advantage".

The West also refuses to acknowledge the key philosophical insight that, even for a liberal society, the concept of freedom must come hand in hand with the concept of responsibility. Indeed, as I argue in the essay entitled *What do US Capitol attack and the West's Covid-19 death rates have in common?*, one crucial factor underlying both the storming of the US Capitol on 6 January 2021 and the high death rates from Covid-19 was that liberty was pursued without due regard for other important philosophical principles like responsibility and equality.

In part II of this volume of essays, I try to document how the evidence shows clearly that the world is experiencing the "return" of Asia. Indeed, our experience with Covid-19 in the year 2020 shows that overall the East Asian societies have handled Covid-19 much better than either the US or European societies. This is why I was happy to accept the invitation by the Economist, a leading Western publication, to explain why the East Asian societies have performed better. Indeed, I also argue that the better performance of East Asian societies confirms that we are seeing the dawn of the Asian century.

I have actually been writing about the return of Asia for several decades now, since the early 1990s. Indeed, the very first essay I published to discuss the return of Asia was in the year 1992 when I published an essay entitled *The West and the Rest* in another prestigious Western journal, *The National Interest*. In that essay, I said:

> The stark picture of an affluent West and a poor Third World is complicated and confused by the increasing importance of the East Asians, the only non-Westerners already in, or poised to enter, the world of developed nations… For Japan and the other East Asian success stories are setting off ripples of development in the Third World in a way that no Western society has ever succeeded in doing.

Many readers of this volume are probably aware that I have written a lot about the reemergence of China and why the West should accept, not try to block, the return of China. Several essays in this volume, including for example *The West Should Heed Napoleon's Advice and Let China Sleep* and *What China Threat?* discuss the reluctance of the West to accept the return of China. However, the Asian story is not just about China. It is also about other parts of Asia, including India and Southeast Asia. This is why this volume discusses the surprising resilience shown by the Association of Southeast Asian Nations (ASEAN) and also discusses how India can play a valuable role by serving as a moral leader in the world. In these essays, including *Why 'the India Way' May be the World's Best Bet for Moral Leadership*, *ASEAN's Quiet Resilience* and *Can Asia Help Biden?*, I argue that both ASEAN and India can play a trusted role as a mediator between the US and China and as supporters for free trade and multilateralism.

Future historians will try hard to understand why the underperforming societies of Asia in the nineteenth and twentieth centuries bounced back in the twenty-first century. The answers will be complex. However, one key reason why Asian societies have done so well in recent decades is that they were brave enough to take full advantage of the opportunities provided by globalization. This wasn't an easy decision to make. There were risks. President Xi Jinping described these risks well when he addressed the World Economic Forum in Davos in January 2017. I was present in the room when he spoke there. I was particularly struck by the following paragraph in his speech:

> There was a time when China also had doubts about economic globalization and was not sure whether it should join the World Trade Organization. But we came to the conclusion that integration into the global economy is a historical trend. To grow its economy, China must have the courage to swim in the vast ocean of the global market. If one is always afraid of bracing the storm and exploring the new world, he will sooner or later get drowned in the ocean. Therefore, China took a brave step to embrace the global market. We have had our fair share of choking in the water and encountered whirlpools and choppy waves, but we have learned how to swim in this process. It has proved to be the right strategic choice.

Globalization was in many ways a gift from the West. For globalization to succeed, it had to rest on three pillars. First, for countries to interact and trade with each other, they needed to have a common set of rules. The West provided this when it created a rules-based order, centered around the United Nations (UN) in 1945. The World Trade Organization (WTO) is also part of the UN family. Thanks to the WTO, global trade has exploded from USD 61 billion in 1950, three years after the General Agreement on Tariffs and Trade (GATT), the legal predecessor of the WTO, was created, to USD 19 trillion in 2019, an increase of over 300 times. Significantly, China's economic growth rate increased sharply after it joined WTO in 2001.

Second, for trade to succeed countries had to accept the law of comparative advantage. This law was gifted to us by a Western economist, David Ricardo, who explained comparative advantage in the following way:

> To produce the wine in Portugal, might require only the labour of 80 men for one year, and to produce the cloth in the same country, might require the labour of 90 men for the same time. It would therefore be advantageous for her to export wine in exchange for cloth. This exchange might even take place, notwithstanding that the commodity imported by Portugal could be produced there with less labour than in England. Though she could make the cloth with the labour of 90 men, she would import it from a country where it required the labour of 100 men to produce it, because it would be advantageous to her rather to employ her capital in the production of wine, for which she would obtain more cloth from England, than she could produce by diverting a portion of her capital from the cultivation of vines to the manufacture of cloth.[1]

This is why after World War II, the biggest champions of free trade were the Western countries. When Lee Kuan Yew, the former Prime Minister of Singapore, addressed a joint session of the US Congress on 9 October 1985, he paid tribute to the West for convincing the world of the virtue of free trade. He said:

> When the war ended in 1945, the US set out, with her European allies, to establish an open and fair trading system under the General Agreement on Tariffs and Trade (GATT) (in force since 1 Jan 1948), and a stable system of currency exchange under the original IMF Agreement at Bretton Woods. These agreements led to the huge growth in trade, banking, and finance throughout the world... In the 1950s and 60s, trade with the US of all countries in the Western Pacific, except communist China, North Korea, and North Vietnam, increased. Many received US investments. The US was the dynamo which hastened economic developments.

The US was the biggest promoter of the law of comparative advantage.

Third, in addition to the theory explaining the virtues of free trade, we also needed in practice some champions who could provide leadership in opening borders and persuading other countries to open up. Indeed, the main reason why the global trading system progressively opened up from the 1950s to the 1980s was because both the US and EU (who represent the core of the West) championed free trade and pushed for the successful completion of global trading rounds, with the last round completing successfully in 1994 when the Uruguay Round was completed in Marrakesh.

Sadly, even though these three pillars, created by the West, have delivered decades of global prosperity (and which consequently led to the reduction of global poverty) the leading Western countries have walked away from these three pillars. When Lee Kuan Yew addressed the joint session of the US Congress in 1985, the US Congress

---

[1] Ricardo, David. *On the Principles of Political Economy and Taxation.* Cambridge: Cambridge University Press, 2015.

was the global champion of free trade. Today, the US Congress has become the chief opponent of free trade deals.

Equally dangerously, the US Congress has also become an opponent of the rules-based order, especially the UN. I experienced this personally when I served as the Singapore Ambassador to the UN from 1984 to 1989 and 1998 to 2004. In both instances, I saw the US take the lead in trying to reduce the budgets of the UN and its affiliated agencies. Recently, the World Health Organization (WHO) has come under a lot of attention as a result of the surge of Covid-19 in 2020. The Trump Administration was ferocious in its attacks on WHO and accused it of incompetence in handling Covid-19. The Trump Administration used this as a justification for pulling out of the WHO. Yet, the criticism by the Trump Administration of the WHO was manifestly unfair because it was the US that had effectively weakened the WHO for several decades. Anyone who doubts this should read an excellent book on the WHO by Professor Kelley Lee.[2] In it, she documents how the Western countries, led by the US, reduced the compulsory assessed contributions to the WHO from 62% in 1970–1971 to 18% in 2017.

Since this campaign by Western governments to weaken or sideline UN organizations had been going on for decades, it would be natural to assume that this big and obvious truth would surface in the "open" Western societies. Hence, every well-informed Western intellectual, especially those who write on global issues, should be aware of this massive Western campaign to weaken multilateral institutions, including crucial global multilateral institutions like the WHO.

Yet, sadly, there is no awareness of this big truth in the West, even though I published an entire book to document this in 2013. The book was entitled *The Great Convergence: Asia, the West and the Logic of One World*. Indeed, this book was endorsed by the late UN Secretary-General, Kofi Annan, who said, "In exploring the tensions that arise as our global community draws ever closer together, Kishore Mahbubani provides a compelling reminder that humanity is strongest when we work together for the benefit of all."

Kofi Annan was very prescient when he spoke of the necessity for humanity to "work together for the benefit of all." This is actually the big message that Covid-19 is trying to send to humanity. Fortunately, some Western intellectuals acknowledge that Covid-19 is telling us that humanity as a whole should cooperate. Yuval Noah Harari has emerged as one of the most influential Western intellectuals of our time. On 27 February 2021, he wrote a brilliant essay in the Financial Times describing well the lessons that humanity should learn from Covid-19. The most obvious lesson is that humanity needs to cooperate as a whole to prevent future pandemics. As he said, "we should establish a powerful global system to monitor and prevent pandemics. In the age-old war between humans and pathogens, the frontline passes through the body of each and every human being. If this line is breached anywhere on the planet, it puts all of us in danger. Even the richest people in the most developed countries have a personal interest to protect the poorest people in the least developed countries. If

[2] Kelley Lee, *The World Health Organization (WHO)* (London: Routledge, 2014).

a new virus jumps from a bat to a human in a poor village in some remote jungle, within a few days that virus can take a walk down Wall Street."

He then goes on to make another obvious point: we can work with the WHO. As he said, "The skeleton of such a global anti-plague system already exists in the shape of the World Health Organization and several other institutions. But the budgets supporting this system are meager, and it has almost no political teeth. We need to give this system some political clout and a lot more money so that it won't be entirely dependent on the whims of self-serving politicians."

This observation by Yuval Noah Harari is truly shocking. He makes the factually correct point that the budget for the WHO is "meager". However, he doesn't say who has made the WHO budget meager. Clearly, it was the Western governments who did so. Did he not say this because he was unaware of this? If someone as well informed and as influential as Yuval Noah Harari is not aware that Western governments, led by the US, have systematically tried to weaken UN and UN-affiliated multilateral organizations over several decades, this is truly shocking. This shows that the Western media, which claims to be free, open, and objective, has occasionally hidden large truths which prove to be inconvenient to Western governments. To ensure that we can achieve the goal that Yuval Noah Harari has set of strengthening the WHO, the Western governments, therefore, need to be honest and confess publicly that they had been trying systematically to deprive the UN-affiliated organizations of resources.

Why did the West try to reduce the compulsory assessed contributions and increase the voluntary contributions? The simple answer is that the Western countries were the largest "voluntary" contributors. They wanted to use their "voluntary" contributions to control the agenda of the WHO (and other similar UN organizations, like the IAEA). I can also speak with some confidence about the efforts of Western governments to starve the IAEA of badly needed funding. In 2007/8, I was invited both by the former President of Mexico, Mr Ernesto Zedillo, and Mr Mohamed ElBaradei, the Director General of IAEA, to join a Commission of Eminent Persons and review the future of the IAEA and provide recommendations on how to strengthen it. This Commission included many renowned personalities, including the distinguished Sam Nunn, former United States Senator (1972–1997), Wolfgang Schüssel, former Federal Chancellor of Austria (2000–2007), Gareth Evans, former Australian Foreign Minister (1988–1996), and Qian Qichen, the former Foreign Minister of China (1988–1998).

I thought that it would be an easy exercise to persuade the West to provide more resources to IAEA since the Western countries are terrified of nuclear proliferation. The IAEA is the prime UN vehicle to prevent nuclear proliferation since only the IAEA has the legitimacy and resources to conduct intrusive inspections of nuclear facilities all around the world. To conduct nuclear inspections effectively, the IAEA had to recruit and retain for their lifetime careers extremely competent and capable nuclear inspectors. Since the IAEA could only fund lifetime nuclear inspectors from long-term guaranteed and compulsory assessed contributions, it would be logical for the Western governments to support more assessed and less voluntary contributions for the IAEA. Instead, the West did the opposite. Hence, the IAEA has reported that it "has been experiencing limited growth in its Regular Budget", and even saw a "decrease in real terms" in its Regular Budget in 2019. As a result, this unwise Western policy had resulted in a weakening of the IAEA, in the same way, that the WHO had been weakened.

When the West tried to do this, they didn't ask themselves a simple question. The West represents 12% of the world's population. The rest represent 88% of the world's population. Was it ethical for the West to use its financial clout to control the agenda of a global organization, like the WHO, which is supposed to represent the interests of humanity and not the interests of a Western minority?

The failure of the West to answer this big moral question points to a huge paradox about Western behavior on the world stage. Domestically, all Western countries believe in democratic governance and insist that all domestic government institutions must represent the wishes and interests of the majority of the people. Globally, all Western countries believe in dictatorial governance and insist that all global governance institutions must reflect the wishes and interests of the minority, 12% who live in the West and not the 88% who live outside the West.

Sadly, in working to weaken or undermine global multilateral institutions, especially those in the UN family, the West is actually acting against its own interests. The only Western leader who has the courage to say this is former President Bill Clinton. In a speech he gave in Yale University in 2003, he said that the US "should be trying to create a world in which rules and partnerships and habits of behavior that we would like to live in when we're no longer the military, political, economic superpower in the world".[3] The West should heed the advice of Bill Clinton.

Since this volume of essays is entitled *The Asian 21st Century*, it would be useful to conclude this introduction by recommending three concrete steps that Asian countries, including China, can adopt to ensure that we have a peaceful and prosperous Asian century. All these three concrete steps will build on the key argument that in the small interdependent global village we live in, today (as demonstrated by the common global challenges we face like Covid-19 and global warming), humanity as a whole should come together to strengthen global multilateral institutions. Since Asians make up the largest share of the global population, representing 60% of humanity, it would be natural for Asians to take the leadership in proposing three concrete steps that can strengthen multilateralism.

The first step is to restore the primary role of the UN General Assembly (UNGA) to serve as the global parliament for humanity. Indeed, the only body that can legitimately claim to represent the voices of all humanity is the UNGA. Hence, if we really want to know what humanity thinks of an issue, we should table this for discussion at the UNGA. This is exactly what the ASEAN countries and China did after Vietnam invaded Cambodia in December 1978 and the Soviet Union invaded Afghanistan in December 1979. China and ASEAN supported resolutions that call for the overturning of these invasions. In the end, since the large majority of countries supported the resolutions proposed by the ASEAN countries and China, the invasions were overturned.

---

[3] Kishore Mahbubani, *The Great Convergence: China, Europe and the Making of the Modern World Economy* (New York: Public Affairs, 2013), 8.

The UNGA also does not support interference in the internal affairs of countries. The West has been very critical of the actions taken by the government of the Special Administrative Region (SAR) of Hong Kong to restore law and order after the violent demonstrations in Hong Kong. Many Western governments claim that the "international community" is critical of the actions taken by Carrie Lam, the Chief Executive of Hong Kong. Yet, if the Western governments were to table a resolution in the UNGA criticizing the actions taken by the Hong Kong government, they would get no support at all from the vast majority of countries in the world. The UNGA is therefore one vehicle that Asian countries can use to demonstrate that Asian perspectives on the world now enjoy far more support than Western perspectives. The Asian countries should therefore work together to strengthen the UNGA.

The second step that Asian countries can take is to strengthen key multilateral organizations, like the WHO and IAEA (as indicated above) by providing them with more resources. In some cases, we may not need to spend more money to strengthen them. In the case of the WHO, for example, it was a mistake to reduce the compulsory assessed contributions from 62% in 1970/1 to 18% in 2017. Without spending more money, we should revert to the old formula of funding and increase the compulsory assessed contribution back to 62%. This would strengthen the WHO enormously because it would enable the WHO to make reliable long-term plans and also recruit more long-term expert staff to handle future pandemics.

One key point needs to be emphasized here. The amount of money needed to strengthen the UN family of institutions is "peanuts". Yet, many Western governments keep trying to reduce funding for the UN. When I served as the Singapore Ambassador to the UN from 1998 to 2004, the US Ambassador to the UN, Richard Holbrooke, led a ferocious campaign in the UN to reduce the US contribution to the UN from 25 to 22%. He succeeded. So how much money did he save for the US each year? He saved USD 69.6 million. How significant of a sum is USD 69.6 million? It amounts to only 0.01% of the annual US Defence budget for 2020. Yet, as we have learned from the experience of Covid-19, the huge amount of money spent in the US Defence budget could not save the lives of over 537,000 Americans who died from Covid-19. Indeed, Covid-19 killed more Americans than all the Americans who died from fighting wars since World War II. And yet the US happily spends over USD 700 billion a year on its Defence budget while complaining about the USD 70 million it contributes in assessed contributions to the entire UN system.

Fortunately, the Asian share of the global GNP has been steadily rising. Hence, Asian countries can take the lead in calling for more financial resources to the UN system while paying their fair share of the global burden. This is the second concrete step that Asian countries can take to strengthen global multilateralism.

The third step for the Asian countries to take is to share with the world one of the best models of regional multilateral cooperation. To some extent, ASEAN has already done this, as documented by my co-author, Jeffry Sng and I, in our book *The ASEAN Miracle*, which was fortunately translated into Chinese by the Peking University Press. We can build on the success of ASEAN by strengthening the Regional Comprehensive Economic Partnership (RCEP). RCEP was proposed by the ten ASEAN countries and also includes five other East Asian countries -

China, Japan, South Korea as well as Australia and New Zealand. Unfortunately, India decided not to join at the last minute, even though it had been participating in the negotiations for over ten years.

The RCEP can therefore be strengthened in two ways. First, a major effort should be made to persuade India to join RCEP. This should be possible since India will benefit from integrating its economy with the dynamic economies of East Asia. Second, we should accelerate the concrete implementation of the RCEP. The goal should be to significantly increase the volume of trade conducted among the 15 RCEP member countries to ensure that it becomes by far the largest free trade agreement in the world. Right now, the total trade among the three countries in NAFTA amounts to just over USD 2.3 trillion, and that among the 27 countries of the EU amounts to USD 2.3 trillion. By contrast, the total trade among the 15 countries of RCEP amounts to USD 2.5 trillion.

One simple goal of the RCEP should be to ensure that the total trade conducted among the 15 RCEP countries is larger than the combined trade conducted by NAFTA and EU. If RCEP can achieve this, it would send a clear and powerful signal of the validity of two key points emphasized at the beginning of this Introduction. Firstly, we are reaching the end of the era of Western domination of world history. Secondly, in the twenty-first century, we will see the return of Asia. Hence, without a shadow of doubt, we will soon be sailing full steam ahead into the Asian twenty-first century.

The End of the Era of Western Domination

The 21st century will mark the end of the era of Western domination. The major strategic error that the West is now making is to refuse to accept this reality. The West needs to learn how to act strategically in a world where they are no longer the number 1.

The Hypocrisy of the West

Abstract One of the great gifts of Western civilization is the philosophical wisdom bequeathed by its great thinkers. At a time when torture and Guantanamo still exist, the West should revive its commitment to using reason to understand and improve the world.

One of the greatest joys of my life was studying Western philosophy, absorbing the wisdom of great Western thinkers from Socrates to Wittgenstein. The dedication of all those great thinkers, over thousands of years, to the power of logical reasoning, was truly inspiring. Hence, for me, the power of the West was always associated with this commitment to using reason to understand and improve the world.

Western logic was always irrefutable. Plain logic would create irrefutable statements. Hence if the premise was "all dogs are animals", the consequence of the claim "Fido is a dog" was the irrefutable statement that "Fido is an animal". A similar rigor applied to moral reasoning. Hence, if a human being called X said "Human beings should not torture other human beings", the irrefutable conclusion was that X was obliged to also say "I should not torture human beings". The rigor of this logic is absolute. No exceptions are possible. Anyone who made the first claim and denied the second claim would be justifiably accused of hypocrisy.

In Theory, the West Condemns Hypocrisy—In Practice, It Indulges in it

In theory, the West condemns hypocrisy. In practice, sadly, it indulges in hypocrisy massively. A few major contemporary examples will illustrate this. For several decades, after the US Congress passed legislation instructing the US State Department to publish annual reports on the human rights performance of all states in the world (except the US), the US State Department would painstakingly record the

---

Originally published in IAI, Dec 16, 2020

K. Mahbubani, *The Asian 21st Century*, China and Globalization,
https://doi.org/10.1007/978-981-16-6811-1_2

cases of torture practiced in other countries.[1] For example, the State Department condemned "near drowning" and "submersion of the head in water" as torture in reports on Sri Lanka and Tunisia. By the logic of moral reasoning, the US was declaring that it did not practice torture.

In 2001, after 9/11 happened, the US went on a global campaign against the radical Islamist terrorists that had attacked it. Under international law, this campaign was justified, especially since it was legitimized by a UN Security Council resolution.[2] However, after the US captured some terrorist suspects, it took them to Guantanamo and tortured them. By so doing, the US was clearly declaring that it had shifted its moral stance from "Thou shalt not torture human beings" to "Thou shalt torture human beings". The US never said this verbally, but by the logic of moral reasoning, it had made this statement even more loudly with its actual behavior.

One of the greatest modern works of moral philosophy is the book "The Language of Morals" by the English philosopher, R.M. Hare (Note: as an aside, let me mention that he wrote parts of this book on toilet paper when he was a prisoner of war of the Japanese in Singapore in World War II). The opening line of this volume is very powerful. It says "If we were to ask of a person 'What are his moral principles?' the way in which we could be most sure of a true answer would be studying what he did."[3]

"Thou Shalt Torture Human Beings"?

In short, since Western moral reasoning is brutally ironclad and allows no exceptions, when the US began torturing human beings, it was declaring "Thou shalt torture human beings". Since this was undoubtedly the moral position taken by the US, the logical consequence should have been for the US State Department to stop issuing annual reports "condemning" torture in other countries. Clearly, this would be hypocritical. Quite amazingly, the US State Department did not stop. Even more amazingly, the largest and most powerful "moral industry" in the world is in the US: No country can match the output of moral judgments that spew out from the editorial pages of the *New York Times* and *Washington Post* and from the reports of the greatest think tanks and universities in the world. This massive "moral industry" should have exploded in outrage at this blatant hypocrisy of the State Department Reports. None of this happened. The annual State Department reports continued to be published and reported and cited in, for example, the *New York Times*. If Socrates

---

[1] Under the Foreign Assistance Act of 1961. These annual country reports have been published since 1977.

[2] UN Security Council Security Council resolution 1373 (2001) [on threats to international peace and security caused by terrorist acts], 28 September 2001, S/RES/1373 (2001), available at: https://www.refworld.org/docid/3c4e94552a.html

[3] Richard Mervyn Hare. The language of morals. No. 77. Oxford Paperbacks, 1991: 1.

were alive today, he would have made the next logically irrefutable statement: the *New York Times* was abetting the hypocrisy of these reports.

The second largest "moral industry" in the world, outside the US, can be found in Europe. Most European governments have not hesitated to condemn countries like Russia and Iran when they received reports of "torture" in these countries. By the logic of moral reasoning that flows from the statement "thou shalt not torture", the same European governments should have immediately condemned the US for practicing torture. Amazingly, to this day, not one European government has done so. Neither have they been called to account by their "moral industry" over their failure to be logically consistent and condemn the US. Here too, we saw a massive dose of hypocrisy.

Even more importantly, all moral philosophers have emphasized that the best way to demonstrate one's fidelity to moral principle is not when it is convenient to do so, without any sacrifice involved. Hence, when European governments condemned, for example, the dictatorial rule of, say, Mugabe in Zimbabwe or Hugo Chavez in Venezuela, they could do so happily as they would not pay any political and economic price for taking these correct moral stances. Since no costs are involved, there is no real demonstration of moral commitment. This is why the non-condemnation of the US practice of torture is very significant. By failing to condemn when the costs of doing so were high (as there could have been retribution from the US), the European governments were showing their real moral stand by, as R.M. Hare says, what they did. Hence, when they did not condemn, they were essentially saying that their true moral position was "thou shalt torture human beings".

In 2021, we will be marking the twentieth anniversary of 9/11 and the subsequent moral distortions it unleashed in major Western societies. Since sufficient time has passed after the US exploded in anger when it was attacked, this may be a good time for all major Western governments, including those of the US and the European Union, to reflect deeply on their clear failure to abide by some of their most cherished moral principles. One point is clear. One of the heinous acts one could carry out on a human being is to practice torture. Indeed, before 9/11, there was a solid consensus among all the Western countries that torture was unjustified in all circumstances.

End the Hypocrisy

The world would be a better place if all Western governments would once again demonstrate, in words and deeds, their total adherence to the strong moral statement "Thou shalt not torture". Guantanamo should be shut down. All the European governments, which were silently complicit in this torture campaign by providing "rendition" centers, should make a clean break with these practices by declaring openly all that had been done so that the chapter on this painful episode in the history of the West can be closed.

At the end of the day, one of the greatest strengths of Western civilization is the large oceans of philosophical wisdom bequeathed by the greatest Western thinkers. Fidelity to the great principles left behind by these great Western philosophers would help to repair the damage done to the standing and prestige of the West after its unholy flirtation with torture. This stain can and should be removed from the West.

Trump, Macron and the Poverty of Liberalism

Abstract The great paradox of our time is that billionaire Trump is supported by the American working class, while middle-class Macron is reviled by the bottom half of French society. One explanation for this great paradox is that modern liberal society overemphasizes individual liberties at the expense of equality and the material livelihoods of its people.

No Western liberal would disagree that Mr Donald Trump's election was a disaster for American society, while that of Mr Emmanuel Macron was a triumph for French society. In fact, the opposite may well be true, as heretical as that sounds. But the first question to ask is why people are engaged in violent street protests in Paris, but not in Washington, DC. I have personally experienced these Paris protests, and the smell of tear gas on the Champs-Élysées reminded me of the ethnic riots I experienced in Singapore in 1964. And why are the yellow vests protesting? For many, at least initially, it was because they did not believe that Mr Macron cared for or understood their plight.

The French President is trying to implement sensible macroeconomic reform. The proposed increases in taxes on diesel fuel would have reduced France's budget deficits and helped lower its carbon dioxide emissions. His hope was that a stronger fiscal position would increase confidence and investment in the French economy so that the bottom 50 percent of society would eventually benefit. But for people to endure short-term pain for long-term gain, they must trust their leader. And Mr Macron, it appears, has lost the trust of much of that bottom 50 percent.

By contrast, Mr Trump retains the trust and confidence of the bottom half of American society, or at least the white portion of it. At first sight, this seems strange and paradoxical: Billionaire Trump is socially much further from the bottom 50 percent than the middle-class Mr Macron is.

But when the American President attacks the liberal and conservative US establishments, he is seen as venting the anger of the less well off toward an elite that has ignored their plight. His election may, therefore, have had a cathartic effect on the

Originally published in Project Syndicate, Jan 22, 2019

bottom 50 percent, which may explain the lack of street protests in Washington or other major US cities.

And these Americans have much to be angry about. Most tellingly, the US is the only major developed society where the average income of the bottom half has not just stagnated but also declined markedly, as Professor Danny Quah of the National University of Singapore has documented. Even more shockingly, the average income of the top 1 percent was 138 times that of the bottom 50 percent in 2010, up from 41 times higher in 1980. There is no single explanation for why inequality in the US has rocketed, while the economic interests of the bottom 50 percent have been ignored.

But we can obtain at least a partial answer by looking at the two principles of justice that Harvard philosopher John Rawls articulated in his 1971 book, *A Theory Of Justice*. The first principle emphasizes that each person should have "an equal right to the most extensive liberty", while the second says that social and economic inequalities are to be arranged so that they are to "everyone's advantage".

The undeniable fact is that Western liberals have emphasized the first principle over the second in both theory and practice, prioritizing individual liberty and worrying far less about inequality. They believe that as long as elections take place and people can vote freely and equally, this is a sufficient condition for social stability. It follows, therefore, that those who fail economically do so because of personal incompetence, not social conditions.

Yet there was no doubt when China joined the World Trade Organization in 2001 that "creative destruction" in developed economies would follow, entailing millions of job losses. These economies' elites - whether in the US, France, or elsewhere – had a responsibility to help those who were losing their jobs. But no such help was forthcoming.

Conventional macroeconomic theory remains sound. Mr Trump's policy of running larger budget deficits in good times will bring pain later, while Mr Macron's economic policies will eventually pay off if the French remain patient. And Mr Macron may yet back reforms that address inequality. But he is clearly not trusted by the bottom 50 percent, while Mr Trump is. For this reason, liberals may have made a strategic mistake by focusing their anger on Mr Trump himself. Instead, they should ask themselves why much of the bottom 50 percent trust him. And if they were honest, liberals would admit that they have effectively let the bottom half of society down.

If liberals want to defeat Mr Trump utterly, there is only one route: Regain the trust of the voters that form much of his base. This will require them to restructure their societies so that economic growth benefits the bottom half more than the top 1 percent.

In theory, this can be done easily. In practice, however, major vested interests will invariably seek to block reform. The choice for liberals is clear: They can feel good by condemning Mr Trump, or they can do good by attacking the elite interests that contributed to his election. If liberals can do the latter, Mr Trump's election would be seen by future historians as a necessary wake-up call, while Mr Macron's merely created the illusion that all was well.

These historians might then conclude that Mr Trump's election was ultimately better for American society than Mr Macron's was for France.

Democracy or Plutocracy? America's Existential Question

Abstract Americans are proud of their democratic political system. But the facts show that America has increasingly come to resemble a plutocracy, where society is governed "of the 1%, by the 1%, for the 1%".

Is the United States of America still a functioning democracy or has it become, for all practical purposes, a plutocracy? And why is this question important? It's important because the answer to the question of whether America has a dark or shining future will depend on whether it's a democracy or plutocracy. Indeed, this question may well be the most existential question America has to address.

The Difference Between "Democracy" and "Plutocracy"

Let's begin to answer this question from the very beginning. What is the actual difference between a democracy and a plutocracy? In a democracy, the masses broadly determine their future. Equally critically, in terms of the economy, society, and political system there is a level playing field where the working classes, middle classes, and affluent elites compete. The term "level playing field" is absolutely critical here. Many Americans believe that their economic and political systems create a level playing field in which the poor and disadvantaged can rise to the top. This is also why there is no social resentment of billionaires in America. Most Americans believe that they have an equal opportunity to become billionaires. So the first big question we need to address is this: is there a level playing field for the poor and rich?

The honest answer is no. Today, when working class or even middle-class Americans have to compete with the affluent elites, they are not competing on a level playing field. They have to run uphill to score goals. By contrast, the affluent elites run downhill as the playing field is tilted in their favor. Writing in the Financial Times in June 2019, Edward Luce provides one statistic to drive home this point: "Studies show that an eighth grade [i.e., a 14-year-old] child from a lower income bracket

Originally published in Horizons, Autumn, 2020

who achieves maths results in the top quarter is less likely to graduate than a kid in the upper income bracket scored in the bottom quarter. This is the reverse of how meritocracy should work."

There is no shortage of data to drive home the point that there is no longer a level playing field in America. Anand Giridharadas, a former *New York Times* columnist, has documented in great detail in his book *Winners Take All* (2018) how the dream of the American middle class has effectively evaporated. As he says:

> A successful society is a progress machine. It takes in the raw material of innovations and produces broad human advancement. America's machine is broken. When the fruits of change have fallen on the United States in recent decades, the very fortunate have basketed almost all of them. For instance, the average pretax income of the top tenth of Americans has doubled since 1980, that of the top 1% has more than tripled, and that of the top 0.001% has risen more than sevenfold—even as the average pretax income of the bottom half of Americans has stayed almost precisely the same. These familiar figures amount to three and a half decades' worth of wondrous, head-spinning change with zero impact on the average pay of 117 million Americans.

Giridharadas claims that the American people are beginning to "feel" that the system is unfair:

> Thus many millions of Americans, on the left and right, feel one thing in common: that the game is rigged against people like them. [...] There is a spreading recognition, on both sides of the ideological divide, that the system is broken, that the system has to change.

Giridharadas is right. To create a level playing field, the system has to change. But it will not change. Why not? What are the obstacles to change? And, if there are obstacles, why hasn't the world's freest media, the American media, revealed these obstacles? This is where the story becomes complex. We also have to venture into politically controversial territory to understand the obstacles to change.

Main Obstacle to Change

The main obstacle to change is a myth. An example from history will help. For centuries, European serfs accepted a feudal system in which they were second-class citizens (if not slaves) in a system dominated by feudal lords. Why didn't the majority of serfs overthrow the minority of feudal lords? A huge myth was created to generate a belief that this system was just. The kind and gentle feudal lords reinforced the myth. At the risk of quoting a politically controversial philosophical concept, let me mention a term used for this phenomenon: false consciousness. According to Daniel Little, Chancellor Emeritus and Professor of Philosophy at University of Michigan-Dearborn, "false consciousness" is a concept derived from Marxist theory of social class. [...] Members of a subordinate class (workers, peasants, serfs) suffer from false consciousness in that their mental representations of the social relations around them systematically conceal or obscure the realities of subordination, exploitation, and domination of those relations embody. Marx asserts that social mechanisms

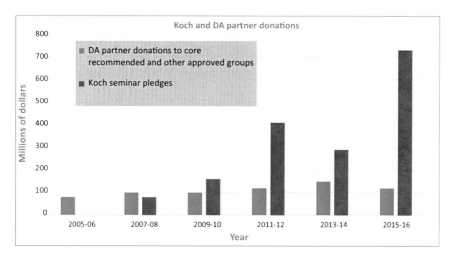

Fig. 1 Democracy Alliance Figures and Koch and DA Partner Donations *Source* Democracy Alliance figures from LeMarche 2014, supplement with correspondence from the Democracy Alliance. Koch seminar figures from media reports of seminars

emerge in class society that systematically creates distortions, errors, and blind spots in the consciousness of the underclass. If these consciousness-shaping mechanisms did not exist, then the underclass, always a majority, would quickly overthrow the system of their domination (Fig. 1).

Yet, even if contemporary Americans were to accept that there was "false consciousness" in the feudal era, they would contest the possibility of it emerging in modern American society, where the unique combination of the world's freest and fiercely independent media, the best universities, the best-funded think tanks and the spirit of open and critical inquiry would expose any big "myth" that enveloped American society. Many Americans would assert no myths can survive in the robustly open environment of American society. Only facts survive.

To be fair, many American writers have written about the several dimensions of plutocracy in American society. In addition to Giridharadas, who was cited earlier, distinguished American writers like Nobel Laureate Joseph Stiglitz and Robert Reich have documented, for example, the growing inequality in America. In his brilliant May 2011 Vanity Fair article entitled, "Of the 1%, by the 1%, for the 1%," Stiglitz opines that it's no use pretending that what has obviously happened has not in fact happened. The upper 1% of Americans are now taking in nearly a quarter of the nation's income every year. In terms of wealth rather than income, the top 1% control 40%. Their lot in life has improved considerably. Twenty-five years ago, the corresponding figures were 12% and 33%.

Yet what most of these articles emphasize is the growing "inequality" in America. And if the problem is "inequality," then fortunately the problem can be solved. As America has the world's most robust democratic system, where the broad masses elect the leaders who in turn take care of the interests of the broad masses, any problem of "inequality" could eventually be fixed. In short, if America has a problem, it also has a solution: democracy.

This brings us to the heart of the argument of this essay. To put it simply, the solution has become part of the problem. While all the democratic processes remain in place, with Americans going to the polls every two or four years (depending on the elected office) to select their leaders (who will, in theory, take care of them), the results of all those processes are that Americans elect leaders who will take care of the 1%, not the 99%.

How did this happen? How did America, which on the surface still functions as a democracy, become a plutocracy, which takes care of the interest of the 1%? *[Note: the term 1%is used metaphorically here. The real reference is to a tiny elite that benefits from a non-level playing field].*

There was one great American who anticipated the effective hijacking of the American democratic system by the very affluent. He is America's greatest political philosopher of recent times, John Rawls. Rawls warned that "if those who have greater private means are permitted to use their advantages to control the course of public debate," this would be the corrupting result:

> Eventually, these inequalities will enable those better situated to exercise a larger influence over the development of legislation. In due time they are likely to acquire a preponderant weight in settling social questions, at least in regard to those matters upon which they normally agree, which is to say in regard to those things that support their favored circumstances.

This is precisely what has happened over the past few decades: the affluent have gained "preponderant weight [...] in regard of those things that support their favored circumstances." There has been a relative transfer of wealth and political power from the vast majority of America's population to a privileged super minority.

The practical effect of transferring power to a super minority is that the political system responds to the needs and interests of the top 1%, not to the 99%. Fortunately, there have been strong, peer-reviewed academic studies that confirm this political reality. Two Princeton University professors have documented how ordinary American citizens have lost their political power and influence. Martin Gilens and Benjamin Page studied the relative influence that the views of average Americans and mass-based interest groups have on policy outcomes versus the views of the economic elite in 1,779 cases. They found that: "economic elites and organized groups representing business interests have substantial independent impacts on US government policy, while average citizens and mass-based interest groups have little or no independent influence. [...] When the preferences of economic elites and the stands of organized interest groups are controlled for, the preferences of the average American appear to have only a minuscule, near-zero, statistically non-significant impact upon public policy. [...] Furthermore, the preferences of economic elites (as measured by our proxy, the preferences of "affluent" citizens) have a far more independent impact upon policy change than the preferences of average citizens do. [...] In the United States, our findings indicate, the majority does not rule—at least not in the causal sense of actually determining policy outcomes."

They reach the following alarming conclusion: "Americans do enjoy many features central to democratic governance, such as regular elections, freedom of speech and association, and a widespread (if still contested) franchise. But we believe that if policymaking is dominated by powerful business organizations and a small number of affluent Americans, then America's claims to being a democratic society are seriously threatened."

In the past, the broad middle classes of America had a strong say in determining the fundamental direction of American society. Today, they no longer do. The decisions of the US Congress are not determined by the voters; they are determined by the funders. As a result, America is becoming functionally less and less of a democracy, where all citizens have an equal voice. Instead, it looks more and more like a plutocracy, where a few rich people are disproportionately powerful.

These conclusions have been reinforced by other academic studies. A 2018 study by scholars Alexander Hertel-Fernandez, Theda Skocpol, and Jason Sclar of the School of International and Public Affairs at Columbia University further argued that since the mid-2000s, newly formed conservative and progressive donor consortia—above all the Koch seminars [founded by brothers Charles and David Koch] and the DA [Democracy Alliance]—have magnified the impact of wealthy donors by raising and channeling ever more money not just into elections but also into full arrays of cooperating political organizations. […] The Koch seminars […] allowed donations to be channeled into building a virtual third political party organized around AFP [Americans for Prosperity], an overarching political network able not only to electorally support the Republican Party but also to push and pull its candidates and office holders in preferred ultra-free-market policy directions. […] To the degree that wealthy donor consortia have succeeded in building organizational infrastructures, they have shifted the resources available for developing policy proposals, pressing demands on lawmakers, and mobilizing ordinary Americans into politics. […] When plutocratic collectives impose new agendas on political organizations seeking to attract financial resources, the funders reshape routines, goals, and centers of power in US politics well beyond the budgetary impact of particular grants. This has resulted in hundreds of millions of dollars that wealthy donors have raised annually within the donor consortia to finance their political interests.

The authors thus conclude: "Our analysis of the Koch and DA consortia highlights that a great deal of big-money influence flows through mechanisms other than individual or business donations to the electoral and lobbying operations. […] To understand how the wealthy are reshaping US politics, we need to look not just at their election and lobbying expenditures but also at their concerted investments in many kinds of political organizations operating across a variety of fields and functions. Only in this way can we account for the stark inequalities in government responsiveness documented by [various] researchers."

So what triggered this massive transfer of political power from the broad masses to a tiny elite in America? This question will be hotly debated by political scientists and historians for decades. Yet it is also clear that one seminal ruling by the US Supreme Court made a huge difference. In a landmark ruling in Citizens United v. Federal

Election Commission (2010) as well as in other decisions, many of the legislative restraints on the use of money to influence the political process were overturned.

A report by the Center for Public Integrity reported that: "The Citizens United ruling, released in January 2010, tossed out the corporate and union ban on making independent expenditures and financing electioneering communications. It gave corporations and unions the green light to spend unlimited sums on ads and other political tools, calling for the election or defeat of individual candidates." The impact of this and other Supreme Court decisions was monumental. Effectively, they ended up transforming the American political system. Martin Wolf says that "the Supreme Court's perverse 2010 Citizens United decision held that companies are persons and money is speech. That has proved a big step on the journey of the US toward becoming a plutocracy."

Now, Martin Wolf is one of the most influential columnists in the world. He also describes himself as being fiercely pro-American. In a column written in 2018, Wolf said "the US was not just any great power. It embodied the causes of democracy, freedom, and the rule of law. This made [my father] fiercely pro-American. I inherited this attitude." America is an open society. Therefore, when major voices like Martin Wolf and Joseph Stiglitz describe America as having become a "plutocracy," the logical result should have been a major public debate on whether this claim is true.

Instead, the opposite happened. This comment by Martin Wolf was buried. The psychological resistance in America to use the term "plutocracy" is deep. Leading newspapers like the *New York Times* and *Washington Post* do not use it. Leading columnists like Richard Cohen and Paul Krugman do not use it. Nor do distinguished historians like Simon Schama mention plutocracy. Certainly, no American politician uses it.

So, what is in a name? Shakespeare once famously said, "a rose by any other name would smell as sweet." I sometimes doubt this piece of wisdom. If someone were to change the name of "rose" to "skunk-flower," we might approach a rose with some caution. Choosing the right name makes a huge difference. As the philosopher Ludwig Wittgenstein said, "the limits of my language mean the limits of my world."

The sad reality about the US is that, functionally, there is absolutely no doubt that the political system has gone from functioning as a democracy (a government of the people, by the people, for the people) toward becoming a plutocracy (a government of the 1%, by the 1%, for the 1%). Yet, while this political reality is undeniable, it is also unspeakable.

Just and Unjust Inequality

What is the real danger that flows from this refusal to describe the American political system as a "plutocracy"? Many dangers! Firstly, it perpetuates the myth that American society has a "level playing field." Anybody can succeed. Hence, if a person fails it is because of his individual defects. It is not because the social environment is rigged against the person. Secondly, by refusing to describe it as a plutocracy, the fundamental difference between "just inequality" and "unjust inequality" falls to the surface.

The term "just inequality" may seem to be an oxymoron. Yet, it was John Rawls who highlighted this difference. It was he who said that inequality was not the problem. The fundamental question was whether rising inequality resulted in an improvement or deterioration of the living conditions of the people living at the bottom. He states this clearly and categorically: "the higher expectations of those better situated are just if and only if they work as part of a scheme which improves the expectations of the least advantaged members of society."

The best way to illustrate the difference between "just equality" and "unjust equality" is to compare concrete examples. Both the United States and China have about the same level of inequality. By the latest estimates, the gini coefficient in America is 0.41 and in China is 0.39. There is no significant difference here. However, there is a significant difference between how the bottom 50% have fared in America and China. America is the only major developed society where the average income of the bottom 50% has declined over a 30 year period from 1980 to 2010, as documented by my colleague of the National University of Singapore, Professor Danny Quah. By contrast, the bottom 50% of the Chinese population has seen the greatest improvements in their standard of living in recent decades. Indeed, the past 40 years of social and economic development that the Chinese people have enjoyed have been the best 40 years in four thousand years of Chinese history.

The story here is not just about economic failures and economic successes. These economic failures and successes have profound effects on the state of psychological and social well-being of societies. In America, this stagnation of income has also resulted in a lot of human pain and suffering, as documented by two Princeton University economists, Anne Case and Angus Deaton. The white working classes of America used to carry the American dream of getting a better life in their hearts and souls. Today, as Case says, there is a "sea of despair" among them. She and Deaton conclude: "Ultimately, we see our story as about the collapse of the white, high-school-educated working class after its heyday in the early 1970s, and the pathologies that accompany that decline." The detailed study of Case and Deaton documents how poor economic prospects "compounds over time through family dysfunction, social isolation, addiction, obesity, and other pathologies."

In China, the situation is almost exactly the opposite. A Chinese-American psychology research from Stanford University, Jean Fan, visited China in 2019. She observed that "China is changing in a deep and visceral way, and it is changing fast, in a way that is almost incomprehensible without seeing it in person. In contrast to America's stagnation, China's culture, self-concept, and morale are being transformed at a rapid pace—mostly for the better."

One obvious counter-argument to the different social conditions of America and China is that the American people are still better off because they enjoy freedom while the Chinese people do not. It is true that the American people enjoy political freedom. This is undeniable. However, it is also true that a person from the bottom 50% of American society is more likely to lose their personal freedom and end up in jail. The chance of being incarcerated in America (if one is born in the bottom

10%, especially among the black population) is at least five times higher than China. America sends 0.655% (or 2.12 million) into jails. By contrast, China sends 0.118% (or 1.65 million) into jails. A 2019 study tried to understand which ethnic group in America had the greatest percentage of individuals with family members in jail or prison. The average figure for all Americans was 45%. The figure for whites was 42%, Hispanics 48%, and blacks 63%.

Any American who has doubts about the dangers posed by plutocracy should pause and reflect on these figures. Let's repeat the figure: 45% of Americans have family members in jail or prison. These high levels of incarceration did not happen because the American people have psychological characteristics that make them more likely to become criminals. This is a result of the socio-economic conditions of the bottom 50% that have steadily deteriorated.

If it is manifestly obvious that the American political system is facing a crisis, why is there no consensus on the American body politic on what has gone wrong? Surely the best newspapers and universities, and the best-known students and professors in the world, should be able to arrive at a clear consensus on the real problems faced by American society?

In the year 2020, we can understand why there was no consensus. The liberal elites were distracted by one major issue: the possible reelection of Donald Trump. They believe that it would be a disaster if Donald Trump is reelected. They also believe that many of America's problems would be solved if Joe Biden wins. I share the hope that Biden will win. Yet, even if he wins, the systemic issues that led to the development of a plutocracy in America will not go away. Money will still dominate the political system.

If anyone doubts this, the following data from an important 2018 study written by Thomas Piketty, Emmanuel Saez, and Gabriel Zucman that appeared in the Quarterly Journal of Economics confirms this very clearly: First, our data show a sharp divergence in the growth experienced by the bottom 50% versus the rest of the economy. The average pretax income of the bottom 50% of adults has stagnated at about USD 16,000 per adult (in constant 2014 dollars, using the national income deflator) since 1980, while average national income per adult has grown by 60% to USD 64,500 in 2014. As a result, the bottom 50% income share has collapsed from about 20% in 1980 to 12% in 2014. In the meantime, the average pretax income of top 1% adults rose from USD 420,000 to about USD 1.3 million, and their income share increased from about 12% in the early 1980s to 20% in 2014. The two groups have essentially switched their income shares, with eight points of national income transferred from the bottom 50% to the top 1%. The top 1% income share is now almost twice as large as the bottom 50% share, a group that is by definition 50 times more numerous. In 1980, top 1% adults earned on average 27 times more than bottom 50% adults before tax, while they earn 81 times more today.

There are two ways of viewing this great divergence. It could be a result of the fact that the top 1% of Americans are becoming smarter and the bottom 50% of Americans are becoming less smart. Or it could be a result of the fact that America has become a plutocracy where there is no longer a level playing field. All the evidence points to the latter conclusion. Many Americans sense that the system does not work for them.

Deteriorating socio-economic conditions mean that people will suffer. All this is brought out by the latest Social Progress Index which was released in September 2020. Quite astonishingly, out of 163 countries assessed worldwide, America, Brazil, and Hungary are the only three countries where people have become worse off. The index collects several metrics of well-being, including nutrition, safety, freedom, the environment, health, education, and others to measure the quality of life in a country. America slipped from number 19 to number 28 in the world. Writing with reference to the aforementioned results, *New York Times* columnist Nicholas Kristof corroborates deteriorating quality of life with "rising distress and despair." Quite shockingly, Kristof describes how one-quarter of the children with whom he went to school on the same school bus is now dead from drugs, alcohol, and suicide. His personal experience mirrors what Case and Deaton have documented on the "sea of despair" among white working classes.

Tyranny of Money

Clearly, something has gone fundamentally wrong with American society. Many Americans are also beginning to sense that the system isn't working for them. Marvin Zonis, a University of Chicago economist has written an article that describes how "the American system is facing a crisis of legitimacy." The level of confidence that American people have in their key institutions has been declining. Confidence in the US presidency has fallen from 52% in 1975 to 37% in 2018. Confidence in the US Congress has plummeted more sharply from 42% in 1973 to 11% in 2018. The explanation that Zonis gives for this declining confidence is credible. As he says, "the central factor in the growing lack of trust and confidence in our institutions has been the realization that our American democracy does not function commensurately with the ideals of the founders or the Constitution. Money has become the key to American political life."

The keyword he uses is "money." If money dictates outcomes in politics, it means that a society has become a "plutocracy." After documenting how the amount of money spent in a US presidential election year has gone from USD 3 billion in 2010 to USD 6.5 billion in 2016, Zonis adds that the "contributors of those many billions expect a return on their investments—and they usually get it. Congressional action on gun legislation, sugar subsidies, policies toward Israel, drug pricing, and countless other issues is best explained by the financing of political campaigns and not by the political preferences of ordinary voters, or even of members of Congress."

Please read the above paragraph again, carefully. It says clearly that the decisions of the US Congress are decided by "contributors of billions" and not by the "political preference of ordinary voters." This observation confirms what Gilens and Page documented earlier. In short, there is no doubt that functionally America has become a plutocracy. Yet, equally significantly, Zonis does not use the term "plutocracy" once in his article.

In Denial

There is an old fashioned adage that says: one must call a spade a spade. Similarly, one must call a plutocracy a plutocracy. The reluctance to do so brings out the key problems facing American society. If America refuses to accept that it has functionally become a plutocracy, how can it possibly find a way out of this challenge? Just as no oncologist can cure a patient of cancer if he or she refuses to submit himself or herself to treatment, similarly America cannot be cured of its plutocracy problem if it remains in denial that such a problem exists.

All this means that there are two possible outcomes. The first is a revolution against the establishment in Washington, DC. Paradoxically this may have been what the working classes thought they were doing when they elected Trump in 2016. They wanted to elect someone outside the establishment and one who would shake up the establishment. When Hillary Clinton responded in 2016 by calling Trump's supporters a "basket of deplorables" it showed that she, together with the rest of the Washington establishment did not understand what the broad masses of Americans were trying to convey. Unfortunately, in electing Trump, the working classes voted in a plutocrat. In office, Trump acted like a plutocrat. He cut taxes for the rich again. The conditions for the bottom 50% didn't improve.

The second possible outcome is the arrival of enlightenment. At some point in time, the top 1% in America must come to realize that if they are going to protect most of their personal economic gain in America, and not make an effort to improve the conditions of the bottom 50%, they will only damage the very body politic— American society—that is enabling them to become so wealthy.

Fortunately, many wealthy Americans are coming to realize this. Ray Dalio is one of them. Dalio runs the largest, most successful hedge fund in the world, which has succeeded through rigorous empirical research. Dalio has now applied this research to understanding poverty and inequality in America. On his LinkedIn page, Dalio spells out the dramatic decline in the living standards of the majority of Americans and points out that "most people in the bottom 60% are poor" and cites "a recent Federal Reserve study [that showed that] 40% of all Americans would struggle to raise USD 400 in the event of an emergency." Worse, Dalio notes that "they are increasingly getting stuck being poor [...]. [T]he odds of someone in the bottom quintile moving up to the middle quintile or higher in a 10-year period [...] declined from about 23% in 1990 to only 14% as of 2011."

The data on social deterioration in America is undeniable. It undercuts the claims that America is a society where hard work brings rewards. For most people, the rewards have dried up. The platitude that "virtue is its own reward" turns out to be grimly and limitingly true.

Five Hard Steps Forward

Yet, even if the top 1% in America, which includes Dalio, were to wish that American society return to its condition of the 1950s and 1960s, when the broad mass of American society was also lifted up as America's economy grew, what should they do? Is there a magic button they can press? Is there a simple "silver bullet" solution to America's problem with plutocracy? Sadly, there are no easy solutions. There are only painful solutions. This article will therefore conclude by suggesting what some of them might be. The first step would be for the Supreme Court's Citizens United decision to be reversed. As Martin Wolf said, this court decision started the slippery slope toward plutocracy in America.

The second step would be for America to emulate the example of its fellow democracies in the European Union and impose strict limits on the amount of money that can be spent on elections. Fortunately, the American people also want to limit the influence of money. A Pew Research Institute survey in 2018 found that "an overwhelming majority (77%) supports limits on the amount of money individuals and organizations can spend on political campaigns and issues. And nearly two-thirds of Americans (65%) say new laws could be effective in reducing the role of money in politics."

The third step is to change American ideology in a fundamental way. It should go back to the wisdom of its founding fathers. The founding fathers of America were all disciples of great European philosophers of the Enlightenment period (including John Locke and Montesquieu) and emphasized both Freedom and Equality—as did the aforementioned Rawls. Of late, however, American politicians, starting with Ronald Reagan, have emphasized Freedom and not mentioned Equality in the same breath.

The fourth step is to acknowledge that market forces alone cannot create a level playing field for all Americans. Government must step in to redress major social and economic inequalities. Therefore, Americans should openly declare that Reagan was totally wrong when he said, "government is not the solution to our problems; government is the problem." Instead, Americans should accept the wisdom of Nobel Laureate Amartya Sen who said that for societies to progress they need the "invisible hand" of the free market and the "visible hand" of good governance. Americans have not used the "visible hand" in recent decades, especially since the Reagan-Thatcher revolution.

Fifthly, the American government should declare that the main goal of American society is to go from being number 28 on the Social Progress Index toward becoming number one on this index. Hence, instead of trying to become the number one military power (and wasting trillions fighting unnecessary wars), America will spend its trillions improving the living conditions of Americans measured in the Social Progress Index.

The bottom line is that solutions are out there, and they're available. But these solutions will only work if Americans agree on what the problem is. And the problem is, quite simply, plutocracy.

Can America Escape Plutocracy?

Abstract The first step in solving a problem is to admit it exists. If the US is to escape plutocracy, it must first ask itself painful questions about the pervasive influence of wealth in its politics.

Throughout human history, wise men have warned of the dangers of plutocracy. In Plato's *Republic*, Socrates warned of the dangers of selecting captains of ships by their wealth. Teddy Roosevelt also warned, "of all forms of tyranny, the least attractive and most vulgar is the tyranny of mere wealth, the tyranny of a plutocracy." Yet despite these warnings, America has gone from democracy toward becoming, for all practical purposes, a plutocracy, moving away from a government of the people, by the people and for the people to a government "of the 1%, by the 1% and for the 1%," as noted by the Nobel Laureate Joseph Stiglitz.

What's the evidence for this claim? It's massive. The wealthy have seized most of the new wealth. Anand Giridharadas, a former *New York Times* columnist, has observed that in terms of income increase since 1980, "that of the top 1% has more than tripled and that of the top 0.001% has risen more than seven fold—even as the average pretax income of the bottom half of Americans has stayed almost precisely the same." But the wealthy are not satisfied with seizing more wealth. They are also seizing political power. Two Princeton University political scientists, Gilens and Page, have documented in detail how political outcomes in America reflect the interests of the wealthy, not the mass voters. Hence, they sadly conclude "in the United States, our findings indicate, the majority does not rule—at least not in the causal sense of actually determining policy outcomes."

How did the 1% seize both greater political and economic control in America? The answer is complex. The slide began with Ronald Reagan saying that "government is not the solution; government is the problem." In most countries, especially in Europe, governments play a critical role in counter-balancing market forces and ensuring a level playing field for all citizens. By weakening the government, America has also taken away equality of opportunity. The result, as Edward Luce says, is that "studies show that an eighth grade (14-year-old) child from a lower income bracket who

Originally published in The Diplomat, Sept 28, 2020

35
K. Mahbubani, *The Asian 21st Century*, China and Globalization,
https://doi.org/10.1007/978-981-16-6811-1_5

achieves maths results in the top quarter is less likely to graduate than a kid in the upper income bracket scored in the bottom quarter. This is the reverse of how meritocracy should work."

The power of money in determining political outcomes in America was given a major boost by the Supreme Court's "Citizens United" decision of January 2010. It gave those with money the green light to spend unlimited sums on ads and other political tools to ensure the election of candidates sensitive to their interests. Martin Wolf says the "the Supreme Court's perverse 2010 'Citizens United' decision held that companies are persons and money is speech. This has proved a big step on the journey toward becoming a plutocracy."

Living in Athens 2400 years ago, Socrates warned that cities that allowed themselves to be ruled by the wealthy would have a "poor voyage." This is exactly what has happened to America. The latest Social Progress Index, which measures well-being in societies across several dimensions, shows that America is the only major developed society that has seen a deterioration in human well-being in many areas. It slipped from number 19 position in 2011 to number 28 in 2020. Nicholas Kristof links this deterioration to "deaths of despair," commenting sadly that one-quarter of the kids who rode his school bus are now dead from drugs, alcohol, and suicide. Two Princeton university economists, Case and Deaton, have also documented that there is a "sea of despair" among working-class Americans.

The existential question that American society faces today is whether it can escape from the clutches of plutocracy after it has taken hold of American society. The only brutally honest answer that one can give to these painful questions is no. Why not? To deal with a problem, one must first acknowledge that there is a problem to deal with. Currently, even though America has the world's freest and most freely independent media, no major newspaper calls America a plutocracy. Neither do the best universities in the world. Americans believe in calling a spade a spade. Yet, if any leading American politician were to call the American plutocracy a plutocracy, he would be committing political suicide. No physician can heal a patient who fails to take the necessary bitter medicine.

America will certainly have to administer bitter medicine to itself to escape from plutocracy. It will have to overturn the Citizens United Supreme Court decision. Like its fellow democracies in Europe, it will have to impose strict limits on the use of money in elections. It will also have to reverse the Reagan-Thatcher intellectual revolution and reach a rock solid consensus that "government is the solution, not the problem." To make government the solution, the pay and prestige of senior government officials will have to be increased. The leading graduates of Harvard and Yale should aspire to join the government, not Goldman Sachs or Chase Bank. Sadly, none of this will happen. America will remain a plutocracy.

What Do US Capitol Attack and the West's Covid-19 Death Rates Have in Common?

Abstract Philosophical concepts can help us to understand key historical moments. The storming of Capital Hill in America and the Covid-19 death rates in the West highlight a different balance between "rights" and "responsibilities" when compared to Eastern societies.

At the end of the day, the root cause of many of the social and political problems we face is the failure to understand the real meaning of key philosophical concepts.

I write these words with some personal satisfaction. Fifty years ago, in 1971, when I graduated from the University of Singapore with a Bachelor of Arts in philosophy, some of my friends and family members secretly believed that I had wasted four good years of my life studying useless things.

Yet, as recent developments have shown, a failure to understand key philosophical concepts can lead to a large amount of human suffering and social and political turmoil.

Two surprising recent negative developments will be studied by historians for decades, if not centuries, to come. The first is the remarkable failure of the most advanced societies in our world, especially the United States and several European Union members, to lower the death rate from Covid-19 in their societies.

The second was the storming of the US Capitol on Jan 6. Both these developments are a result of a failure to understand how key philosophical concepts cannot be understood in isolation.

Future historians will certainly be astonished to see the great disparity in the death rates from Covid-19 between leading Western societies and East Asian societies. The gap is enormous.

Originally published in The Straits Times, Feb 2, 2021

K. Mahbubani, *The Asian 21st Century*, China and Globalization,
https://doi.org/10.1007/978-981-16-6811-1_6

Disparity in Societies

So what explains this great disparity in death rates? The answer is surely complex. One root cause, however, has been the insistence of Western societies to emphasize "rights" while Asian societies focus on both "rights and responsibilities".

One reason why casualties from Covid-19 have been much higher in many Western countries is that citizens emphasize their "right" not to wear masks while never mentioning their "responsibility" to wear masks to save lives of fellow citizens. Fortunately, in most Asian societies, there is a greater acceptance of such responsibilities. This is why underlying philosophical assumptions are so important for social well-being.

I know from direct firsthand experience that many Western societies are reluctant to give equal importance to "rights" and "responsibilities". In 1998, the United Nations had a special session to commemorate the 50th anniversary of the adoption of the Universal Declaration of Human Rights (UDHR).

The UDHR is a truly moving and inspiring document. As human beings, we should worship and cherish it. Thanks to it, human rights standards in the world have improved significantly since it was launched in 1948, as documented, for example, in chapter "Asia, Say No to NATO" of psychologist Steven Pinker's book, *Enlightenment Now*.

Emphasizing Responsibilities

Yet, for centuries, Western and Asian philosophers have also emphasized the equal importance of "responsibilities". Economist and philosopher Friedrich Hayek, in *The Constitution Of Liberty*, states that "liberty and responsibility are inseparable".

Philosopher and Holocaust survivor Victor Frankl said: "Freedom, however, is not the last word. Freedom is only part of the story and half of the truth. Freedom is but the negative aspect of the whole phenomenon whose positive aspect is responsibleness. In fact, freedom is in danger of degenerating into mere arbitrariness unless it is lived in terms of responsibleness. That is why I recommend that the Statue of Liberty on the East Coast be supplemented by a Statue of Responsibility on the West Coast."

Fortunately, many leading statesmen of the world, led by the legendary former German chancellor Helmut Schmidt, decided to draft a "Universal Declaration of Human Responsibilities" to accompany the UDHR. Indeed, Mr Schmidt drafted such a declaration, which was then endorsed by several other global statesmen, including Mr Malcolm Fraser, Mr Lee Kuan Yew, Mr Pierre Trudeau and Mr Mikhail Gorbachev.

Mr. Schmidt's declaration was drafted in 1997. The perfect opportunity to have launched this Universal Declaration of Human Responsibilities was when the UN celebrated the 50th anniversary of the Universal Declaration of Human Rights. Since the West believes in the virtues of free speech and open debates, I thought that

Western governments and non-governmental organizations would support a free and open discussion of Mr Schmidt's initiative. Instead, they mounted a strong campaign to suppress all discussions of the document. I know that all this happened. I was personally present and saw all this with my own eyes.

Two decades after this suppression of the discussion of responsibilities, the time has come for the West to make a massive U-turn away from its prevailing ideology of emphasizing rights only, without giving equal emphasis to equivalent responsibilities. Such a U-turn will save lives. Indeed, many lives lost to Covid-19 could have been saved.

The second shocking development was the storming of the US Capitol last month. What was the fundamental underlying cause of the anger displayed by the predominantly white working classes on that day? One clear answer is that a "sea of despair" has emerged among white working classes in America, which Nobel laureate in economics Angus Deaton and his wife, economist Anne Case, have documented well in their book, *Deaths Of Despair And The Future Of Capitalism.*

This sea of despair is also a result of failure to understand some key philosophical concepts. In the US, for example, most politicians and pundits emphasize only the importance of "freedom". Yet, philosophers have always used the term "freedom and equality" together.

The best proof of this is provided by American philosopher John Rawls. In his classic book, *A Theory Of Justice*, he emphasizes that two principles of justice go hand in hand. The first principle emphasizes individual liberty. Yet, the second principle emphasizes that any inequality that arises from "most extensive basic liberty" must nonetheless result in a society that works to "everyone's advantage".

Unlike the concept of strict egalitarianism, which calls for the allocation of equal material goods to all members of society, Dr. Rawls' principle allows for inequalities if it helps the bottom 10% improve their lives.

This is what happened in the US for many decades, from the 1950s to 1970s. Yet, from the 1980s, the incomes and standard of living of the bottom 10%, indeed bottom 50%, have stagnated or declined. The result has been the "sea of despair", which is the result of ignoring key philosophical precepts. And, in turn, the "sea of despair" has generated 74 million votes for Mr Donald Trump and, when he lost, the violent storming of the US Capitol.

In short, when we see societies in trouble, we should not just focus on personalities and events. We should take a deep dive and try to discover the underlying structural causes.

In so doing, we will often discover that the structural cause is a failure to understand the direct and necessary correlation between key philosophical concepts, like those between rights and responsibilities and between freedom and equality.

Was Trump Right or Wrong on China? Biden's Answer Will Shape the Future

Abstract Even though Washington now agrees that the policies of the Trump Administration were a failure, a consensus has emerged that Trump was right to confront China. But after four years of worsening US-China relations under the Trump Administration, the Biden administration needs to seriously rethink Washington's approach to Beijing.

The most important question that US President Joe Biden's administration needs to ask in formulating its China policy is a simple one: was Donald Trump right or wrong on China? Right now, the overwhelming consensus in Washington is that even if he was wrong on everything else, Trump was right on China. Indeed, the only Trump policy that enjoyed bipartisan consensus was his China policy, with senior Democrats such as Nancy Pelosi and Chuck Schumer praising the president on China. There is therefore a real danger that the Biden administration will retain many elements of Trump's policies toward China. If so, America is heading toward a disaster.

The goal of this essay is a simple one: to suggest that the Biden administration should first stop and do a cool, dispassionate analysis of US-China relations and then work out a coherent, credible, and comprehensive long-term strategy toward Beijing. Currently, America lacks a strategy. Henry Kissinger confirmed this to me personally. The absence of dispassionate analysis and cool strategic calculation has effectively meant that American policy toward China has swung from one delusion to another; from the delusion of the Obama/Clinton era that American engagement would transform China into a liberal democracy to the Trump/Pompeo delusion that American pressure on China would lead to the collapse of the Chinese Communist Party (CCP). In swinging from one extreme to another, without stopping at the middle path of realism, American policy toward China is headed for failure.

Yes, the Trump administration was "right" in one sense. Chinese foreign policy had become very assertive, even arrogant, after the Global Financial Crisis of 2008, when the West looked weak. Resentment toward China, including among the key constituency of US business, had been building up in the American body politic. Hence, when the Trump administration lashed out at China, it had a healthy cathartic

---

Originally published in Global Asia, Mar 2021

K. Mahbubani, *The Asian 21st Century*, China and Globalization,
https://doi.org/10.1007/978-981-16-6811-1_7

effect. China would have also noticed that no major American voices spoke up for China when the Trump administration unleashed its anti-China frenzy.

Acknowledging a Harsh Reality

With that catharsis over, reason must return to American policymaking. What exactly did Trump accomplish with China? Did his administration's policies raise America's standing in the world, weaken China significantly, and lead to the progressive isolation of China from the vast majority of countries? The answer to all three questions is a resounding no. The reality is that the Trump administration's policies on China damaged America's standing, did no real harm to China, and did not arrest China's growing trade and economic links with the rest of the world. Therefore, the thesis of this article is very simple: If the Biden administration continues the Trump administration's policies on China, it will only result in a weakened America, a strengthened China, and a world where far more countries will have more substantive ties with China than with America.

There's a simple reason why Trump's policies on China failed. They were not based on a realistic assessment of the adversary that America was dealing with. So, here's a simple and easy step the Biden administration can take. There are six billion people living outside America and China. If America were to take the sensible step of showing a "decent respect for the opinions of mankind," what would it learn from the perceptions of other countries toward China?

First, none would agree with the Trump administration's belief that the CCP will disappear. Instead, they would agree with the considered assessment of the Harvard Kennedy School that support for the CCP among the 1.4 billion Chinese grew from 86.1% in 2003 to 93.1% in 2016. Second, more importantly, none see China as an exporter of communism to undermine democracy. Many Americans blithely claim that the CCP represents a threat to American democracy. So why don't the world's two largest democracies, India or Indonesia, or even the European democracies, see the CCP as a threat to their democracies? The biggest mistake in geopolitical calculations is to allow ideology to triumph over realistic analysis. Third, most serious leaders around the world see Xi Jinping as a capable, competent, and constructive leader. He may be close to exercising absolute power at home, however, he is capable of making compromises abroad (as with the Europeans on the China-EU investment deal and with India on the border agreement). The demonization of Xi, particularly in the Anglo-Saxon media, has been damaging because it will lead Americans to underestimate him. The undeniable reality is that American leaders are dealing with a thoughtful and strategic leader who is making careful long-term calculations. In contrast, the Trump administration was engaged in grandstanding that neither harmed China nor benefited America. Significantly, even though Trump was praised in America for bashing China, no major country supported his policies toward China. They could see these policies heading toward failure.

If this analysis is correct (and the facts prove that it is), the first critical step that the Biden administration needs to take is to acknowledge that Trump failed on China. Given the toxic anti-China political environment in Washington, it may not be wise to say this publicly. However, internally, the Biden administration must reach a considered consensus that Trump failed on China. With that consensus in hand, the Biden administration should chart an alternative path toward Beijing. Such an alternative path can be taken with five steps.

The first step is to press the "pause" button on the US-China geopolitical contest. Why? Two reasons. The whole world would cheer this "pause" because most countries want to focus first on fighting immediate challenges, such as Covid-19. Also, this "pause" would give the Biden administration time to reverse policies that haven't worked, for example, Trump's tariffs and export restrictions. The goal of those was clearly to weaken China's economy. And was it weakened? The data says no. Here's one key statistic on which US policymakers should reflect: In 2009, the size of China's retail goods market was USD 1.8 trillion while that of America was USD 4 trillion, more than double. By 2019 (after three years of Trump's trade war), the size of China's market was USD 6 trillion, more than tripling, while that of America only rose to USD 5.5 trillion, an increase of less than 1.5 times. On this trade war, Fareed Zakaria has observed that "The Biden campaign described Trump's trade war with China as 'an unmitigated disaster' that cost Americans money and jobs. When Biden was asked in an August interview whether he would keep Trump's tariffs, he answered 'no' and offered a wholesale critique of Trump's China policies. But none of that is being reversed. It's all 'under review.'" Biden was right in saying the trade war was a disaster. Hence, the rational response is to stop it.

The second step, during this "pause" period, is to do a realistic assessment of which actions by Trump may have inadvertently strengthened Xi and China. The "Longer Telegram," an anonymous essay by a former US official published earlier this year, claims that President Xi is accumulating detractors among Chinese elites. It argues: "The political reality is that the CCP is significantly divided on Xi's leadership and his vast ambitions. Senior party members have been greatly troubled by Xi's policy direction and angered by his endless demands for absolute loyalty. They fear for their own lives and the future livelihoods of their families." If this is true, America's strategy should be to deepen these Chinese divisions. Instead, because America lacks a strategy toward China, the Trump administration has effectively enhanced Xi's standing in China through the launch of the erratic trade war and, even more damagingly, by the detention in Canada of Meng Wanzhou, the daughter of the founder of Chinese telecom giant Huawei and the company's chief financial officer. Meng's detention has strongly reinforced the solidarity of the Chinese regime because it recalls powerful memories of China's "Century of Humiliation," when Western laws were applied on Chinese soil. Many Chinese leaders must have thought: what happens if my daughter is also detained by America?

Many Americans may balk at the idea that Meng should be released. Americans believe in the rule of law. Anyone who breaks American domestic laws should be punished. I agree. Yet Meng committed no crimes on American soil. Indeed, she didn't violate any American domestic laws. She was caught by the "extraterritorial" application of American laws against Iran. It's a fact that America routinely makes exemptions from such extraterritorial laws. The Biden administration should give a quiet wink to the Canadian government to release her. This would serve America's national interests. This is what geopolitical cunning is all about.

The third and most difficult step that the Biden administration will have to take is to develop a realistic understanding of the real strengths and weaknesses of its strategic adversary. Indeed, this is the most important step in any strategic competition, as emphasized by Sun Tzu in his most important maxim: "know thyself, know thy enemy; fight a hundred battles, win a hundred battles." In this context, "know thy enemy" means "know China."

In trying to understand China, the Biden administration should bear in mind a key point made by one of America's greatest strategic thinkers, George Kennan. He said that the outcome of any geopolitical contest would depend on the following: "It is rather a question of the degree to which the United States can create among the peoples of the world generally the impression of a country which knows what it wants, which is coping successfully with the problems of its internal life and with the responsibilities of a World Power, and which has a spiritual vitality capable of holding its own among the major ideological currents of the time."

If Kennan were alive today, the first question he would pose would be: which society enjoys greater "spiritual vitality," America or China? Actually, if he were alive today, he would not be able to pose this question because the very idea that a communist-run China could enjoy greater "spiritual vitality" than the world's greatest democracy is inconceivable to an American mind.

There's no question that overall, America is still today a more successful society and ahead of China in many areas. This is why my most recent book, Has China Won? begins with a fictional memo to Xi Jinping, emphasizing that China should never underestimate America. However, it would be an equally big mistake for America to underestimate China. Those Americans who believed that American engagement with China would transform China were guilty of this. Indeed, future historians will be very puzzled that a young American republic, barely 250 years old, believed that it could single-handedly transform a 4000-year-old civilization with a population four times its size. Curiously, most Americans are not even aware that this belief is somewhat arrogant.

Arrogance inhibits understanding in other ways. Few Americans are aware that for the Chinese people, especially for the bottom 50%, the past 40 years have been the best in the 4000 years of Chinese history. The Stanford University psychologist, Jean Fan, has documented that "in contrast to America's stagnation, China's culture, self-concept, and morale are being transformed at a rapid pace—mostly for the better." The overall question of whether American or Chinese society is stronger and more resilient is a massive one. It cannot be answered in a brief essay such as this one. This is why I had to write an entire book to discuss it fully. The sad reality is that most Americans just don't understand China, even though it has been around for more than four millennia. Most Americans believe that 1.4 billion Chinese people are unhappy. Hence, they cannot even conceive of the realistic possibility that the Chinese people may be swimming happily in an ocean of Chinese norms and values, which create both a sense of a well-ordered moral society and psychological well-being. By historical standards, the vast masses of Chinese people have never been better off.

Long-Term Strategy

The fourth step to take after developing a realistic understanding of China's strengths and weaknesses is to work out a comprehensive long-term strategy to manage the competition with China. This will not be easy. Some past options are not available. Containment, for example, will not be possible. More countries trade more with China than with America. Indeed, much more. Nor can America assume military superiority, especially close to China's shores. All the Pentagon war games show that American aircraft carriers and battleships are vulnerable to Chinese hypersonic missiles. Fortunately, the Mutually Assured Destruction (MAD) doctrine will prevent all-out war between America and China.

The Biden administration has been wise in reaching out to allies and friends in formulating a new China policy. Many allies and friends, including Japan, India, the UK and Australia, share American strategic concerns about the rise of Chinese power. They are worried. This is real. Yet none will join a containment policy. This is not just for economic reasons. All countries around China are asking a question that is unmentionable in American strategic circles: which economy will be bigger in a decade or two: America's or China's? Most realistic analysts expect the American economy to become number two within a decade or two. Surely, the strategic calculations of the whole world, including of America, will change when America's economy goes from being No. 1 in the world to becoming No. 2. Any serious strategic planner in America must consider this possibility. But only few brave souls dare discuss this publicly in America. It is politically taboo for any American politician to talk of this almost inevitable outcome: America could become No.2 in the world. This is another key reason why the Biden administration needs to carry out a massive strategic recalculation before proceeding full steam ahead with Trump's policies.

The fifth and final step that the Biden administration needs to take may look simple: Stop insulting China (in the way Vice President Mike Pence and Secretary of State Mike Pompeo used to do). Given the American propensity to pass judgment on other countries, this may be difficult. But the Biden administration should consider not insulting China for two reasons. First, even today, America is the only country that insults China. No other government in the world does so. In such a context, it is not China that will look isolated. America will. Second, the public insults of China feed an unconscious strain in the Western body politic that could seriously complicate Sino-American relations: the fear of the "yellow peril." This fear has surfaced from time to time, contributing to the rise of anti-Asian violence in America.

At the end of the day, what most of humanity would like to see is a rational understanding and a rational discourse between the world's two leading powers, America and China. Insults never help. One of the best definitions of a good diplomat is that he or she is someone who can tell you to go to hell in such a way that you feel you are going to enjoy the journey. Diplomacy has been around for several thousand years. It's the best weapon the Biden administration can use to build a new relationship with China, with the right balance of competition and cooperation.

Why the Trump Administration Has Helped China

Abstract With the United States riven by the Trump administration's mishandling of the coronavirus pandemic and the George Floyd protests, China is now perceived as the more competent country in the world.

Undoubtedly, the Trump administration was the most aggravating administration that China had to deal with since the normalization process that Henry Kissinger began in 1971. It launched a trade war that has damaged the Chinese economy a little. Restrictions were placed on technology exports to China. A massive effort was undertaken to cripple Huawei. Yet, the most galling move was the effort to extradite Meng Wanzhou. Applying Western laws to Chinese citizens reminds the Chinese people vividly of the Century of Humiliation when Western laws were applied on Chinese soil.

Yet, if the Chinese leaders think long-term and strategically, as they are wont to do, they could also calculate that the Trump administration may have helped China. Clearly, the Trump administration lacked any thoughtful, comprehensive, and long-term strategy to manage an ever-rising China. Nor did it heed the wise advice of key strategic thinkers, like Kissinger or George Kennan. Kennan, for example, advised that the long-term outcome of the contest with the then Soviet Union would depend on "the degree to which the United States can create among the peoples of the world" the impression of a country "which is coping with the problem of its internal life" and "which has a spiritual vitality." Post-Coronavirus and post-George Floyd, America is delivering the opposite impression. In relative terms, the Trump administration succeeded in raising the stature of China, which is now perceived as the more competent country in the world.

To be fair, America's internal problems preceded President Donald Trump. It is the only major developed country where the income of the bottom 50% has gone down for a thirty-year period leading to the creation of a "sea of despair" among the white working classes. John Rawls would have been appalled to see this. Indeed, as Martin Wolf of the Financial Times says, America has become a plutocracy. By

Originally published in The National Interest, Jun 8, 2020

contrast, China has created a meritocratic governing system. A meritocracy could well outperform a plutocracy.

Equally importantly, Kennan emphasized that America had to assiduously cultivate friends and allies. The Trump administration seriously damaged relationships with friends and allies. In private, the Europeans were appalled. Walking away from the World Health Organization (WHO) when the world never needed the WHO more, especially to help poor African countries, was massively irresponsible. Not one American ally followed the United States out of the WHO. The Trump administration also threatened tariffs on allies like Canada and Mexico, Germany and France. All this does not mean that the rest of the world will rush to embrace China. Indeed, the Europeans have developed new reservations about working closely with China. Yet, there is no doubt that diminishing global respect for the United States opens more geopolitical space for China. Madeleine Albright once said "We are the indispensable nation. We stand tall and we see further than other countries into the future." The Trump administration may very well have succeeded in making America a dispensable nation, presenting another geopolitical gift to China.

The Trump administration also ignored another wise piece of advice of George Kennan: to not insult one's adversaries. No other Administration has insulted China as much as the Trump administration. Trump has said "China's pattern of misconduct is well known. For decades, they have ripped off the United States like no one has ever done before."

In theory, such insults could have damaged the standing of the Chinese government in the eyes of its own people. The effect has been the opposite. According to the latest Edelman Trust Barometer, the country where the people have the highest trust in their government is China. It is 90%. This is not surprising. For the vast majority of Chinese people, the past 40 years of social and economic development have been the best in four thousand years. Kennan spoke of domestic "spiritual vitality." China enjoys it today. A Stanford University psychologist, Jean Fan, has observed that "in contrast to America's stagnation, China's culture, self-concept, and morale are being transformed at a rapid pace—mostly for the better." The Chinese people are also acutely aware that China has handled the coronavirus crisis better than America. If America had the same rate of fatalities as China, then it would have had one thousand deaths instead of one hundred thousand. Against this backdrop, the constant insults hurled at China have only provoked a strong nationalistic response, boosting the standing of the Chinese government. One small but critical point needs to be added here: no other government in the world hurls insults at China. America stands alone in this dimension, ignoring once again Kennan's valuable advice: "And if there were any qualities that lie within our ability to cultivate that might set us off from the rest of the world, these would be the virtues of modesty and humility."

If he were alive today, then Kennan would first advise his fellow Americans to step back and thoughtfully work out a comprehensive long-term strategy before plunging into a major geopolitical contest against China. Any such strategy, heeding the advice of thinkers like Sun Tzu, would first require a comprehensive evaluation of the relative strengths and weaknesses of both parties.

There is no doubt that America retains many magnificent strengths. It remains the most successful society humanity has created since human history began. No other society has sent a man to the moon. No other society has produced a Google and Facebook, Apple and Amazon, in short order. Even more remarkably, two of its biggest corporations, Google and Microsoft, are run by foreign-born citizens. No major Chinese corporation is run by a non-Chinese. China can tap the talent of 1.4 billion people; America can tap the talent of 7.8 billion, including talented Chinese. It would be a huge mistake for any Chinese leader to underestimate America. Fortunately, or unfortunately, that is not likely to happen.

By contrast, in evaluating China's relative strengths and weaknesses, the Trump administration made the mistake of underestimating China. Here the supreme ideological conviction that democracies will always triumph against a communist party system creates particular ideological blindness in America. In reality, functionally, the CCP does not stand for the Chinese Communist Party. It stands for the Chinese Civilization Party. The key goal of the CCP is not to revive communism globally. It is to revive the world's oldest civilization and make it again one of the world's most respected civilizations. This is the goal that energizes the Chinese people and explains the unusual vibrancy and vitality of Chinese society. Equally importantly, the Chinese civilization has historically been the most resilient civilization. As Professor Wang Gungwu says, it is the only civilization to have been knocked four times over four thousand years. Each time it stood up again. There is no doubt that Chinese civilization is now a great renaissance.

It is therefore unwise for any American strategic thinker to assume that Americans cannot lose. It's true that America hasn't lost a major contest in over a hundred years but it has never had to deal with a competitor as formidable as China. Equally importantly, if the primary goal of the CCP is to improve the well-being of its people (and thereby revive Chinese civilization), there need not be a fundamental contradiction with the primary goal of any new American administration: to once again improve the well-being of the American people. Hence, when the Trump administration goes and America tries again to work out a more thoughtful long-term strategy toward China, it should consider a now unthinkable option: a strong Chinese civilization and a strong America can live together in peace in the twenty-first century. If this happens, the world will be relieved and even cheer for the outcome. And the American people will be better off.

Why American Presidents Matter

Abstract The zeitgeist of the world is infused by the character of the US leader. Biden will bring back the civility and generosity that the American spirit is associated with.

The first American president to enter my personal consciousness was John F. Kennedy. It wasn't his stirring rhetoric that reached me as a child in Singapore. It was the news of his assassination. The sense of loss was globally palpable. History has been kind to him.

He was succeeded by Lyndon Baines Johnson. As a child, I was puzzled. How could someone so ugly succeed someone who was so attractive? Indeed, he was boorish. Legend has it that he would summon his staff to meetings while sitting on his toilet seat, doing his business.

Still, history will be kind to him. His bold and massive civil rights legislation changed the course of US history. This may explain why he has the most voluminous and still unfinished biography of any recent American president, in the four volumes by Robert Caro.

History has been unkind to Richard Nixon, his successor. Watergate killed him. The liberal media has not forgiven him. Yet there's no doubt that he changed the course of human history. Without Mr. Nixon, Henry Kissinger could not have gone to China.

Mr. Lee Kuan Yew named Mr. Nixon as the greatest American president he had met, saying: "But for the misfortune of Watergate, I would say Richard Nixon. He had a realistic view of the world. He was a great analyst, realistic, but also a tactician to get things done."

When Mr. Nixon stepped down, Mr. Lee lost a true friend in the White House, a major asset for the leader of a small country.

This partially explained the contempt Mr. Lee had for Jimmy Carter, whom he considered naive. In Tom Plate's book, *Giants Of Asia: Conversations With Lee Kuan Yew*, Mr. Lee named Mr. Carter the worst president, saying of him: "Your job as a

---

Originally published in The Straits Times, Nov 10, 2020

K. Mahbubani, *The Asian 21st Century*, China and Globalization, https://doi.org/10.1007/978-981-16-6811-1_9

leader is to inspire and to galvanize, not to share your distraught thoughts. You make your people dispirited."

Fortunately, Mr. Carter was succeeded by the two-term Ronald Reagan, another admirer of Mr. Lee. I was present when they met in the White House. Still, as a Singapore diplomat in Washington and New York during Mr. Reagan's era, I experienced the condescension the liberal media displayed toward him. However, history has been very kind to Mr. Reagan, especially because of his spectacular victory over the Soviet Union.

Mr. Reagan was succeeded by another great friend and admirer of Mr. Lee, George H. W. Bush. I was present in a small room in St Petersburg, Russia, in the late 1990s when Mr. Bush confirmed that the No. 1 leader he admired in the world was Mr. Lee. I reported this to him. Sadly, Mr .Bush became a one-term president, and his departure was another huge blow to Mr. Lee.

The point of these stories is a simple one. The selection of an American president has huge consequences for the world, including Singapore.

What Biden Offers

Indeed, given the overwhelming power of America, especially in the media and communication dimensions, the zeitgeist of the world is infused by the character and personality of the American president.

Donald Trump's narcissistic and self-absorbed personality has deprived the world of a major source of inspiration, especially after Barack Obama. So what does the election of Joe Biden bring to the world? Will good times return? The short answer is yes and no. Mr. Biden is a truly decent human being. He will bring back the civility and generosity that the American spirit is associated with. However, Mr. Biden also knows that he is taking over a deeply divided country, as demonstrated by the huge numbers who voted for Mr. Trump even though he was defeated. His priority is to heal his country, not create a better world.

Nonetheless, Mr. Biden has at least three opportunities he can capitalize on to retain his positive glow. First, he can bring back some boredom to the White House. Both America and the world have become exhausted by Mr. Trump's tweets and in-your-face presence. Some calm and reticence by the Biden administration will help to return the world to a certain degree of normalcy. Mr. Biden knows that he cannot do this alone. Fortunately, he has assembled a formidable transitional team of real American heavyweights. They share Mr. Biden's distress over the divisions in the country. Repairing the wounds in American society and bringing back a happy America will be the main priority.

The second opportunity is geopolitical. Mr. Biden cannot reverse the US-China geopolitical contest, for reasons I have documented in my book, *Has China Won?* He would be persecuted if he is seen to be soft on China. Yet, even if he cannot reverse course on China, he can press the pause button on the contest. Americans believe in common sense. Simple common sense would say that Americans should first deal with the pressing challenges of Covid-19 and economic slowdown, not to mention global warming. All these problems would be better handled with some degree of cooperation with China. Just as Winston Churchill partnered an adversary, Joseph Stalin, to defeat Adolf Hitler, Mr. Biden can partner a competitor, China, to defeat Covid-19. Both Mr. Nixon and Mr. Lee would have approved such a Machiavellian maneuver against a common foe.

The third opportunity lies in stopping America's drift toward a plutocracy. One key reason why Mr. Trump was elected in 2016 was because of the "sea of despair" among the white working classes. This is because America is the only major developed economy where the average income of the bottom 50% has gone down. The anguish of these white working classes must be dealt with. Some redistribution must take place.

Mr. Reagan delegitimized taxes. Mr. Biden must re-legitimize them. And, if America's many plutocrats are wise, they would support him.

In short, Mr. Biden can apply some gentle soothing balm on the many wounds generated by the Trump presidency. His greatest asset is his decency. Plain decency will bring a lot of healing to America. Mr. Trump may have been cruel to call him "Sleepy Joe". Yet a "Sleepy Joe" and calm American presidency may be good for America and the world.

What Biden Will Mean for the Rest of the World

Abstract The decisions facing President Biden will be complex and multifaceted, but if he acts shrewdly, the US-China relationship can still lead to a more stable global environment. How can the world navigate the US-China relationship, and what should Biden learn from the rest of the world?

Project Syndicate You've warned that "the international order has lagged dangerously behind shifting global power dynamics." Will US President-elect Joe Biden's administration improve prospects of reform?

Kishore Mahbubani Sadly, the answer is no. The combination of intellectual laziness and political inertia has fueled the belief in Washington, DC, that weaker multilateral institutions are better for America's national interests. But, while that logic may have had some merit in a unipolar world, it does not suit the multipolar world in which we live. As Bill Clinton put it in 2003, the United States should be trying to create the kind of world in which it would like to live when it is "no longer the military, political, and economic superpower."

America's proclivity for constraining multilateral institutions goes back decades, perhaps as far as Ronald Reagan's presidency. For example, the US has long fought to reduce its contributions to the United Nations, and has even withheld payments, even though the money saved is a drop in the bucket of the US budget.

If the Biden administration is truly committed to multilateralism—and, more fundamentally, to being a good global citizen—it should immediately pay all US arrears. This would send a powerful message, opening the way for a broader rethink of the twentieth-century multilateral order and make it fit for purpose in the (Asia-led) twenty-first century.

PS In January 2019, you noted that President Donald Trump was trusted by much of the bottom 50% of earners. Trump's opponents thus faced a choice: "feel good by condemning Trump" or "do good by attacking the elite interests that contributed to his election." Biden stuck to the first path. But by running largely on the platform that he wasn't Trump, he will enter the White House with the US as politically polarized

Originally published in Project Syndicate, Nov 24, 2020

K. Mahbubani, *The Asian 21st Century*, China and Globalization,
https://doi.org/10.1007/978-981-16-6811-1_10

as ever. Are there lessons in building trust and broadly credible institutions that the Biden administration should take from East Asia?

KM The first lesson that the Biden administration should take from East Asia begins with a look at the relative distribution of income. The latest data for Japan (2012) show that 12.3% of the country's total income goes to the top 1% of earners, while 19.6% of the total goes to the bottom 50%. In South Korea, the latest comparable figures (2015) are 14 and 19.3%.

In the US, the figures are reversed, with the top 1% claiming 18.7% of total income, and the bottom 50% getting just 13.5% (as of 2019). The simple explanation for this imbalance is that the US has become a plutocracy, in which the super-wealthy have hijacked the political system to advance their own interests. As the political scientists Martin Gilens and Benjamin Page wrote in 2014, "Economic elites and organized groups representing business interests have substantial independent impacts on US government policy, while average citizens and mass-based interest groups have little or no independent influence."

This has contributed significantly to the despair and frustration that have enveloped the white working class, fueling support for the supposedly "anti-establishment" Trump. But, far from breaking economic elites' hold over government, Trump's actions—from hiring industry insiders to lead regulatory agencies to cutting taxes for the wealthiest Americans—reinforce plutocracy.

If Biden wants to build the kind of public trust and credible institutions seen in East Asia, he will need to reject plutocracy unequivocally. This means, first and foremost, introducing tough new regulations on money in politics. Here, Australia also provides a model worth emulating.

PS Perhaps the only matter on which US Democrats and Republicans agree is that China's rise represents a threat to US interests—a simplistic and dangerous view that you condemned in 2018. While Biden will presumably act less crudely and impetuously than Trump, do you think this will actually leave China better off? Or do you envision Biden taking a more methodical approach—possibly with the support of once-alienated allies—to "containing" China?

KM On China, Biden's hands are tied. Given the overwhelming bipartisan consensus, appearing weak on China would be political suicide. Biden is well aware of this: he called Chinese President Xi Jinping a "thug" during the election campaign, precisely to dispel any doubts about his willingness to take a tough line.

Yet, as former US Secretary of State Henry Kissinger once pointed out to me, the US lacks any real strategy for dealing with China. If Biden is truly shrewd, he will devise one that advances core American interests (such as protecting US businesses in China) and permits cooperation on shared challenges, like the Covid-19 crisis. If Winston Churchill could cooperate with Josef Stalin to fight Adolf Hitler, the US can certainly manage to work with China to end a pandemic.

At the same time, Biden should recognize that China still represents massive economic opportunities for the US. American farmers have been badly hit by Trump's reckless trade wars. They would be far better off if Biden gradually reduced the trade sanctions on China and improved US farmers' access to Chinese markets. Beyond the economic benefits, this would help to erode Trump's base, improving Democrats' electoral prospects in the coming years.

PS On the Chinese side, to what extent have policymakers grasped the intensity of the shift in US public and elite opinion, and reconsidered their "calm and rational policies toward the US"? How might their calculations change under the Biden administration, and how should they change?

KM China has one big strategic advantage: it always plays the long game. As Kissinger notes in his 2011 book On China, the Chinese play Wei Qi, not chess. And, as he puts it, "Wei Qi is about the protracted campaign." So, while the US lurches from one administration to another, China has been quietly executing its long-planned maneuvers, gradually and consistently strengthening its position.

Deepening international ties—including with faraway countries—is central to China's strategy. Consider Brazil. In 2000, it took six months for the country to trade $1 billion worth of goods with China; today, it takes 72 h. Moreover, a Brazilian is at the helm of the New Development Bank, established by the BRICS countries (Brazil, Russia, India, China, and South Africa). Such ties have bolstered the bilateral relationship, even as Brazil's right-wing populist president, Jair Bolsonaro, has emulated the China-bashing Trump in other ways.

But China has also made serious strategic mistakes. A tsunami of anti-China sentiment engulfed India after last June's clashes on the Himalayan border, which left 20 Indian soldiers dead. And some ASEAN countries remain troubled by China's territorial claims in the South China Sea.

China's leaders are astute enough to recognize that if Biden does restore America's reputation as a reliable ally, a formidable group of countries might join the US in confronting China. Given this, China's leaders should work hard to establish constructive, mutually beneficial relations with the Biden administration, remaining all the while "calm and rational."

PS In your recent book, *Has China Won? The Chinese Challenge to American Primacy*, you note that when you served in the Singapore Foreign Service, you learned a "big lesson" from Singapore's three exceptional geopolitical masters (Lee Kuan Yew, Goh Keng Swee, and S. Rajaratnam): The first step to formulate any long-term strategy is to frame the right questions. As US strategists attempt to develop "new analytical frameworks to capture the essence of the competition with China," what questions must they answer first?

KM In *Has China Won?*, I spell out ten major questions, all of which the Biden administration should consider. Here is another big one: What happens if China's economy surpasses America's in the next decade or two?

For many in Washington, DC, this scenario is unthinkable. But the truth is that it's entirely possible. It's also possible that the US can remain the world's most influential country, even if it becomes the number two economic power. George Kennan, the master strategist who shaped US policy toward the Soviet Union during the Cold War, explained how in 1947: the US creates "among the peoples of the world generally" the impression that it is successful domestically and enjoys a "spiritual vitality."

If he were alive today, Kennan would heartily disapprove of US strategists' belief that the country's global primacy is more important than the interests of its people. He would also strongly oppose the relentless growth of defense spending. After all, Kennan would surely recognize, the outcome of the US-China geopolitical contest will be determined not by bullets and bombs, but by the two countries' relative "spiritual vitality." That is why the Biden administration should shift America's focus from maintaining global primacy to improving human well-being.

PS In May, you said that Hong Kong had become a "pawn" in the geopolitical chess match between the US and China. Have China's decisive moves to assert the mainland's control there given it an advantage in the game? Where does that leave the people of Hong Kong?

KM All "great powers" put their national interests ahead of those of smaller autonomous territories. US Republicans block Puerto Rico from becoming a state because they worry that the extra votes would go largely to Democrats. Similarly, China's central government will not allow instability in Hong Kong to destabilize China and undermine its strategic position vis-à-vis the US. That is why the National Security Law was passed.

The conventional wisdom is that Hong Kong will suffer mightily as a result of increased central government control. But it is just as likely that the increased stability will leave Hong Kong's people better off, especially if the city government can finally overcome vested interests and expand its public housing program significantly. This would go a long way toward addressing a major source of popular anger in Hong Kong.

PS What advice do you have for the leaders of other territories and countries that are likely to get caught in the crossfire of the Sino-American rivalry?

KM Don't make the same mistake as Australia. In Asian cultures, including China's, saving face is important. When Australia publicly called for an international inquiry into China's handling of the Covid-19 crisis, it put China on the spot. With so many eyes on the standoff, China cannot blink—or it will risk more confrontations with more countries. So, all Australia will get from its initiative is a slow, painful war of economic attrition.

Fortunately, most countries have made clear that they don't want to take sides in the US-China rivalry. Neither the US nor China should try to force them to.

PS You note in Has China Won? your diverse array of cultural connections that extend across Asia. But your description of those linkages reveals an active interest in searching for them, such as through your name's Arabic-Persian roots. How, if at all, did this inclination influence your decade of service as an ambassador to the UN, and what does it tell us about the conceptual limits of the nation-state?

KM The personal cultural connectedness I have felt across a wide range of countries, from Morocco to South Korea, has been a huge advantage in my career as a diplomat and writer. In Morocco, I heard my favorite singer, Mohammad Rafi, perform in a remote village. In Korea, I encountered the story of the Indian princess who landed on the peninsula in the first century AD.

This cultural connectedness makes me a keen optimist. I believe that, over time, we will look at shared challenges like global warming and the Covid-19 pandemic, and recognize that we belong to common humanity. Nation states have become like small cabins on a larger global boat. Having the most luxurious cabin means nothing if the boat sinks.

East and West: Trust or Distrust?

Abstract The return of Asia to the center stage of world history can be explained in part by its absorbing of the wisdom and ideas of Western civilization. But to stem the rising distrust between East and West, the West must now learn some critical lessons from China's Asian neighbors on how to manage the rise of China.

The world stands at one of its most important crossroads in human history. As we move inexorably away from the brief era of Western domination of human history, societies from the East and the West will have to find a new balance. And there are two clear paths that the East and West can take: toward convergence or divergence.

In theory, there should be divergence. Many Asian societies and civilizations still have strong memories of Western domination. At its peak, the West trampled on the Islamic world, effortlessly colonized India and humiliated China. As once downtrodden societies recover their civilizational strength and vigor, it would be perfectly natural to return with a desire to wreak vengeance on the West. As Samuel Huntington once famously predicted, the world should be experiencing a clash of civilizations.

Instead, the opposite has happened. Thanks to the generous gifts of Western wisdom, especially the gift of Western reasoning, there is a fundamental convergence taking place in the dreams and ambitions of young people in both East and West. As Larry Summers and I observed in our 2016 essay "The Fusion of Civilizations," "most people around the world now have the same aspirations as the Western middle classes: they want their children to get good educations, land good jobs, and live happy, productive lives as members of stable, peaceful communities. Instead of feeling depressed, the West should be celebrating its phenomenal success at injecting the key elements of its worldview into other great civilizations."

A few years later, Yuval Noah Harari reached the same conclusion when he observed in Sapiens that nearly all humans today share the same geopolitical, economic, legal, and scientific systems. As he argues, "today when Iran and the United States rattle swords at one another, they both speak the language of nation states, capitalist economies, international rights, and nuclear physics." There is no

Originally published in Edelman Trust Barometer, Jan 19, 2020

K. Mahbubani, *The Asian 21st Century*, China and Globalization, https://doi.org/10.1007/978-981-16-6811-1_11

better living proof of the possible psychological convergence between Iran and America than the foreign minister of Iran, Mohammad Javad Zarif. His deep knowledge and understanding of Western history and culture would put many great Western minds to shame.

Thanks to the spread of Western wisdom and the global convergence on norms such as the rule of law, the societies with the highest levels of trust in both government and business today are China, Indonesia, India, and the UAE, much higher than in many Western countries including the United States, United Kingdom, Germany and France.

The magical benefits of greater convergence between Eastern and Western minds can be seen in the most competitive human laboratory of the world. When young entrepreneurs flock to Silicon Valley in search of the next start-up and when young freshmen enroll in the greatest Ivy League universities, they are barely aware that they come from the East or the West. Instead, they speak a common language of aspirations and see no problem collaborating across cultures in search of achieving extraordinary excellence. Similarly, when Chinese university presidents strive to create the best universities in the world, they know that they have to emulate the best practices of American and European universities. In short, many forces are pushing the 7.5 billion people of the world toward greater convergence. All this should naturally lead to greater trust between the East and the West.

Yet, there are also equally strong forces pushing humanity toward divergence. One has already broken out: the geopolitical contest between the US and China. This will be a multidimensional contest, in economics and politics, in the military and cultural spheres. Kiron Skinner, the former director of policy planning in the State Department, astutely observed that this would be the first struggle that the US would have with a "non-Caucasian power." She put her finger on a key factor that would lead to distrust between the US and China.

This distrust explains how the forces of science and technology, which have been propelling humanity toward a common understanding of our natural world and which have built bridges across cultures, can now become a divisive force. If a German or French (or even Japanese or Indian) telecommunications company had been the leader in developing 5G technology, the US would have acquiesced. However, when a Chinese company, Huawei, became the technological leader, the US balked and decided to throttle Huawei. As Tom Friedman presciently observed, "However much justified, this move was the equivalent of China freezing out Apple and Microsoft. It was an earthquake in China's tech lands… Lots of Chinese tech companies are now thinking: We will never, ever, ever leave ourselves again in a situation where we are totally dependent on America for key components. Time to double down on making our own."

The struggle over Huawei is only the tip of a massive iceberg. The US will make a major effort to "decouple" itself from Chinese technology, perhaps in the hope that this will stall China's development. It could. But it would be unwise to bet on it. As Asia's leading historian Professor Wang Gungwu has wisely observed, China is the only major civilization that has fallen down four times and stood up again each time.

Right now, it has only just begun to revitalize its civilizational sinews. The return of China is unstoppable.

Having defeated the mighty Soviet Union without firing a shot, it would be perfectly natural for American strategic planners to believe that America will prevail again. And it well could. However, the world of 2020 is vastly different from the world of 1950 when the Cold War began. All around the world, strong and self-confident societies are emerging. The 6 billion people of the world who live outside the US and China will not be easily dragooned to join one side or another. They will make their own choices.

America and the West could well learn some valuable lessons from how China's Asian neighbors manage the rise of China. Many of these neighbors share some Western concerns about the rise of China. However, having lived with China for thousands of years, they also know it would be futile to stop China. Instead, each of the neighbors, including major and middle powers like India and Japan, South Korea and Vietnam, will make pragmatic adjustments: pushing back against China when necessary, cooperating when it is mutually beneficial.

As the twenty-first century progresses steadily toward a multicivilizational world, the West could well learn a lesson or two from supple Asian minds. Instead of seeing the world in black and white terms, where binary choices are made between trust and distrust, the West could learn to live with successful non-Western societies, which were both similar and different from Western societies. They will share some key Western attitudes and retain their unique civilizational identities in other dimensions. This may well be the biggest test for Western societies in the realm of trust: can they "trust" societies that will never be fully Western in their identity?

Great Battles Require Strategic Discipline—And Washington Needs It in This Crisis

Abstract The US must learn tact and discipline in the style of Churchill and Kissinger to weather the Covid-19 storm and come out of this crisis on the right side of history.

At a dark moment of World War II, in August 1942, British Prime Minister Winston Churchill flew to Moscow to have dinner with Soviet Premier Joseph Stalin. The ideological gap between them was far greater than the gap between the US and China today. Yet Churchill didn't hesitate to cooperate with Stalin. Why not?

An old strategic adage holds that in any great war, one should focus on the main battlefield and not get distracted by secondary issues. The great Prussian military theorist Carl von Clausewitz wrote, "The talent of the strategist is to identify the decisive point and to concentrate everything on it, removing forces from secondary fronts and ignoring lesser objectives." US Secretary of State Mike Pompeo, who graduated first in his class from West Point, should know this strategic adage well.

Today, if Churchill were leading America's war against a pandemic, he would advise focusing on the main battlefront, Covid-19, rather than getting distracted by the ongoing geopolitical contest with China. Indeed, just as he dined with Stalin, Churchill would advise America to cooperate with China. Sadly, few voices in America are recommending such Churchillian wisdom.

Only President Trump, with his usual flair for unusual moves, could put in a phone call to Chinese President Xi Jinping on March 27, 2020. Yet, at the same time, the Trump administration has been sending contradictory signals. Its campaign against Huawei has not abated; the Trump administration is considering additional measures to restrict the supply of chips to the Chinese technology giant. On March 27, President Trump also signed a law obliging Washington to raise global support for Taiwan, a direct slap in the face for Beijing. Churchill, if he were alive today, would disapprove of these contradictory approaches. He would have said, "Focus on the main battlefront."

America has seen huge spikes in Covid-19 cases. Indeed, America now has more cases than any other country in the world. More dangerously, the number

Originally published in The Hill, Apr 10, 2020

K. Mahbubani, *The Asian 21st Century*, China and Globalization,
https://doi.org/10.1007/978-981-16-6811-1_12

of fatalities could run from as high as 200,000 to 1.7 million, as per projections based on the Centers for Disease Control and Prevention (CDC) scenarios. Off and on, America has desperately needed masks, ventilators, gowns, gloves, and other personal protective equipment (PPE) for health care personnel and other workers.

On March 29, 2020, a plane from Shanghai landed at JFK Airport in New York, carrying 12 million gloves, 130,000 N95 masks, 1.7 million surgical masks, 50,000 gowns, 130,000 hand-sanitizer units, and 36,000 thermometers. Yet, these amounts were a drop in the ocean. Even France ordered a billion masks, a vast majority of them from China.

Instead of relying on domestic commercial channels, the US government should work with the Chinese government. To foster such effective government-to-government cooperation, a few simple steps should have been taken. The first would have been to stop insulting China; it was unwise, for example, for the Trump administration to try to persuade the G-7 countries to call Covid-19 the "Wuhan virus." The main lesson we should take away from this massive global outbreak is that all 7.5 billion inhabitants of Planet Earth have become like the passengers on the ill-fated cruise ship off Japan, the Diamond Princess: Our destinies, especially our health destinies, are intertwined. We have to work together to solve this crisis. It's not smart to argue about who sprung the leak when a boat is sinking; what matters is how we respond to it. A clear signal from the Trump administration should have been to stop scapegoating China, which would calm countries and markets all around the world, including the US.

There's one other simple step that Churchill would advise the US to take: President Trump should announce that he will immediately rescind all the tariff and non-tariff measures he imposed on China, with the understanding that China will do the same. This may not lead to a major boost in trade or economic growth immediately. It will, however, send a powerful signal to the markets that when Covid-19 begins to retreat, both the economic growth and the international trade will bounce back faster.

President Trump will lose nothing from making such an announcement. And he could extend it further by withdrawing all threats to raise tariffs on allies such as the European Union, Japan, Canada, and Mexico. The markets will take note of these soothing measures. We all feel nostalgic for the world before the pandemic. By sending signals that the world will eventually return to the status quo ante, we will build up confidence in the future that will come when Covid-19 recedes, as it surely will.

When we return to the status quo ante, we may well return once again to a resumption of the US-China geopolitical contest. Before America do so again, however, it may wish to heed the advice of its own strategic thinkers, like Henry Kissinger and George Kennan. It was unwise of America to plunge headlong into a geopolitical contest against China without first working out a comprehensive long-term strategy, as I argue in the book, *Has China Won?*

If America presses the "pause" button on the US-China geopolitical contest now, as Churchill would advise it to do, this pause should provide American strategic thinkers the time to ponder all the dimensions of this contest before plunging in again. It also would provide Americans an opportunity to discover where the rest of the world stands on this issue. During the Cold War, all of Europe enthusiastically supported America. Today, it is unclear that Europe would do so: Some Italians in Rome played the Chinese National Anthem on public loudspeakers, and Serbia's president cried and kissed the Chinese flag, after urgently needed medical supplies arrived in both countries from China; in Spain, citizens trended "Gracias China" on Twitter to thank China for sending medical supplies and personnel; the French foreign minister expressed his gratitude to China for providing much-needed medical supplies, including surgical masks, protective suits, and gloves.

This doesn't mean that all will be lost for America in this geopolitical contest. It only means that America will have to emulate the wisdom of great strategic thinkers, like Churchill, Kissinger, and Kennan—and think hard before making its next, critical moves.

The Asian Renaissance

From the years 1 to 1820, the largest economies in the world were Asian. After 1820 and the rise of the West, however, great Asian civilizations like China and India were dominated and humiliated. The 21st Century will see the return of Asia to the centre of the world stage.

On the Dawn of the Asian Century

Abstract The recent pandemic has revealed the strengths of Asian societies and the weaknesses of Western societies. The West's incompetent response to the pandemic will hasten the power shift to the East and herald the dawn of the Asian Century.

History has turned a corner. The era of Western domination is ending. The resurgence of Asia in world affairs and the global economy, which was happening before the emergence of Covid-19, will be cemented in a new world order after the crisis. The deference to Western societies, which was the norm in the nineteenth and twentieth centuries, will be replaced by growing respect and admiration for East Asian ones. The pandemic could thus mark the start of the Asian century.

The crisis highlights the contrast between the competent responses of East Asian governments (notably China, South Korea and Singapore) and the incompetent responses of Western governments (such as Italy, Spain, France, Britain, and America). The far lower death rates suffered by East Asian countries is a lesson to all. They reflect not just medical capabilities, but also the quality of governance and the cultural confidence of their societies.

What has shocked many in Asia is the reluctance of some Western governments to allow science—and basic epidemiological modeling—to determine the policy responses. After its initial missteps in Wuhan (which were clearly disastrous), China firmly deployed good science and robust public policy measures to break the back of the problem. It responsibly released the genetic data as soon as Chinese scientists sequenced the genome of the virus on January 12th.

A half century ago, had a similar global pandemic broken out, the West would have handled it well and the developing countries of East Asia would have suffered. Today the quality of governance in East Asia sets the global standard. The leaders who turned their countries around, such as Deng Xiaoping in China and Lee Kuan Yew in Singapore, planted the seeds of knowledge, internationalism, and order in their societies. These have blossomed into respect for science and technology, a culture of pragmatism, a willingness to learn best practices from around the world,

---

Originally published in The Economist, Apr 20, 2020

© The Author(s) 2022
K. Mahbubani, *The Asian 21st Century*, China and Globalization,
https://doi.org/10.1007/978-981-16-6811-1_13

and a desire to catch up with the West. These went along with deep investments in critical public goods such as education, health care, and the environment.

The result is that the post-Covid-19 world will be one in which other countries look to East Asia as a role model, not only for how to handle a pandemic but how to govern more generally.

Ever since Ronald Reagan declared, "Government is not the solution to our problem; government is the problem," in his inaugural address in 1981, there has been a progressive delegitimization and consequently, demoralization, of public services in America. President Donald Trump didn't create this problem. He aggravated it. The Centers for Disease Control and Prevention (CDC) in Atlanta was one of the most globally respected agencies. Yet Mr Trump proposed to cut the CDC's budget even after Covid-19 emerged. The world gasped in horror.

By contrast, East Asian societies have believed in the wise insight of Amartya Sen, a Nobel laureate in economics, that for societies to succeed they need the invisible hand of free markets and the visible hand of good governance. China now arguably has the most meritocratic government in the world. The post-Covid-19 world will see China accelerate both for the public's benefit—and the balance of strong markets and good governance will be an appealing model for other countries.

China was a feudal society for thousands of years and the brains of the vast majority at the bottom of society were never used. Given the tribulations it suffered in its "century of humiliation" from the mid nineteenth and twentieth centuries, China understands well the dangers of a weak government. And because the Chinese psyche fears chaos more than any other force, the people welcome a strong state. The public's trust in its leaders has been enhanced by the successful response to Covid-19.

Clearly, there are sharp differences between the communist system of China and the societies of South Korea, Japan, Taiwan, and Singapore. Yet one feature they share in common is a belief in strong government institutions run by the best and the brightest. This emphasis on meritocracy also has deep roots in Confucian culture. The entry bar to the Chinese Communist Party is set very high: only the top graduating students are admitted. Equally importantly, the rising levels of competent governance are both fueled by, and contribute to, rising levels of cultural confidence. All this is gradually eroding the natural deference to the West that used to be the norm in Asia.

Taken together, the competence and confidence of East Asia will reshape the world order. It has already begun. Twenty years ago, no Chinese national ran any United Nations Organization. Today they oversee four: the Food and Agriculture Organization, the International Telecommunication Union, the UN Industrial DevelopmentOrganization and the International Civil Aviation Organization. If the International Monetary Fund and World Bank remain bastions of Western power, insisting that only Europeans and Americans can run the shop, they will progressively lose their credibility unless they allow Asians (as well as Africans and Latin Americans) to manage them. Failure to adapt hurts any organism—including international organizations.

The rules-based global order was a gift by the West to the world after the Second World War. Will China overturn it when it becomes the world's undisputed economic power, as it eventually will? Here is the good news. As the current, biggest beneficiary of this order (since China is already the world's largest trading power), the country will preserve the rules. However, China will systematically try to reduce American influence in international organizations. In early 2020 China put up a candidate to run the World Intellectual Property Organization. America campaigned ferociously against her. In the end, a neutral candidate from Singapore won. This provides a foretaste of fractious battles to come.

Even Europeans are becoming disenchanted with American-led world order. Few will forget that in the same week that the Trump administration banned travel from Europe (without any advance notice), the Chinese government sent medical equipment including masks, ventilators, protective suits, and doctors to Italy and Spain. This is why the Group of Seven countries resisted pressure by America to call Covid-19 the "Wuhan virus" in a communique after a virtual meeting in March.

However, this does not mean the world will shift to a solely China-led order. Countries do not want to be forced to choose between China and America, as I document in my latest book, *Has China Won?* (Public Affairs, 2020). There will still be concerns over China's rise, especially among its neighbors. No one feels comfortable sharing a small room with an elephant, no matter how benign.

Most would welcome a continuing American presence to balance China's influence. Yet they wish to see a competent and careful American presence, not one that forces them to choose between the two systems—as if America's "with us or against us" ethos were the only options.

To maintain its role and its respect, America will have to demonstrate remarkable diplomatic dexterity. Yet its foreign service has never been more demoralized; the Chinese one never more confident. Fortunately, all is not lost for America. In South-East Asia, for example, there remain huge reservoirs of goodwill after many years of American engagement in the region, which its diplomats can tap.

As China's weight in global affairs grows, it will have to take on greater responsibilities. America has progressively walked away from the family of United Nations institutions. China has not, and may use its new confidence to take on a larger role. For example, before the pandemic the World Health Organization (WHO) had been weakened by an effort led by the West, starting in the 1970s, to reduce the share of funding that member states are obliged to pay and make the majority of its budget come from voluntary contributions. Today, some 80% of WHO's budget is voluntary. China could demonstrate global leadership by calling for a charge to restore the mandatory funding to its earlier level of around 60%, since WHO can only develop long-term capabilities on the basis of predictable, compulsory contributions.

But that may just be a start. The world after the crisis may see a hobbled West and a bolder China. We can expect that China will use its power. Paradoxically, a China-led order could turn out to be a more "democratic" order. China doesn't want to export its model. It can live with a diverse multipolar world. The coming Asian century need not be uncomfortable for the West or the rest of the world.

ASEAN's Quiet Resilience

Abstract Many expected ASEAN to falter under the strain of rising geopolitical tensions. But as its leadership on the Regional Comprehensive Economic Partnership shows, ASEAN has quietly managed to deliver peace and economic growth to Southeast Asia, helping to uphold a global, multilateral trading order.

ASEAN should have begun to crack and fall apart from the strain of the rising geopolitical rivalries in Asia between the United States and China, if what critics say about its fragility were true. But ASEAN steadily marched through another difficult and challenging year and quietly delivered many positive results that will improve the well-being of its 650 million people.

Most importantly, there were no wars or conflicts. Indeed, not even serious political tensions. ASEAN did not experience any aerial battles like the ones between India and Pakistan in February 2019 or a major military assault like the drone attack on the Saudi Arabian oil installations that took 5% off global oil supplies.

ASEAN consistently and quietly delivers peace to one of the most Balkanized regions in the world. Yet, no one notices. ASEAN economies continue to grow moderately but steadily. A few years ago, Western media reported with great fanfare that India had surpassed China as the fastest-growing major economy in the world. There will be no such fanfare when the results show that ASEAN grew faster than India in 2019. Nor are many people aware that ASEAN is already the fifth-largest economy in the world with a combined GDP of USD 3 trillion.

More remarkably, the understated and quiet leadership of ASEAN managed to pull off one of the biggest coups in recent economic history by announcing the completion of negotiations on the Regional Comprehensive Economic Partnership (RCEP), the world's largest free trade area. RCEP's 15 member states make up 30% of the world's population and 29% of the world's GDP.

Singapore's Minister for Trade and Industry Chan Chun Sing observed that 'RCEP is more than just an economic agreement. It is a strategic signal to the rest of the world that this part of Asia continues to believe in upholding a global, multilateral trading order'. India's last-minute decision not to join could have stalled and broken

---

Originally published in East Asian Forum, Dec 8, 2019

K. Mahbubani, *The Asian 21st Century*, China and Globalization, https://doi.org/10.1007/978-981-16-6811-1_14

down the RCEP process and could have been as distracting as Brexit. Instead, the wisdom of the 'ASEAN minus X' formula shone through.

ASEAN has always believed that perfection is the enemy of the good. If not all participants can join, the rest will proceed first. India will come to realize that its 'Look East' and 'Act East' policies will mean absolutely nothing if it does not join RCEP.

The completion of RCEP was particularly critical against the backdrop of the escalating trade war and the larger geopolitical contest between the United States and China. ASEAN could have been paralyzed or broken apart by this rivalry due to a struggle between its more pro-China members and the more pro-American members. Yet, the culture of accommodation and pragmatism prevailed.

The Prime Minister of Singapore Lee Hsien Loong spoke for many in the region when he said at the Shangri-La Dialogue on 31 May that the region should not be divided by geopolitical contests. He insisted that regional cooperation initiatives proposed by other countries 'should strengthen existing cooperation arrangements centered on ASEAN. They should not undermine them, create rival blocs, deepen fault lines, or force countries to take sides. They should help bring countries together, rather than split them apart'.

Significantly, ASEAN launched its own ASEAN Outlook on the Indo-Pacific due to fears that the US Free and Open Indo-Pacific strategy could divide the region. Indonesian President Joko 'Jokowi' Widodo argued for the need to cooperate with China within ASEAN's Indo-Pacific framework and to build connectivity and infrastructure between ASEAN and China.

In recent years, the South China Sea issue has been divisive. Against this backdrop, it was significant that on 31 July 2019, China revealed that ASEAN and China had completed the first reading of the single draft negotiating text for a Code of Conduct ahead of schedule. This was commended at the ASEAN–China Summit in Bangkok on 3 November.

While Beijing continued its steady and constant engagement with ASEAN, Washington remained domestically distracted. US President Donald Trump did not attend the ASEAN–US Summit in Bangkok on 4 November 2019. Neither did US Vice President Mike Pence nor US Secretary of State Mike Pompeo.

Only the US National Security Adviser Robert O'Brien turned up. As a result, only three of the ten ASEAN leaders—Thailand, Vietnam, and Laos—attended the meeting. Washington was miffed, but as Hoang Thi Ha observed, the United States missing meetings with ASEAN was a classic case of déjà vu for Asia. Each such absence is a geopolitical gift to China.

It would be a mistake, however, to believe that ASEAN will drift inexorably into a Chinese sphere of influence. Over the years, ASEAN has accumulated quiet geopolitical wisdom. It will keep all windows open and also take advantage of unexpected geopolitical opportunities.

In recent years, South Korea has been in a tough spot. It has experienced difficult relations with China over THAAD, Japan over 'comfort women' and the United

States over base funding. It made sense for ASEAN to reach out to South Korea—leading to a tremendously successful summit between ASEAN and South Korea on 26 November 2019 in Busan.

The wisdom and resilience that ASEAN revealed again in 2019 took years to develop. The Indonesian culture of *musyawarah* (consultation) and *mufakat* (consensus) has become embedded into the DNA of ASEAN and has proven to be a major asset. Perhaps the time has come for other regions to come and study this ASEAN 'miracle'. Emulating ASEAN may be a productive approach for other regions to adopt.

Asia, Say No to NATO

Abstract Since the end of the Cold War, NATO has turned from a stabilizing force to a destabilizing force. The Pacific, which has managed to maintain a degree of peace, has no need for the destructive militaristic culture of the Atlantic alliance.

Something very dangerous happened a few weeks ago when the North Atlantic Treaty Organisation (NATO) held its meeting in Brussels. In its communique after the meeting on June 14, it identified China as a "systemic challenge" to areas "relevant to Alliance security".

The implicit message was clear: NATO would like to expand its tentacles beyond the Atlantic to the Pacific Ocean. All of us who live close to the Pacific Ocean, especially in East Asia, should be deeply concerned. If NATO comes to the Pacific, it only means trouble for us. Why? Three reasons.

First, NATO is not a geopolitically wise organization. It did a brilliant job in the Cold War, deterring Soviet expansion into Europe. During the Cold War, it was careful and restrained, building up military capabilities and avoiding direct military conflicts.

The Cold War ended 30 years ago. In theory, after "mission accomplished", NATO should have shut down. In practice, it desperately looked for new missions. In the process, it destabilized Europe.

It bears remembering that relations between Russia and NATO used to be much better, so much so that in 1994, Russia officially signed up to the Partnership for Peace, a program aimed at building trust between NATO and other European and former Soviet countries. But things fell apart because NATO rejected Russia's repeated requests to refuse to accept new members in its "backyard". Then, in April 2008, NATO pushed things further, opening the door to membership for Georgia and Ukraine at the Bucharest summit.

As US commentator Tom Friedman noted: "There is one thing future historians will surely remark upon, and that is the utter poverty of imagination that characterized US foreign policy in the late 1990s. They will note that one of the seminal events of this century took place between 1989 and 1992—the collapse of the Soviet Empire…

Originally published in The Straits Times, June 25, 2021

K. Mahbubani, *The Asian 21st Century*, China and Globalization,
https://doi.org/10.1007/978-981-16-6811-1_15

Thanks to Western resolve and the courage of Russian democrats, that Soviet empire collapsed without a shot, spawning a democratic Russia, setting free the former Soviet republics and leading to unprecedented arms control agreements with the US. And what was America's response? It was to expand the NATO Cold-War alliance against Russia and bring it closer to Russia's borders."

The result was inevitable. Russia had tried to be a friend of the NATO countries after the Cold War ended. Instead, it was slapped in the face with NATO expansion. Many Western media reports portray Russia as a "belligerent, aggressive actor". They fail to mention that NATO actions generated this response.

A truly dangerous moment surfaced in 2014 when it looked as if NATO was about to encroach into Ukraine with the ouster of its pro-Russian president Viktor Yanukovych by Western-supported demonstrators. For President Vladimir Putin, that was the last straw, and soon after came the seizure of Crimea, which the Russians consider part of their cultural heartland.

The dangers of Western expansion into Ukraine were well known. Dr Henry Kissinger had pointed out that the Ukrainians "live in a country with a complex history and a polyglot composition. The Western part was incorporated into the Soviet Union in 1939 when Stalin and Hitler divided up the spoils. Crimea, 60% of whose population is Russian, became part of Ukraine only in 1954, when Nikita Khrushchev, a Ukrainian by birth, awarded it as part of the 300th-year celebration of a Russian agreement with the Cossacks. The west is largely Catholic; the east is largely Russian Orthodox. The west speaks Ukrainian; the east speaks mostly Russian. Any attempt by one wing of Ukraine to dominate the other—as has been the pattern—would lead eventually to civil war or break-up. To treat Ukraine as part of an East–West confrontation would scuttle for decades any prospect to bring Russia and the West—especially Russia and Europe—into a cooperative international system".

Sadly, since 2014, Ukraine has become a divided country. If NATO had shown greater geopolitical restraint, these problems could have been avoided.

The second major weakness of post-Cold War NATO is that its behavior reflects the old adage: If you are a hammer, every problem looks like a nail.

Curiously, during the Cold War, NATO dropped very few bombs on foreign countries. Since the end of the Cold War, NATO has dropped a massive amount of bombs on many countries. Between March and June 1999, NATO bombing campaigns were estimated to have killed 500 civilians in the former Yugoslavia. NATO also dropped several thousand cluster bombs there, despite their use being illegal under the 2010 Convention on Cluster Munitions Treaty.

NATO airstrikes in Libya in 2011 resulted in 7700 bombs dropped, and killed an estimated 70 civilians.

Many of the bombing missions were illegal under international law. I vividly remember having dinner at the home of a former Canadian diplomat in Ottawa when NATO decided to bomb Yugoslav forces in 1999. This Canadian diplomat was deeply worried. Since this military campaign was neither an act of self-defense nor authorized by the United Nations Security Council, it was clearly and technically illegal under international law.

Indeed, Ms Carla Del Ponte, a former special prosecutor in the International Criminal Tribunal for Yugoslavia, tried to investigate whether NATO committed war crimes in the former Yugoslavia. Even though most NATO countries believe in the sanctity of international law, they applied so much political pressure that Ms Del Ponte could not carry out her investigations.

Even worse, NATO has often started a military campaign and then walked away from the disastrous consequences of its intervention. Libya is a classic example of this. The NATO countries were exultant when Muammar Gaddafi was removed from Libya. However, after the country split apart and became caught up in a civil war, NATO just walked away. Many years ago, a wise former US secretary of state, Mr Colin Powell, warned against such military interventions by citing a common statement in crystal shops: "If you break it, you own it." NATO failed to own the wreckage it left behind.

This leads to the third danger: East Asia has developed, with the assistance of ASEAN, a very cautious and pragmatic geopolitical culture. In the 30 years since the end of the Cold War, NATO has dropped several thousand bombs on many countries. By contrast, in the same period, no bombs have been dropped anywhere in East Asia.

This is therefore the biggest danger we face in NATO expanding its tentacles from the Atlantic to the Pacific: It could end up exporting its disastrous militaristic culture to the relatively peaceful environment we have developed in East Asia.

Indeed, if NATO was a wise, thinking, and learning organization, it should actually be studying the East Asian record—especially the ASEAN record of preserving peace—nand learning lessons from it. Instead, it is doing the opposite, thereby creating real dangers for our region.

In view of the risks to East Asia through the potential expansion of NATO culture, all of East Asia should speak with one voice and say no to NATO.

East Asia's New Edge

Abstract Work ethic, social consciousness, and belief in institutions are key elements of East Asia's "edge". This edge was strikingly illustrated during the Covid-19 pandemic when East Asian countries responded far better to the virus than its Western counterparts.

A deep determination to battle against great odds may explain why East Asia has so far responded much better to the Covid-19 pandemic than most Western countries. And if the region's economies also recover faster, they may well offer a glimmer of hope to a world currently drowning in pessimism.

Death tolls don't lie. The most striking disparity in Covid-19 fatalities to date is between East Asian countries, where the total number of deaths per million inhabitants is consistently below ten, and much of the West, where the numbers are in the hundreds. For example, as of May 25, 2021, Japan has so far reported 96.9 deaths per million, followed by South Korea (37.34), Singapore (5.6), China (3.5), and, most remarkably of all, Vietnam, with nearly zero deaths (0.4). By contrast, Belgium now has 2167.6 confirmed deaths per million, and the United Kingdom has 1916.2, followed by Spain (1695.8), Italy (2037.4), and the United States (1778.5).[1]

What accounts for this extraordinary difference? The answers are complicated, but three possible explanations stand out. First, none of the East Asian states believe that they have "arrived," much less achieved the "end of history" at which they regard their societies as being the apotheosis of human possibility. Second, East Asian countries have long invested in strengthening government institutions instead of trying to weaken them, and this is now paying off. And, third, China's spectacular rise is presenting its regional neighbors with opportunities as well as challenges.

It's always dangerous to oversimplify. Yet, the evidence shows that whereas Europeans tend to believe in state-sponsored social security, East Asians still believe that life is composed of struggle and sacrifice. French President Emmanuel Macron is battling to overhaul his country's pension system and decrease retirement benefits in

---

Originally published in Project Syndicate, July 22, 2020

[1] Data updated, https://www.who.int/publications/m/item/weekly-epidemiological-update-on-covid-19---25-may-2021.

© The Author(s) 2022
K. Mahbubani, *The Asian 21st Century*, China and Globalization,
https://doi.org/10.1007/978-981-16-6811-1_16

order to achieve much-needed reductions in budget deficits. As a result, France was convulsed for months by "Yellow Vest" protests. But when South Korea faced a far more serious financial crisis in 1997–98, old ladies donated jewelry to the central bank in an effort to help.

East Asians are aware that their societies have done well in recent decades. But constant adaptation and adjustment to a rapidly changing world is still the norm—even in Japan—and huge investments in public institutions have helped these countries to fulfill it.

Here, the contrast with the US could not be starker. Ever since President Ronald Reagan famously declared in his 1981 inaugural address that, "government is not the solution to our problem, the government is the problem," the very phrase "good governance" has been an oxymoron in America. We have again seen the consequences of this mindset in recent weeks, with the weakening even of globally respected institutions such as the US Federal Aviation Administration, the US Food and Drug Administration, and the US Centers for Disease Control and Prevention. Even today, with America beset by multiple crises, no prominent US leader dares to say the obvious: "Government is the solution."

East Asian societies, on the other hand, retain a strong and deeply-held belief in good governance, reflecting the traditional Asian respect for institutions of authority. Vietnam's spectacularly effective pandemic response, for example, can be attributed not only to one of the world's most disciplined governments but also to wise investments in health care. Between 2000 and 2016, per capita, public-health expenditures increased by an average of 9% per year. This enabled Vietnam to establish a national public-health emergency operations center and surveillance system in the wake of the 2002–03 SARS epidemic.

Vietnam's track record is all the more astonishing given the country's low starting point. When the Cold War ended three decades ago, and Vietnam finally stopped fighting wars after almost 45 years of near-continual conflict, it had one of the world's poorest populations. But by emulating China's economic model and opening up to foreign trade and investment, Vietnam subsequently became one of the world's fastest-growing economies.

As then-World Bank President Jim Yong Kim pointed out in 2016, Vietnam's average annual growth rate of nearly 7% over the previous 25 years had enabled the country "to leapfrog to middle-income status in a single generation." And during the same period, Kim noted, Vietnam had managed the "especially remarkable achievement" of reducing extreme poverty from 50% to just 3%.

The country's success did not happen in isolation. After the Soviet Union collapsed, Vietnam integrated itself into many of East Asia's existing regional bodies, including the Association of Southeast Asian Nations (ASEAN) and the Asia–Pacific Economic Cooperation (APEC). There, it learned quickly from its neighbors, including China. More recently, Vietnam joined the Comprehensive and Progressive Agreement for Trans-Pacific Partnership, an 11-country trade pact.

China's spectacular resurgence has naturally heightened Vietnamese insecurity, given that the two neighbors have fought as recently as 1979. But rather than paralyzing Vietnamese policymakers, that insecurity has fostered a sense of strategic discipline and vigilance, which has contributed to the country's extraordinary performance during the pandemic. China's rise has had a similar galvanizing effect on some of its other neighbors, including Japan and South Korea.

Singaporean Prime Minister Lee Hsien Loong has often cited the former Intel CEO Andy Grove's mantra that "only the paranoid survive." Paranoia is usually a negative emotion, but it can also trigger a powerful impulse to fight and survive. A deep determination to battle against great odds may explain why East Asia has so far responded far better to the pandemic than most of the West. And if the region's economies also recover faster, they may well offer a glimmer of hope to a world currently drowning in pessimism.

Why the 'India Way' May Be the World's Best Bet for Moral Leadership

Abstract The growing US-China geopolitical contest makes India well placed to provide a leading ethical voice on the international stage.

India is entering a geopolitical sweet spot. What does this mean? In a world crying out for a strong, independent voice to provide moral guidance to a troubled planet, the only realistic candidate is India.

None of the three other obvious candidates—the United States, the European Union, and China—can step up to the plate now.

The US is a deeply troubled country, even after the election of Joe Biden. It has traveled the full moral arc from a John F. Kennedy, who famously said, "Let every nation know, whether it wishes us well or ill, that we shall pay any price, bear any burden, meet any hardship, support any friend, oppose any foe to assure the survival and the success of liberty", to a Donald Trump, whose proclaimed goal was to "Make America Great Again". In short, America went from caring for the world to caring for itself only.

The EU is faring no better, bogged down with the technical details of Brexit, while struggling to deal with Covid-19, terrorism, and a surge of migrants. China is sadly distrusted by the Western world as it is increasingly seen as a threat, not an opportunity. By a process of elimination, that leaves India as the only realistic candidate.

This is why the book by the Indian Foreign Minister, Dr. S. Jaishankar, *The India Way*, is so timely. It provides valuable glimpses of the thinking behind many of India's policies.

It is very rare for sitting foreign ministers to write books. To avoid offending countries, they can only offer platitudes. Fortunately, Jaishankar avoids them (although he does indulge in elliptical allusions, some of which may be beyond the reach of lay readers).

He makes it clear, for example, that India will not be beholden to one side in the growing US-China geopolitical contest.

Originally published in South China Morning Post, Nov 19, 2020

K. Mahbubani, *The Asian 21st Century*, China and Globalization,
https://doi.org/10.1007/978-981-16-6811-1_17

As he writes: "If India drove the revived Quad arrangement, it also took membership of the Shanghai Cooperation Organization. A long-standing trilateral with Russia and China coexist now with one involving the US and Japan. These apparently contradictory developments only illustrate the world in which we now operate."

Yet while Jaishankar's many geopolitical observations are fascinating, the most powerful chapter in his book is the one on the Mahabharata, a significant ancient Sanskrit text.

> "The Mahabharata is indisputably the most vivid distillation of Indian thought on statecraft," he states categorically. "As an epic, it dwarfs its counterparts in other civilizations, not just in length but in its richness and complexity. Focusing on the importance of the sense of duty and sanctity of obligations, it is also a description of human frailties."

It is truly brave of Jaishankar to try to distill the life lessons of the mighty Mahabharata into one chapter. But he succeeds in drawing out the complexity of the epic, which narrates the rivalry of two groups of cousins.

While Jaishankar points out all the deceptions waged by both sides, he also emphasizes the advantages of being ethical.

> "Where the Pandavas consistently scored over their cousins was the ability to shape and control the narrative," he writes. "Their ethical positioning was at the heart of a superior branding."

In short, ethical power enjoys a key advantage. He concludes the chapter by saying: "Being an ethical power is one aspect of the India way."

Providing ethical leadership has been part of India's DNA. Indeed, of the two greatest ethical leaders in the twentieth century, Mahatma Gandhi and Nelson Mandela, one came from India.

Mandela was often inspired by Gandhi. He once said: "[Gandhi's] philosophy contributed in no small measure to bringing about a peaceful transformation in South Africa, and in healing the destructive human divisions that had been spawned by the abhorrent practice of apartheid."

He also said: "Gandhi remained committed to non-violence; I followed the Gandhian strategy for as long as I could."

This is why it was right for Prime Minister Narendra Modi to tell the UN General Assembly last year on September 25th—Mahatma Gandhi's birthday—that "whether it's climate change or terrorism, corruption or selfishness in public life, Gandhiji's ideals are the guiding light for us when it comes to protecting humanity. I believe that the path shown by Gandhiji will lead to a better world".

One simple path India could take in our challenging world is to ask what Gandhiji would say about a vexing contemporary question.

Take the case of the terrorist killings in France. Gandhi would have unreservedly condemned the killings. Yet, he would also have counseled an understanding of the deep sensitivities of the 1.4 billion Muslims of the world.

He would have echoed the message by Canadian Prime Minister Justin Trudeau, who defended free speech but said it should not "arbitrarily and needlessly hurt" people with whom "we are sharing a society and planet".

The world has come a long way from leaders of the caliber of John F. Kennedy and Margaret Thatcher, Francois Mitterand and Helmut Schmidt, Jawaharlal Nehru and Lee Kuan Yew, who never hesitated to speak out when the world needed a strong moral voice.

In the book, Jaishankar writes: "The Singaporean leader Lee Kuan Yew once paid India's rise a backhanded compliment of being the more reassuring one [as compared with China's]."

India's rise is "reassuring" because it is not perceived as a threat by other powers. Given this trusted position, India can take advantage of it by providing the world ethical leadership, of the kind that Gandhiji would have provided if he were alive today.

One ethical step India can take is to become the global champion of multilateralism. As Jaishankar says, "our own growth model and political outlook intrinsically favor rules-based behavior".

Rules-based behavior has sadly declined in the Trump era. It can return in the Biden era. Yet, it also needs a fervent champion. Emmanuel Macron has been one such champion. However, no Western leader today can enjoy the same level of trust in the non-Western world (who make up 88% of the world's population) that India does.

Jaishankar is right to lament the fact that India has not yet been made a permanent member of the UN Security Council (UNSC). Indeed, as I have argued consistently, India should be made a permanent member immediately. Many others agree. Martin Wolf observed in 2009: "Within a decade a world in which the UK is on the UN Security Council and India is not will seem beyond laughable."

A decade has passed. The UNSC does look laughable.

India has been campaigning strongly to get its permanent seat. Yet the best way to achieve this is to get a global consensus that the world's most ethical power deserves a seat on the UNSC. Indeed, India could even exercise a veto today by refusing to implement the UNSC resolutions which are clearly unjust.

The "best" India way forward is to project itself as the leading ethical voice on planet earth. This is also what Krishna would whisper into the ears of Arjuna as they ride their chariot together into battle.

As Jaishankar says about the Mahabharata: "The courage required to implement policy is, perhaps, its most famous section—the Bhagavad Gita." India can provide this courage.

India's Tryst with the Asian Century

Abstract As the Asian Century draws near, India faces three choices for how it can navigate geopolitically turbulent times. It can align closely with the US and the Quad, integrate itself into an Asian ecosystem of trade and peace, or become an independent pole in new multilateral world order.

Geopolitics is a cruel game. It rewards cunning and calculating moves and punishes emotional responses. In the twenty-first century, as we move into an era of massive power shifts, geopolitical nimbleness will become even more critical for all countries. In this regard, India is one of the most fortunate countries. Given its size and political heft, it has more choices than most. Yet, it too has to choose wisely. Each choice has benefits but also costs.

The first choice is obvious. To balance China's growing weight and influence, especially after the tragic clash at the Sino-Indian border in June, India could drift toward becoming an ally of the US. Many influential voices are advocating this option, which has many merits. Despite its problems, the US remains the world's number one economic and military power. By joining the Quadrilateral Security Dialogue, or the Quad, together with Australia and Japan, India is sending a strong signal that it is moving in that direction. Undoubtedly, the US has been generous to India, especially under former president George W. Bush, under whose leadership the US signed the civil nuclear agreement with India, thereby paving the way for global recognition of India as a nuclear power.

By aligning itself with the US, India would be making a choice similar to one made by China, which aligned itself with the US and Pakistan against the Soviet Union and India in the Cold War. It was truly cunning of China to forget its differences with the US when Henry Kissinger visited them in 1971. China simply ignored the fact that the US still recognized Taiwan as the official government of China. In return, China got many benefits. The CIA stations in Xinjiang provided some protection from the Soviet threat. Equally crucial, the US generously opened up its market and integrated China into the liberal rules-based order. As a result, China's gross national product,

Originally published in India Today, Jul 18, 2020

K. Mahbubani, *The Asian 21st Century*, China and Globalization,
https://doi.org/10.1007/978-981-16-6811-1_18

one-tenth the size of the US in purchasing power parity terms in 1980, became bigger than the US in 2014. China should thank the US for its exceptional economic success.

Sadly, in 2020, the US can no longer be as generous. It is the only major developed society where the average income of the bottom 50% has gone down over a 30-year period, creating, as two Princeton University economists have documented, a "sea of despair" among the white working classes. Local jobs are protected. Hence, in mid-2020, the Trump administration canceled H1B visas and visas for overseas students, hurting many Indians. Equally importantly, Adam Garfinkle, the long-time editor of The American Interest, has wisely warned many Asian countries to not expect the US to continue playing a major role in Asia. He says, "It's too bad that it's all over now. Yes, it's gone, not coming back." He is right. History teaches us that great powers recede when their domestic problems take priority, just as the British retreated from East of Suez. So, even though Japan and Australia remain staunch allies of the US today, they might be secretly planning for alternative scenarios.

The second choice for India is to join a new silent ecosystem of peace and prosperity evolving in East Asia. With the US retreating from FTAs (free trade agreements), East Asia is persisting with them, keeping alive even the Trans-Pacific Partnership (TPP) that the US walked away from. This system is ASEAN-centered. The paradox here is that since ASEAN is weak and nonthreatening, everyone trusts it. Hence, ASEAN has signed FTAs with all of its East Asian partners, including India. These FTAs were further consolidated into the Regional Comprehensive Economic Partnership (RCEP), which all partners of ASEAN, except India, have joined. India's concerns over another surge of imports from China after joining RCEP are valid. Yet, a bilateral safeguards agreement can take care of it.

The East Asian ecosystem has delivered prosperity and rests on a culture of peace, pragmatism and competence. Covid has proven how competent East Asian societies have become. As of May 25, 2021, the number of Covid deaths per million is much lower in East Asia (South Korea, 37.34 Japan, 96.9; China, 3.5; Singapore, 5.6; and Vietnam, 0.4 compared to the West (Spain, 1695.8; Italy, 2037.4; Belgium, 2167.6; UK, 1916.2; and US, 1778.5).[1] This confirms that the shift of competence from the West to East Asia is gaining momentum.

Managing the rise of China is the biggest challenge for the East Asian ecosystem. Differences persist over the South China Sea, the Diaoyutai/Senkaku Islands. Wars could break out. Yet, amazingly, the guns have been silent for over three decades. A quiet culture of pragmatism has become the norm. There is one clear point of agreement among the East Asian states: now is the time to focus on economic growth and development and the eradication of poverty. This explains why the ASEAN region, once one of the world's poorest, will become the fourth largest economy of the world by 2030. Pragmatism pays.

The third choice for India is to emerge as an independent pole in new multipolar world order. Clearly, as I document in Has China Won?, the world will be rocked by a major geopolitical contest between the US and China in the coming decades.

---

[1] Data updated, https://www.who.int/publications/m/item/weekly-epidemiological-update-on-covid-19---25-may-2021.

This contest could not come at a worse time. Our imperiled planet faces many challenges, global warming, and a global recession caused by Covid. If the two countries continue with their struggle, future historians may well see them as two tribes of apes fighting each other while the forests around them burn. Common sense would dictate otherwise.

This may also explain why few countries are rushing to take sides. Many traditional Asian allies of the US, including the Philippines and Thailand, Japan and South Korea, do more trade with China than with the US. South Korea and Japan are also alarmed that the economic bill for the US soldiers stationed on their soil has skyrocketed, leading them to ask if they are allied soldiers or mercenaries. Yet, as Garfinkle has pointed out, the US has to take care of its own interests first.

The one country big enough to emerge as an independent pole and provide common sense and calm leadership in a geopolitically turbulent world is India.

India has also been a champion of multilateralism. Working with the European Union, India could provide global leadership by speaking truth to power. The world is yearning for such an independent leader. One story tells it all. In the mid-1990s, Japan ran against Bangladesh for a seat on the UN Security Council and lost. While I was serving as the Singapore ambassador to the UN, I asked the African states why they didn't vote for Japan. They said, "Why give two votes to the US in the UNSC?".

None of these three choices will be easy options for India. Each will have its share of benefits and costs. Hence, it would be wise for India to explore carefully all its options before making its final choice. One advantage India has is that it has a strong leader. Its biggest strength is that it has more choices than virtually any other nation today.

India: A Brave and Imaginative Superpower?

Abstract If India can be as successful domestically as Indians are internationally, it can fulfill its potential to become a leading global superpower.

Fortune favors the brave, the Ancient Romans said.

This is equally true for individuals as it is for nations. India is now about to enter a geopolitical sweet spot. It will have a once in a millennium opportunity to emerge as the world's most respected superpower. The only question is whether it will be able to muster the courage and the imagination needed to seize this opportunity.

So where does this opportunity come from? It comes from many sources. First, we are entering a new historical era. The artificial era of Western domination of world history is coming to an end. Second, we are seeing the natural return of China and India as the world's largest economies. This is perfectly natural as China and India were the largest economies of the world from 1 to 1820 AD, as documented by Angus Maddison. Third, the world has shrunk. As Kofi Annan said, we live in a global village. In the twentieth century, the American century, the United States (US) naturally provided leadership of this global village. Post-Donald Trump, the US has lost its shine. The world is therefore looking for a new guiding light. India can provide a festival of lights.

However, to emerge and be globally acknowledged as a leading superpower, India has to develop a unique combination of three strengths: economic heft, geopolitical shrewdness, and moral courage. All three are within reach of India.

Take economic heft. In theory, India should have the most competitive economy in the world. Empirical evidence backs this claim. The most competitive human laboratory in the world is the US. The best minds from all over the world come to compete in the world's best universities and companies in the US. Guess which ethnic group has the highest per capita income in the most competitive human laboratory? It is the Indian community. Indeed, it is even more striking that if we add up the market capitalization of the American companies that have been run by Indians born in India, including Google, Adobe, Microsoft, MasterCard, PepsiCo, Micron, this sum

Originally published in India On Our Minds, November 2020

could add up to around USD 2 trillion. By comparison, the gross domestic product of India, with a population of 1.3 billion, is USD 2.7 trillion.

Curiously, even though overseas Indians thrive in competition, India, as a country, is still wary of economic competition. This explains, in part, India's reluctance to join free trade agreements, like the Regional Comprehensive Economic Partnership. The reluctance could have also been due to opposition from vested interests. The corollary of the concept of economic competition is creative destruction. The sad reality is that if India tries to protect its current industries (some of which are globally uncompetitive), it is preventing the emergence of dynamic new industries which could be as globally competitive as the American companies run by Indians. Surely, if Indians can run the most competitive companies in the world, they can also develop the most competitive companies in India. This is why India needs to make a courageous leap into the future with its economic policies. If any Indian government official opens up and liberalizes the Indian economy, it will be rewarded by years of rapid growth a decade later, as proven by the bold liberalization moves made by Manmohan Singh and Montek Singh Ahluwalia in the early 1990s. Jeffrey Sachs of Columbia University and a leading expert on the fight against poverty, states this in his book, *The End of Poverty: Economic Possibilities of Our Time*. Before the reforms, "India remained trapped with low and erratic growth…Enter Manmohan Singh, who understood clearly that it was time to end the License Raj. From mid-1991 onwards, India became part of the global wave of market reforms…" These reforms were met with a lot of skepticism. Sachs writes: "My protestations that trade liberalization works—that India's exports were bound to grow—were met with repeated warnings that 'India was different'… To nearly worldwide astonishment, India became the hub of large-scale service-sector exports in the new information technologies." Just as courage paid off in the 1990s, it can also pay off in the 2020s.

Similarly, geopolitical shrewdness is clearly within reach of India. There is now no question that the biggest geopolitical contest in the next few decades will be between China and the US, as I document in great detail in my book, *Has China Won?*, the luckiest country in this geopolitical contest is India. Both the US and China are courting India assiduously as they know that the only country that has the heft to tilt the geopolitical balance one way or another is India. It doesn't take a geopolitical genius to figure out the best place for India to be in this geopolitical context. If an Indian Henry Kissinger or George Kennan were advising India, he would say: just imagine China and the US as two elephants balancing each other on the two ends of a see-saw. The best place for the third elephant to take would be to stand in the middle of the see-saw. Whichever way the third elephant leans will significantly affect the geopolitical balance between the US and China.

This is geopolitical common sense. Yet, it is equally true that a strong head of steam has built up in the Indian body politic against China. Some of it is understandable. China's support of Pakistan against Indian interests has jeopardized Indian security. Yet, this is also where geopolitical shrewdness comes in. During the Cold War, the US supported Taiwan strongly. China claimed Taiwan. The Chinese and American positions were irreconcilable. Mao Zedong and Zhou Enlai could have insisted that Nixon and Kissinger abandon Taiwan completely before China could cooperate with the US. China pragmatically ignored the Taiwan issue and instead used the US to increase its geopolitical leverage. China's rapid emergence as an economic power could not have happened if it had not cleverly taken advantage of all the opportunities provided by the US (big markets, access to science and technology, and university education for China's youth). Clearly, China took advantage of its potential future adversary, the US, to enhance the social and economic transformation of its society. Today, India could take advantage of the economic opportunities provided by China, such as, for example, the Belt and Road Initiative (BRI). Right now, joining the BRI is an unthinkable option in India. Geopolitical shrewdness would recommend that no option be deemed unthinkable.

Finally, moral courage. The country that has produced the most morally courageous leader in the world is India. Mahatma Gandhi epitomizes this moral courage. He didn't just care for India. He cared for humanity as a whole. As Prime Minister Narendra Modi said, "Whether it's climate change or terrorism, corruption or selfishness in public life, Gandhiji's ideals are the guiding light for us when it comes to protecting humanity. I believe that the path shown by Gandhiji will lead to a better world."

What would Gandhi say if he were alive today? He was a great admirer of the US. In 1931, he said, "When real Peace and Disarmament come, they will be initiated by a strong nation like America…" Gandhi would therefore be deeply troubled by the rallying cry of President Trump: "Make America Great Again". He would expect America, the richest and most powerful country in the world, to make the world great again.

Yet, it is equally true that there is a great sense of exhaustion in the American body politic about providing leadership to the world. Domestically, America is a deeply troubled society. It is the only major developed society where the average income of the bottom 50 percent has gone down over a 30-year period. As Anne Case and Angus Deaton, two Princeton University economists, say, the white working classes of America used to carry the American dream of getting a better life in their hearts and souls. Today, however, there is a "sea of despair" among them. In view of this, the US can no longer be the "Shining City on the Hill". Neither can China take this role. The Chinese believe that their civilization is one of the best in the world. However, it is a civilization that can primarily be enjoyed by the Chinese. The Chinese, unlike the Americans, have no universalizing mission.

This provides India with a unique opportunity. As we move away from a monocivilizational world dominated by the West to a multicivilizational world where Asian civilizations are coming back strongly, the world is looking for leaders to provide bridges between the East and the West. India is in a unique position to provide such bridges. It is trusted by both the East and the West.

The world is therefore longing for a moral leader like Gandhi who will point out the follies of the many wars that the West had engaged in. Indian voices do speak out. For example, Shyam Saran, a leading Indian official, has written eloquently about the folly of Western interventions.

In most cases, the post-intervention situation has been rendered much worse, the violence more lethal, and the suffering of the people who were supposed to be protected much more severe than before. Iraq is an earlier instance; Libya and Syria are the more recent ones. A similar story is playing itself out in Ukraine. In each case, no careful thought was given to the possible consequences of the intervention.

Likewise Shivshankar Menon, former National Security Adviser to the Indian government stated, "Unilateral (sometimes covert) interventions, as in Libya or Syria, have led to unexpected and dangerous outcomes… We clearly need to improve, strengthen and use the processes and institutions of multilateral consultation and action available to the international community." Menon is right. Multilateralism is the solution. India is a natural leader in the multilateral arena.

In 1941, Henry Luce exhorted Americans to realize an American century through an imaginative vision:

> No narrow definition can be given to the American internationalism of the 20th Century. It will take shape, as all civilizations take shape, by the living of it, by work and effort, by trial and error, by enterprise and adventure and experience.
>
>   And by imagination!

Luce was right. The American century was brilliant and inspiring because it was driven by imagination. Today, India has that opportunity to be equally imaginative. It should seize the moment.

Can India Become Stronger Than China? Yes, It Can

Abstract The country with the biggest gap between its potential and its performance is India. All India has to do is to learn from its Southeast Asian and Chinese neighbors and open itself up to economic competition.

Introduction

Can India become stronger than China? What do I mean by becoming stronger? Simple: have a bigger economy. The goal of this lecture is to explain why I believe India can have a bigger economy (indeed the biggest economy in the world) and how India can set about achieving it.

I will divide my lecture into three parts. In part I, I will explain why I am confident that India can have the largest economy in the world. In part II, I will explain the principles India can take to become number one. In part III, I will also suggest some concrete steps India can take to develop an economy bigger than China's.

Part I: Why I am Confident

There are two reasons why I am confident. The first reason is historical evidence. As British historian Angus Maddison has documented, from year 1 to 1820, the two largest economies of the world were always China and India.

What happened after 1820? The British arrived. As Shashi Tharoor, a distinguished citizen of Kerala, has documented, when the British arrived, India's share of Global GNP (nominal) was 23%. When they left in 1947, the share fell to around 3%. Today, India's share remains at about 3%. India's share of the global population is 18%. Hence, its share of global GNP should also be 18%, if you assume that the average Indian is as intelligent and capable as the average human being.

Originally published in Lecture at the K R Narayanan Birth Centenary Lecture, 5th August 2021

K. Mahbubani, *The Asian 21st Century*, China and Globalization,
https://doi.org/10.1007/978-981-16-6811-1_20

This is the second reason why I am confident. The average Indian is clearly as intelligent and as capable as other human beings. I hope that this is an uncontroversial statement. But I would also like to make a controversial statement: the average Indian can outperform the average citizen of other communities. You can see why such a statement is inherently controversial. Hence, let me back it up with some evidence.

The most competitive human laboratory in the world is the USA. In an article I wrote for McKinsey, I said, "It's so easy to grasp the gap between India's potential and its performance because you can see the potential of what an ethnic Indian can do in the most competitive human laboratory in the world, which is the United States of America. And when the Indians arrived in America, they thought they might be number five or number six in terms of per capita income. They ended up being number one."

Today, the average per capita income of the Indian residing in the US is US$ 55,298. If Indians in India can achieve the same per capita income, the total GNP of India would be around US$ 71 trillion, making it the largest economy in the world, larger than the US at US$ 21 trillion or China, at US$ 15 trillion. If this figure is unimaginable, let's imagine that the average Indian in India is half as smart as the average Indian in the US. Then India would still have a GNP of US$ 35 trillion, still larger than that of the US at US$ 21 trillion and China at US$ 15 trillion.

Why do I highlight all these figures? I do so because I only want to emphasize one big point at the beginning of my lecture: the country with the biggest gap between its economic potential and its economic performance in India. India's GNP today is US$ 2.6 trillion. It should be at least 10 or 20 times larger.

Let me deal with one objection immediately. The argument can be made that the super-smart Indians ended up in the US. Hence, they ended up with super-high per capita incomes. Even if I acknowledge this as true, how about comparing the per capita income of Indians in India with Indians in other countries? I don't have the data for all overseas Indian communities. However, I have traveled all around the world and met Indians from all corners of the world. Without fail, in almost every country I have visited, the overseas Indian communities have done well and are thriving.

So, why are they thriving? The answer could be complex but let me mention one key factor: Indians are naturally competitive economic animals and thrive in economic competition. In this regard, they are very similar to the Chinese. This brings me to the second important point I want to emphasize in my lecture: the economic fortunes of the Chinese turned after the key reformist leader of China, Deng Xiaoping, asked a very simple question: why were the Chinese people successful in every economy except in China itself? The answer was a simple and obvious one: the Chinese were allowed to compete economically in every country in the world except China. Hence, Deng Xiaoping did the obvious thing: he opened up the Chinese economy and allowed all Chinese, 1.4 billion of them, to compete.

So what were the results? Deng Xiaoping started to open up the Chinese economy in 1980. 1980 is a significant year. In 1980, the size of the Chinese economy (US$ 191 billion) and the Indian economy (US$ 186 billion) were about the same. Today, the size of the Chinese economy is US$ 15 trillion, over five times the size of the Indian economy at US$ 2.6 trillion.

So how did India go from having an economy the same size as China's to having an economy one-fifth that of China? The answer is amazingly simple. China opened its economy to global economic competition and allowed 1.4 billion Chinese to compete. Since the Chinese thrive in economic competitions, the Chinese economy thrived and surged ahead.

By contrast, the 1.3 billion Indians have been deprived of economic competition. Since they have been deprived of economic competition, they cannot thrive. Hence, India's economy has fallen behind.

Let me add another important point here. India's economy has also fallen behind other regions and countries. I come from Southeast Asia. Of the ten ASEAN states, nine have an Indic cultural base. Hence in some ways, we are cultural satellites of India. The total population of ASEAN is 650 million, half that of India's. But the combined GNP of ASEAN in 2020 was about $3 trillion, slightly larger than that of India ($2.8 trillion).

Another statistic is more shocking. In 1971, when India helped Bangladesh to become an independent country, many commentators said that Bangladesh was a hopeless country that would become an economic basket-case, according to Henry Kissinger. Indeed, when I was Ambassador to the UN from 1984 to 1989 and from 1998 to 2004, Bangladesh was a member of the Least Developed Countries (LDCs). India was never a member of LDCs. Yet, by 2020, the per capita income of Bangladesh (US$ 1968) became larger than that of India (US$ 1900).

So why have the ASEAN countries and Bangladesh outperformed India in the economic realm? The simple answer is that ASEAN and Bangladesh plunged into global economic competition. India didn't.

All this brings me to part II of my lecture: what principles should India follow to become the largest economy in the world? My broad answer, of course, is that India needs to unleash the vibrant animal spirits of the 1.3 billion Indian people by exposing them to global economic competition. However, this broad answer has to be implemented with some concrete steps. I will try to spell out some of them.

Part II: Key Principles to Follow

Before spelling out the principles that India can take to become more competitive, let me confirm at the outset that it will not be easy. There will be many political, economic, bureaucratic, psychological, vested interests, and so on, obstacles to overcome. Indeed, China didn't have an easy time either. I was present at the World Economic Forum, Davos meeting in 2017 when President Xi Jinping admitted that the process of opening up the Chinese economy was a difficult one. This is what he said: "There was a time when China also had doubts about economic globalization and was not sure whether it should join the World Trade Organization. But we came to the conclusion that integration into the global economy is a historical trend. To grow its economy, China must have the courage to swim in the vast ocean of the global market. If one is always afraid of bracing the storm and exploring the new world, he will sooner or later get drowned in the ocean. Therefore, China took a brave step to embrace the global market. We have had our fair share of choking in the water and encountered whirlpools and choppy waves, but we have learned how to swim in this process. It has proved to be the right strategic choice."

Hence, India should have no illusion that changing course will be easy. Like China, India will also struggle to swim when it plunges into the ocean of globalization. What will make it even more difficult is that India will have to follow two contradictory principles in trying to open up its economy to global competition. The first principle is to have a radical change of mindset and decide that an open Indian economy will do better than a closed Indian economy. The second principle is that when opening up the Indian economy, India should do it carefully and pragmatically. It should not try either a big bang approach or shock therapy as the experiences of Russia and East Europe have shown that big bang approaches don't work. In short, India will have to follow two contradictory principles. But both are equally important. Hence I will explain both.

The radical change of mindset is important because the general assumption in India is that the best way to protect the poor in India is to keep the Indian economy as close as possible. Hence, the intentions of those who kept the Indian economy relatively closed were noble: to protect the poor. However, the record of recent history shows that poverty reduction happens faster when economies open up faster. The best evidence of this is provided by Vietnam which had a typical Soviet style protected economy. However, as soon as the Cold War ended, it joined its fellow East Asian countries in opening up its economy and the results in poverty reduction were spectacular. As then-World Bank President Jim Yong Kim pointed out in 2016, Vietnam's average annual growth rate of nearly 7% over the previous 25 years had enabled the country "to leapfrog to middle-income status in a single generation." And during the same period, Kim noted, Vietnam had managed the "especially remarkable achievement" of reducing extreme poverty from 50 to just 3%.

Let me use a simple metaphor to explain why opening up India's economy helps the poor. The main reason why I emphasized the super-performance of Indians over-seas is to point out we should view Indians differently. We should see them as 1.3 billion economic tigers, poised to perform well. What is the best way to get tigers to perform well? Keep them in cages where they have limited competition and limited room to grow? Or release them into a wild jungle where they can roam freely and become strong and fierce?

I am using the metaphor of economic tigers to drive home the essential point that generations of Indian policymakers have made a major mistake by underestimating the ability of Indians to compete. This is why, relative to most East Asian economies, the Indian economy is relatively closed. For those who doubt my statement that India's economy is relatively closed, let me provide some statistics: A relatively open economy trades more with the world. A relatively closed economy trades less with the world. Here is the data: China and India have about the same population. Yet China's total trade with the world ($4.5 trillion) is more than five times that of India ($800 billion). Even more shockingly, the population of ASEAN is half that of

India. Yet the total trade of ASEAN ($2.8 trillion) is more than three times that of India.

Here, let me acknowledge one important point. When India opens up its economy, there will be "creative destruction" (as pointed out by the famous economist, Joseph Schumpeter). And "creative destruction" is good. It destroys the inefficient parts of the economy and strengthens the efficient part of the economy. This is exactly what happened to China. Before China joined the WTO in 2001, the State-Owned Enterprises (SOEs) made up two-thirds of China's economy. Now it is down to one-third. In short, there was a lot of "creative destruction" of Chinese SOEs.

Let me add that there was also a lot of trepidation in China when it opened up its economy. This is a story told by the former Foreign Minister of Singapore, Mr George Yeo. As Mr George Yeo recounts, "I was in Doha when China was admitted to the WTO in November 2001. There was great celebration, but the Chinese at the time felt bruised by the negotiating process. The US, working in concert with the Europeans and the Japanese, extracted the maximum from China. And I remember a few years later suggesting to China that they join the TPP. The commerce minister held up his hands and said, we have given so much we can't afford to do this. No one expected, that from 2001 to end of 2019 before COVID, the Chinese economy will grow seven times in PPP terms, nine times in Renminbi terms, and 11 times in US dollar terms."

Since this lecture is named after Mr K.R. Narayanan, I want to pause here and quote a sentence from him. As you all may know, one of the most important government memos he wrote was on the long-term implications of the explosion of a nuclear bomb by China in 1964. In that memo, he had a striking comparison between the economies of China and India. He said: "The left-wing of the CPI [Communist Party of India] has already begun to highlight before the people the spectacular progress made by 'socialist China' as compared to 'capitalist India'."

In 1964, it was absolutely true that India was capitalist and China wasn't. 57 years have passed. Today, China has become more capitalist than the US. This is not my opinion. It is the opinion of an economist called Dr Shan Weijian, who received his Ph.D. in Economics. This is what he said: "[Americans] don't know how capitalist China is. China's rapid economic growth is the result of its embrace of a market economy and private enterprise. China is among the most open markets in the world: It is the largest trading nation and also the largest recipient of foreign direct investment, surpassing the United States in 2020. The major focus of government expenditure is domestic infrastructure. China now has better highways, rail systems, bridges, and airports than the United States does… [The Chinese] don't know how socialist it [America] is, with its Social Security system and its policies to tax the rich by collecting capital gains taxes. China is still in the process of building a social safety net that is largely undefined and underfunded, and it has no tax on personal capital gains. In 2020 China had more billionaires than the US did, and it outpaces the US three to one in minting them."

This also explains why it is almost inevitable that China will overtake the US and become the number one economy within ten years. It also explains how India can overtake both China and the US and become the number one economy in 20 or

30 years. It should open up its economy, trade more with the rest of the world and, as a result, allow more creative destruction to take place at its inefficient sectors.

Hence, the theoretical direction that India should take to make its economy stronger is clear. However, as I indicated earlier, theory is one thing. Practice is another. Russia and a few East European countries thought that they were doing the right thing by opening up their economies with a "big bang". They were seduced by a famous statement which said "You cannot cross a chasm in two leaps". Janos Kornai, a Hungarian economist, said that reform would be "a good deal better if the price system had undergone one brave surgery". Włodzimierz Brus, a Polish economist, said that China should "cross the river as fast as possible to reach the other shore." Sadly, the Russians and some East Europeans fell into a chasm by trying to take one big leap.

The Chinese reformers were wiser. They heeded the advice of Deng Xiaoping, who advised that China should "grope for stones to cross the river steadily". However, the most important point here is not that the river must be crossed cautiously. Instead, the key point here is that the river must be crossed and India must reach the other side.

Part III: Some Concrete Steps

It's sometimes easy to spell out big principles to follow in economic reforms. It's harder to spell out the concrete steps to take. So let me conclude this lecture by suggesting three concrete but cautious steps India can take to start the process. Fortunately, to use another metaphor, there is some low-hanging fruit India can pick. Of course, there will be some risks associated with each step. However, any sober calculation will show that the risk of not taking the steps to cross the river will be even greater. India will continue to fall behind the fast-growing East Asian states.

The first step is an easy one: join the Regional Comprehensive Economic Partnership (RCEP) immediately. Why join the RCEP? Many reasons. Firstly, in today's world, Europe represents the past, America represents the present, and East Asia represents the future. By joining RCEP, India will be betting on the future, not the past. Secondly, with a total population of 2.3 billion and a combined GDP of $38 trillion, RCEP can provide the biggest markets for Indian products. Here's one statistic that explains how markets are growing faster than the rest of the world. In 2009, the size of the retail goods market in China was $1.8 trillion while that of the US was $4 trillion. Yet, by 2019, two years after Trump's trade war, China's market had become bigger at $6 trillion while that of the US was $5.5 trillion.

Thirdly, and most importantly, India spent over six years negotiating entry into RCEP. Many of its concerns have already been addressed. So, why didn't India join? I don't know the exact answer. But I would make an educated guess that some vested interests felt threatened. If this is true, it shows why a radical change of mindset is necessary for India. Is it more important for India to protect a few vested interests? Or is it more important for India to expose 1.3 billion Indian economic tigers to global economic competition? And, to put things more harshly, if India cannot even compete as well as the ten Southeast Asian states, who can it compete with? Certainly, some Indian industries will struggle to compete with RCEP. However, even the most basic economic calculations will show that the Indian economy overall pays a far heavier price (and therefore the poor Indians suffer) when it is not subject to economic competition.

The second concrete step that India can take is to make the South Asian region (including all the SAARC members) as open as the Southeast Asian region. Most countries grow by opening up their economies to their neighbors. Just look at the European Union (EU) and the North American Free Trade Agreement (NAFTA). Now South Asia can never be as open as the EU or NAFTA. These are very high-level and complex agreements. However, there is no reason why South Asia cannot be as open as Southeast Asia.

Here, let me emphasize one important point. In deciding how to open up the region, India doesn't have to reinvent the wheel. All that it does have to do is to pick up a copy of the ASEAN Free Trade Area agreement and share it with all its neighbors. After doing so, India should make a commitment to work with its neighbors and agree to sign a similar agreement among all the SAARC members.

Let me add here that I am not naive. I am aware that there are problems between India and some of its neighbors, especially between India and Pakistan. Both countries don't even have normal trade with each other. Here too one Southeast Asian story is relevant. India and Pakistan fought their last major war in 1971. China and Vietnam (who have been suspicious of each other for 2000 years, longer than India and Pakistan) fought their last major war in 1979. Yet, after Vietnam joined ASEAN (with whom it had been quarreling for decades, in 1995), it then also joined the China-ASEAN FTA in 2002. Since the mid-1990s, trade between Vietnam and China has grown 3000 times. Therefore trade between India and Pakistan can also grow 3000 times. The biggest beneficiaries of this increased trade will be the poor people of India and Pakistan.

The third concrete step India can take is to open the doors to Foreign Direct Investment (FDI) as much as the ASEAN countries have done so. Here is one statistic that Indians should reflect on. The combined GNP of the three dynamic North-East Asian economies (namely China, Japan and South Korea) is $21 trillion. By contrast, the combined GNP of the ten relatively poorer 10 ASEAN economies is only $3 trillion. Logically, since $21 trillion is more than $3 trillion, there should be more American investment in Northeast Asia rather than Southeast Asia. Instead, the figure is the opposite. In Northeast Asia, it is $287 billion and in Southeast Asia, it is $335 billion.

Let me add an important geopolitical point here. Given the growing tensions between the US and China (which I have documented in my book, Has China Won?), many American manufacturers are looking for a China plus one investment destination. Many want to invest in India for geopolitical reasons. However, as soon as they arrive in India and encounter Indian bureaucracy, they get discouraged. So here too there is a simple solution. Many of the Southeast Asian countries, including Indonesia and Vietnam, Malaysia, and Thailand, have produced simple and clear investment brochures. Each state in India should compete to produce investment brochures as good as those in ASEAN. Then they will find that the best and easiest way to boost economic growth is to attract FDI.

In short, it will not take rocket science to make India's economy the largest in the world and larger than even that of China and the US. It will only take simple common sense. There's no need to invent anything new. All India has to do is copy and learn from Southeast Asian countries that have had close relations with India for two thousand years. Prime Minister Manmohan Singh called on India to "Look East". Prime Minister Narendra Modi called on India to "Act East". My message to you is a much simpler one: please come to Southeast Asia and learn from the East.

The West Needs to Rethink Its Strategic Goals for Asia

Abstract When the West had its "End of History" moment at the end of the Cold War, it failed to recognize the return of Asia to the center stage of world history. Now, rather than blaming the rise of China for the myriad of problems it faces, the West should rethink its strategy for dealing with Asia.

Few thinkers can speak about global governance with as much authority as Kishore Mahbubani. A former President of the United Nations Security Council, Permanent Secretary of Singapore's Foreign Ministry, and Dean of the renowned Lee Kuan Yew School of Public Policy at the National University of Singapore, he has been named "the muse of the Asian century" and listed among the top 100 most influential public intellectuals in the world by the Financial Times, Foreign Policy and Prospect.

In his latest book, due this year, Mahbubani plans to tackle the rising tensions between the United States and China, and the former diplomat have some frank advice for the West. As he explains, the election of President Donald Trump and the launching of a trade war with China should be viewed as symptoms of the refusal of the US to accept its inevitable decline as the world's number one economy. Instead of howling at the moon, the US should embrace a more minimalist and strategic approach to foreign policy to maximize its interests in an era of Asian dominance.

Q: In your last book, *Has the West Lost It?*, you point out that there has been a remarkable improvement in the quality of life of people across the world over the past 30 years, but public discourse in the West has become increasingly pessimistic. What is behind this contradiction?

A: The great paradox, as I emphasize in the book, is that the dramatic improvement in the human condition is the result of the generous gifts of the West to the rest, especially the gift of reasoning. And, frankly, future historians looking back at our time would say that the 30 years from roughly 1980 to 2010 saw probably the most dramatic improvement in living standards in human history. So, this should be a moment of great celebration in the West—the great Western project of improving the human condition has succeeded.

Originally publised in Forbes, February 27, 2019

K. Mahbubani, *The Asian 21st Century*, China and Globalization,
https://doi.org/10.1007/978-981-16-6811-1_21

Paradoxically, the West has never been more depressed. I think the one reason for this is that the West made a huge strategic mistake at the end of the Cold War in 1989: it was seduced by the essay of Francis Fukuyama, "The End of History?," which basically said that the West had defeated the Soviet Union and it could just switch on autopilot, whereas the rest of the world needed to make strategic adjustments to this new world.

Fukuyama's essay did a lot of brain damage to the West. He put the West to sleep precisely at the moment when China and India were waking up. For 1800 of the past 2000 years, the world's two largest economies have always been those two countries. The last 200 years have been a major historical aberration. And, of course, all aberrations eventually come to a natural end.

But what no one could have foreseen in 1989 was the speed at which China and India have re-emerged. In 1980, in purchasing power parity terms, the United States' share of global GDP (gross domestic product) was 21.7% and China's share was 2.3%, which means that China's share was around 10% of the US. By 2014, astonishingly, China's share had become bigger. That's why it's such a dramatic period in human history.

Q: You outlined two key factors that have destabilized the West: first, a decline in real wages following the entry of China and Eastern Europe into the global trading system; and second a realization that national governments are becoming powerless to control the forces of globalization. Which of these is the most important?

A: They're both related. I think just as the West made a big strategic mistake at the end of the Cold War, another strategic mistake was made in 2001 when 9/11 happened. I was actually in Manhattan on 9/11, so I understood the shock that was felt by America. What happened as a result of 9/11 was that America decided its biggest strategic challenge was going to come from the Islamic world, so it launched wars in Afghanistan and Iraq.

That was a mistake because the most important strategic event that happened in 2001 was not 9/11 but China's admission into the World Trade Organization. China's entry injected 800 million workers into the global capitalist system and—as Joseph Schumpeter taught us—that would lead to creative destruction. So, it's not surprising that in the decade that followed, lots of people in the US and Europe lost their jobs. But because the elites were benefiting from the expansion of the global economy, they didn't notice that their own masses were suffering.

So, I would say that future historians will see that the election of Donald Trump in 2016 was not a surprise, but an inevitable result of the elites not taking care of their masses. The median income of the American worker had not improved for 40 years. That's shocking. Everything is tied together to China's admission to the WTO.

Q: Recently, many commentators in the US have been debating whether it was a "mistake" to allow China to join the World Trade Organization in 2001. What is your view on this debate?

A: There's a wonderful Western expression, 'there's no point shutting the door after the horse has bolted.' This is a classic demonstration of that saying. China has already joined the WTO; it is part of the global trading system and is incredibly integrated into it. There is nothing you can do about that.

What the West, and especially the US, needs to do is to adjust to this new competitive global system. I think it can adjust and can do well, but it is a question of working with rather than against China, which is why the current trade war is misguided. In fact, any sensible Western economist will tell you that America's trade deficit is not a result of China playing unfairly. It is actually the result of the US having the global reserve currency, which allows it to consume more than it produces. That is actually a privilege.

Q: In a recent article for Project Syndicate, you said you were struck during a recent sabbatical in the US by how decisively sentiment among the US elite has turned against China. What has caused this change?

A: I don't know, it's mystifying, but it has happened. I think there is a growing awareness that China is becoming bigger and stronger. Even though Americans don't like talking about America becoming number two, subconsciously they must realize that America is moving toward that status. Instead of looking in the mirror and asking what mistakes you have made, it's always easier to find a scapegoat, and China is the obvious one. The danger is that when you look for a scapegoat, you ignore the core structural issues that America has to deal with in this new era.

Q: How receptive should China be to the US's complaints about its economic and trade practices?

A: I think the Chinese should figure out which complaints are valid, and which are invalid. The invalid one is that the bilateral deficit is the result of the Chinese playing unfair—that is not true at all. In fact, the trade deficit paradoxically helps American workers in some ways. Even though their income has not gone up, they can buy more things, more cheaply thanks to Made-in-China products.

But, of course, there are also valid complaints. First, China may have been stealing intellectual property from American firms. Second, China has insisted that if American firms invest in China, they are to transfer technology to China. Third, there are non-tariff barriers. China has lowered its tariff barriers and fulfilled its WTO obligations, but there are non-tariff barriers that have hindered Western exports to China.

I think what China needs to do is respond with a certain generosity of spirit because China has done very well thanks to the West opening up its markets. Now, China can reciprocate by opening up its markets even more. That would also give the US and Europe greater strategic interest in maintaining good ties with China.

Q: The US is increasingly focusing its ire on China's Made in China 2025 strategy. What is your view on this strategy?

A: I think it's legitimate for China to aspire to become a technological superpower in its own right. Frankly, I think that China is going to succeed. The US should not complain about what China is doing, and instead, ask itself what the American response should be. But here, the ideology of people like US Trade Representative Robert Lighthizer—who believes that all government-led industrial policies don't work—gets in the way.

If industrial policies don't work, then why not allow this one to fail? If you complain about it, that suggests you believe it's going to work. Now, if it's going to work in China, why doesn't the United States launch its own comprehensive national strategy to maintain its technological lead? Instead of complaining about Made in China 2025, they should have a Made in America 2025.

Q: If China does emerge as the world's leading economy, how do you expect China to reshape the global order?

A: Just as America is reluctant to face the prospect of China overtaking them, I think the Chinese are reluctant to face the prospect of becoming number one. The Chinese should think more about this because it's very important that China makes a big effort to reassure the world that they're going to maintain the current rules-based order that the West has given the world. This is essentially what Xi Jinping promised in his two speeches in Geneva and Davos in January last year. And that's the message that needs to be repeated by China to the world.

It would be wise for China to strengthen the WTO, the United Nations, the International Monetary Fund and the World Bank, but that will require that the West gives up control. There was a rule created over 50 years ago that said the head of the International Monetary Fund should always be European and the World Bank leader should always be American. That rule was credible when the West's share of global GDP was overwhelming, but when your relative share of the global economy declines, and the most dynamic economies are in Asia, why are you disqualifying Asians from running these two organizations?

Q: How should the US and Europe position themselves in a global system dominated by Asia?

A: Europe and the US need to face the fact that the last two centuries of Western dominance have been a historical aberration, and that aberration is coming to a natural end. They need to be ready to deal with a world in which they remain strong, but in which their relative share of global GDP has gone down. If your share of GDP goes down, you need to adopt a new strategic approach, and what I suggest in Has the West Lost it? is a new "three-m" strategy for the West.

The first is "minimalist." The West should ask itself: should it get involved in so many wars? Should it be intervening in Afghanistan, Iraq, Libya, Syria, Yemen, and so on? The Chinese haven't fired a shot in 40 years, since the end of the war with Vietnam in 1979, whereas even during the last year of the presidency of Barack

Obama, a peaceful man who won the Nobel Peace Prize, America dropped 26,000 bombs on seven countries. That's crazy.

The second "m" is multilateral. Here, I build on the advice of former President Bill Clinton, who told his fellow Americans that if you can conceive of a world in which America is number two, then surely it is in America's interests to strengthen the world's multilateral order, which will then constrain the next number one, China. The tragedy is that although the world's multilateral institutions are the West's gift to the world, it is America with the silent collusion of Europe that has been weakening them. That's unwise.

And the third "m" is Machiavellian, which is just short for "be pragmatic." You want to focus on your own priorities and do what's important for you. So, for example, Europe's long-term challenge is not going to come from Russia—Russian tanks are not going to invade Germany. But what you're going to get is a demographic explosion in Africa that's going to be a challenge. You're going to get more refugees coming, and we've seen what has happened to Europe politically because of refugees. Therefore, it is in Europe's interest to see Africa develop, and the best partner to develop Africa is China. America is frightened of China's influence in Africa and condemns Chinese investment there, and the Europeans, because they're subservient to America, also criticize China. But China's long-term strategic investment in Africa is a gift to Europe. That's what I mean about thinking in Machiavellian terms about where your interests lie.

Myanmar Coup Could Jump-Start US-China Cooperation, Through Quiet Diplomacy

Abstract An isolated Myanmar and divided ASEAN are not good for Beijing. The wisest thing Joe Biden can do is show that American diplomacy can once again succeed in Asia.

The sociologist Max Weber once famously said, "it is not true that good can follow only from good and evil only from evil, but that often the opposite is true. Anyone who fails to see this is, indeed, a political infant".

Myanmar proves the sagacity of his statement. The "evil" of the coup was facilitated by the "good deeds" of Western leaders, whose isolation and rejection of Aung San Suu Kyi gave the generals the courage to launch a coup against her. Yet, good may also come out of the evil of the coup.

For a start, it could quietly jump-start discreet geopolitical cooperation between Beijing and the new Biden administration in Washington. Inconceivable? Why should China abandon an isolated military regime in Myanmar that would be safely dependent on it?

The simple answer is that an isolated Myanmar, which in turn divides ASEAN, is not a geopolitical asset for China. A divided ASEAN provides opportunities for Beijing's adversaries. And since Beijing thinks long-term, not short-term, it is acutely aware that keeping ASEAN together is in its interests. Hence, China will quietly support ASEAN's efforts to reverse the coup in Myanmar.

Yes, there will be trade-offs. In my two years as the Singapore ambassador to the UN Security Council (UNSC), I saw almost daily trade-offs among the five permanent members, including the US and China. After invading Iraq, George W. Bush needed China's help to lift UNSC sanctions on the country. Beijing obliged. Subsequently, the Bush administration squeezed the independence-inclined Chen Shui Bian administration in Taiwan.

Shocking? Fortunately, trade-offs among great powers are an old game, although to be honest, they are best done under the table with little public scrutiny.

Originally published in South China Morning Post, Feb 10, 2021

Are such deals ethical? Ask Max Weber. His answer would be that if the military regime is eased out of Myanmar through geopolitical trade-offs, then the outcome is ethical.

Equally importantly, if strong and silent collaboration between Beijing, Washington and key ASEAN capitals eventually results in the reversal of the coup, it would send a powerful signal that the era of military coups is over in Asia. ASEAN governments are not perfect.

Indeed, the range of political regimes within the ten countries is astonishing. Yet the trend toward civilian control of government is undeniable. Indonesia is exhibit A, having successfully created the most resilient democracy in the Islamic world.

Yet, to succeed in Southeast Asia, Washington will have to once again work comfortably with Southeast Asian norms and practices. This has happened before. During the Cold War, after the Vietnamese invasion of Cambodia in December 1978, the Reagan administration wisely allowed ASEAN to take the lead.

When I was sent as a young puppy, at the age of 35, to the UN in 1984, my American counterpart was the legendary ambassador Vernon Walters, who was 67 then. He once asked to see me. I offered to call on him. Instead, he insisted on walking over to my office, despite his age. Such humility won him many friends.

To understand the resilience of ASEAN norms, Americans should remember one significant historical fact. When the US left Vietnam ignominiously in 1975, Southeast Asian countries were supposed to collapse as dominoes. Instead, they developed the second most successful regional organization in the world (with quiet back room American support).

In our new era, as the Asian century gains momentum, it may be best to use Asian methods of solving knotty problems. In the West, domestic political pressures lead to public grandstanding. This was why the West publicly criticized Aung San Suu Kyi. Yet, in Asia, quiet diplomacy works. Even though this current Myanmar coup is a reversal, it is vital to remember that the previous Myanmar military regime was even more stubborn and difficult.

Over time, through silent peer pressure at the thousands of ASEAN meetings that Myanmar military officials attended, the message got through: Myanmar had to open up and integrate if it wanted to succeed and catch up with the rest of Asia. Hence, the wisest thing that the Biden administration could do is to engage in quiet diplomacy with Beijing, ASEAN capitals (as well as Tokyo and New Delhi) to deliver a quiet and consistent message to the Myanmar military regime that the era of military coups is over.

The keyword here is diplomacy. What is the essence of diplomacy? One wag explained it well: a good diplomat is someone who can tell you to "go to hell" in such a way that you feel you are going to enjoy the journey. Certainly, there is an almost universal agreement among all of Myanmar's neighbors, including China, that the current military regime should go to hell. The challenge is to deliver this message quietly and respectfully so that it offers the Myanmar military regime a face-saving way out of the quandary it is in.

Here's a radical proposal for Washington to consider. Why did Indonesia make a smooth transition away from military rule while Myanmar has stepped backward?

One key reason is that even during Suharto's authoritarian rule, Indonesian military officers were trained at American military staff colleges. When the history of Indonesia's democracy is written, there is no doubt that former president Susilo Bambang Yudhoyono (2004–2014) will be given great credit. And why did he support democracy despite being a general under Suharto?

The answer is that he was trained at the US Army Command and General Staff College. There he learned the most important value of American democracy: that civilians must always control the military. So the solution is clear: Washington must invite young Myanmar military officers to train in American military colleges. Impossible?

Then Washington must once again revisit the wisdom of the statement from Max Weber. Instead of just publicly condemning the Myanmar military, the correct and politically courageous thing to do is to go against American conventional wisdom and talk to the Myanmar military, instead of isolating it.

And if the Biden administration quietly succeeds in easing out the military regime, it will demonstrate that American diplomacy can once again succeed in Asia, paving the way for a new and sustained American engagement that is more effective and wiser because it is low-key and understated.

Can Asia Help Biden?

Abstract A strong, self-confident America is needed to resume its leadership role. Asia has a role to play—if the US is prepared to listen.

Ask not what America can do for you! Ask rather what you can do for America.

If US President Joe Biden were in a position to send a sincere and honest message to the rest of the world in his recent inaugural address, these are the words he should have used—echoing the famous words of John F. Kennedy, exactly 60 years ago, when he said: "Ask not what your country can do for you—ask what you can do for your country."

Instead, because American presidents are prisoners of American political tradition, President Biden had to say: "We can make America, once again, the leading force for good in the world."

The sad reality is that the United States can no longer provide the world with unquestioned leadership.

American leadership has benefited the world: The multilateral rules and institutions it generated after World War II have prevented World War III; the open markets of America helped the East Asian tigers and China to succeed; the US Navy enabled freedom of navigation. But all this strong global leadership required a strong, self-confident America, one that Kennedy's stirring rhetoric could rouse 60 years ago.

Sadly, Mr. Donald Trump has left a broken, deeply divided America that has neither the spirit nor the will to lead the world. Any illusions that a strong, self-confident America would bounce back after Mr. Biden's election were wiped out on Jan 6, when the world saw an unruly mob storm the US Capitol, in part because of the implicit encouragement of Mr. Trump himself.

This is why Dr. Richard Haass, president of the Council on Foreign Relations, America's most prestigious foreign policy think tank, tweeted that day: "No one in the world is likely to see, respect, fear, or depend on us in the same way again. If the post-American era has a start date, it is almost certainly today."

Originally published in The Straits Times, Jan 22, 2021

K. Mahbubani, *The Asian 21st Century*, China and Globalization,
https://doi.org/10.1007/978-981-16-6811-1_23

British journalist Martin Wolf is equally pessimistic. As he wrote in the Financial Times: "The US republic has survived the test of Trump. But it still needs to be saved from death."

The big question that the rest of the world, including Asia, faces with President Biden's inauguration, is whether it is in the world's (or Asia's) interest to see America continue to decline and weaken, or if we should instead help America to recover.

The answer is obviously the latter: The world is better off with a strong, self-confident America.

Yet, Asia (or the world) can help America only if it believes that it needs help. Sheer pride will make it difficult for Americans to accept that they need help, even though thoughtful Americans, like political scientist Francis Fukuyama, acknowledge that America has some serious internal healing to do.

Dr. Fukuyama said that the US is "divided, internally preoccupied, and contradicting its own democratic ideals".

America's internal problems are deep and structural. As I document in Has China Won?, they range from the deeply plutocratic political system that has become entrenched to the "sea of despair" that has emerged among the white working classes, who sadly and unwisely supported Mr. Trump in their anger.

No magic wand can wave away all these deep structural problems.

There is no question that President Biden is doing the right things to help America get back on the road. He has announced the following measures in the first 100 days of his term: a US$1.9 trillion (S$2.5 trillion) coronavirus relief package, 100 million vaccine doses, a US$15-an-hour minimum wage increase, extending a pause on student loan payments, and extending nationwide restrictions on eviction. Let's hope that these internal healing measures work.

Equally important, President Biden should avoid painful and demanding external commitments. The wisest thing that he could do to help both America and the world heal from the Covid-19 rampage is to press the pause button on the US-China geopolitical contest. It would be sheer common sense to do this.

Unfortunately, given the toxic anti-China mood in America, his hands are tied. If he is seen to be soft on China, he will be excoriated. Thus, publicly, he must appear to be tough on China.

Surprisingly, President Biden said nothing about China in his inaugural speech.

However, his Cabinet appointees—including Dr. Janet Yellen for treasury secretary, Mr. Antony Blinken for secretary of state, and Ms. Avril Haines for director of national intelligence – have criticized China strongly in their Senate confirmation hearings.

Ms. Haines said: "China is a challenge to our security, to our prosperity, to our values across a range of issues, and I do support an aggressive stance, in a sense, to deal with the challenge that we're facing."

Yet, even though the logical and sensible pause button is out of Mr. Biden's reach, he can still rebalance the US-China contest.

If former president Barack Obama opted for 60% cooperation and 40% competition with China, while Mr. Trump essentially went for 90% competition and

10% cooperation, President Biden can at least go for 60% competition and 40% cooperation.

Golden Opportunity

Yet, President Biden cannot achieve this rebalancing on his own. He needs the help of Asia. All this provides ASEAN (including Singapore) with a golden opportunity.

To win political support for a more rational China policy, Mr. Biden needs political cover. ASEAN can provide political cover by collectively calling on both China and the US to first focus on working together to solve common and pressing problems like Covid-19 and climate change.

The most sensible thing Mr Biden could do is to send his senior diplomats to East Asia on a "listening" mission.

Indeed, all good diplomacy begins with listening and understanding. Here, there is no question what President Biden's diplomats will hear from South-east Asians: They want a strong American presence in South-east Asia, but they also do not want to be forced to choose between America and China.

The former Indonesian ambassador to the US, Dr. Dino Patti Djalal, put it well when he said: "Today, South-east Asians want to get along with the US and China, but they also want the US and China to get along, at least in their region. Is that too much to ask?".

He added: "We don't want to be duped into an anti-China campaign".

Fortunately, President Biden has chosen as his Asian "czar" Mr Kurt Campbell, a seasoned and experienced diplomat. During the Covid-19 lockdown period, he and I partnered together in a debate organized by Intelligence Squared the US to argue in favor of a motion, "Coronavirus will reshape the world order in China's favor".

In the debate, he said: "We expect a country to provide domestic capacity and demonstrate competence in terms of dealing with the pandemic. No one would argue that the US has been able to do anything of this kind. It's been a tragedy to see the incompetence with which the US has dealt with the issue".

"We would expect that the leading nation would be able to provide support in terms of PPE (personal protective equipment) and equipment. We've seen nothing of the sort from the US".

"What we see in contrast is China, even though this is where the virus originated; since that time they've been reaching out, providing equipment and support to a variety of countries around the world".

He added: "After the coronavirus has swept the planet, it is undeniable that China has taken advantage of the situation, has moved forward and everyone sees that America has been missing in action." Changing priorities.

Mr. Campbell is also a good listener. If he came to South-east Asia, he would hear another clear message on the priorities of ASEAN.

All countries have to prioritize politics, economics, and security in their international affairs. America tends to prioritize the security dimension the most, followed by politics and economics. China prioritizes economics, followed by politics and security. There is no question that the priorities of ASEAN are closer to those of China than America.

Given the social and economic travails of the US, and the "sea of despair" faced by its working classes, it would now be in America's self-interest to also put economics ahead of security.

Unwisely, America has spent over US$5 trillion fighting futile post-9/11 wars. If this US$5 trillion had been spent on the bottom 50% of American society, each citizen in this group would have received a cheque for US$30,000. This is a very significant amount, especially since 60% of Americans do not have access to US$400 in case of an emergency.

In short, contrary to the conventional wisdom in Washington, which is strongly in favor of accelerating the geopolitical contest against China, it would be wiser for America to at least press the pause button on this contest and focus on getting both the American and global economies back on track.

ASEAN (and Singapore) has a golden opportunity to help Mr Biden by providing him with the necessary political cover to pursue a more sensible approach in US-China relations. By doing this, ASEAN will also repay America a major debt. Without American support and backing, ASEAN could not have been successfully launched in 1967. Now it is ASEAN's turn to help America successfully re-launch itself.

The Peaceful Rise of China

The balance of power in the world is currently shifting from West to East with the rise of China and other Asian nations. While this rise has been peaceful, it has caused major concern in the West. The tempestuousness of this rise is mainly due to the considerable influence China is having on how a new world order may be shaped.

China: Threat or Opportunity?

Abstract China today is the superpower with the greatest "spiritual vitality". While many in the United States see this as a threat to its primacy, the United States should instead work with China to better the lives of its people.

Is China a threat or an opportunity for America?

Is that a simple question? As a student of philosophy, I have learned that behind a simple question can lurk many others that are more complex. Here are a few for that particular question: Does China intend to weaken or undermine America? Or is its rise driven by domestic factors? Does China have a grand strategy? If so, what are its primary goals? Is China's rise a threat to American primacy or to the American people? And, perhaps most controversially, should America give priority to geopolitical primacy or to its citizens in taking on the challenge from China?

Curiously, there has been little genuine debate on this complex challenge in the US Instead, there has been a dramatic convergence in the opinions of many Americans, despite deep political polarization, toward the view that China is a threat. Nine in ten Americans believe that, according to a recent Pew poll. The "deep state" has also turned against China. As Henry Paulson put it last year: "You have Homeland Security, the FBI, CIA, the Defense Department, treating China as the enemy and members of Congress competing to see who can be the most belligerent China hawk. No one is leaning against the wind, providing balance."

The goal of this essay is to provide some balance and objectivity.

Despite this extraordinary convergence of views, most thoughtful Americans would agree that China has no plan to invade or occupy America. It would be a mission impossible. Nor would China dream of launching a nuclear attack. It has only about 290 nuclear weapons, compared to America's 6000-plus. Nor does China have any desire to close off sea lanes, like Germany tried to do in World War II. China does more international trade than America. Paradoxically, the US Navy is keeping sea lanes open for Chinese commerce.

Yet, it is also true that there has been a significant change in military balance between China and America. In 1996, President Bill Clinton sent two aircraft carriers

Originally published in Noema, Jun 15, 2020

© The Author(s) 2022
K. Mahbubani, *The Asian 21st Century*, China and Globalization,
https://doi.org/10.1007/978-981-16-6811-1_24

to patrol the ocean off the coast of China to dissuade Beijing from being too aggressive toward Taiwan. Today, these two aircraft carriers would be sitting ducks in the face of Chinese hypersonic missiles. The military balance has shifted, creating discomfort in Washington.

Even so, this isn't where the primary challenge will arise from China. In the era of nuclear weapons, superpower primacy is likely to be determined in the economic sphere, not military sphere.

One of America's wisest strategic thinkers was the diplomat George Kennan, who lived from 1904 to 2005. When America embarked on its great geopolitical contest against the Soviet Union, Kennan said the final outcome would be determined by "the degree to which the United States can create among the peoples of the world generally the impression of a country which knows what it wants, which is coping successfully with the problem of its internal life and with the responsibilities of a world power, and which has a spiritual vitality capable of holding its own among the major ideological currents of the time".

Kennan added that with this "spiritual vitality," America should cultivate more "friends and allies." He also counseled "humility" and bravely said America should avoid "insulting" the Soviet Union, as America would still have to deal with it.

Fortunately, Kennan's strategic advice was largely heeded. America won the geopolitical contest against the Soviet Union handsomely. Curiously, even though China will be a far more formidable superpower rival, with four times the population of America and a political resilience that is at least 4000 years old, America has not attempted to work out a comprehensive long-term strategy to deal with it.

If Kennan is right and the contest will be determined by domestic "spiritual vitality," China is winning. America is the only major developed society where the real wages for the bottom half of the working population declined over a 30-year period. In turn, this has generated a "sea of despair" among the white working classes, as documented by Princeton economists Anne Case and Angus Deaton.

By contrast, 1.4 billion Chinese people have experienced an extraordinary improvement in living standards. The past 40 years have been the best the Chinese have experienced in 4000 years. As a result, as the researcher, Jean Fan has documented: "In contrast to America's stagnation, China's culture, self-concept, and morale are being transformed at a rapid pace—mostly for the better." China has spiritual vitality. America, not as much.

If Kennan were alive today, he would be deeply alarmed. He would strongly argue against burning money in useless foreign interventions. In fact, he was alive when the Iraq War began in 2003—and he opposed it. If America had heeded his advice and disbursed the roughly USD 5.4 trillion it spent on post-9/11 wars in the Middle East and Central Asia on its own people instead, each member of the bottom 50% of the population would have received a check for more than USD 33,000. This is why Eisenhower wisely advised in 1953 that "every gun that is made, every warship launched, every rocket fired signifies, in the final sense, a theft from those who hunger and are not fed, those who are cold and are not clothed".

America is still a much richer country than China, with a per capita income of around USD 63,000 compared to USD 9700 for China. Its universities and scientific expertise are clearly superior to China's. Yet when Covid-19 hit, China experienced 0.33 deaths per 100,000 people (as of mid-May). The US figure was 27. One figure cannot tell everything. But it provides a clue that China has been investing in strong domestic institutions, especially in public service, while America has been neglecting them. President Ronald Reagan began this slide when he declared: "Government is not the solution to our problem; it is the problem." China believes otherwise.

All this brings up the key dilemma America faces in taking on the strategic challenge from China: Should it focus on defending American primacy or defending the well-being of its people? Most Americans assume that America is rich and powerful enough to do both. Sadly, the data argue otherwise. As the Nobel Laureate Joseph Stiglitz and Harvard professor Linda Bilmes have said regarding the money spent on Iraq: "[H]ad the taxpayer's taxes been reduced commensurately, or if the money had been spent on providing healthcare, it would have made a difference to hard-pressed middle-class families." With better healthcare, fewer Americans would have died from Covid-19. The price for giving strategic priority to American primacy has been paid by the American people.

Can America change direction and focus on domestic economic and social development instead of wasteful external adventures? In theory, yes. In practice, it will be difficult. America has had many brilliant defense secretaries. None could reduce defense department expenses. Why not? Defense spending results from a complex lobbying system rather than from a comprehensive rational strategy.

Nevertheless, it remains true that there is a strong consensus within the American body politic, especially among the American elite, that America should remain number one. Americans feel an obligation to lead the world. Secretary of State Madeleine Albright expressed this well in 1998: "If we have to use force, it is because we are America; we are the indispensable nation. We stand tall, and we see further than other countries into the future, and we see the danger here to all of us." Americans want America to be the "shining city on a hill," inspiring the rest of the world.

Indeed, the rest of the world would be happy to see a strong, self-confident America inspiring us all. However, its "shine" comes from its domestic record, not its military adventures. Clearly, the "sea of despair" among the working classes, the rise of populism, the election of Donald Trump and the recent incompetency around Covid-19 have dented America's standing in the world. Any empirical study would show that while America's geopolitical influence has been receding, China's has been gradually expanding.

But even if China's influence has grown, it has no desire to step into America's shoes and provide global leadership. China has only one key strategic goal: to become strong enough to prevent another century of humiliation, the period between 1842 and 1949 when Western forces trampled on China with great abandon. China regained its strength by plugging into the rules-based global order that America gifted to the world in 1945.

China has no desire to overturn this order. It would be happy to cooperate with America within it. In short, a prosperous China can live together in peace with a prosperous America, as inconceivable as this thought might seem in the toxic political environment in the US.

Hence, at the end of the day, all is not lost for America. It can reverse its slide in geopolitical fortunes. However, to do so, it must begin to heed the advice of its strategic thinkers, like Kennan. As Kennan said, it should become humble and stop insulting adversaries. It should cultivate friends and allies and focus on its domestic spiritual vitality. Even to a lay observer, this is plain common sense. America can still win—not by investing in military supremacy but in moral supremacy. Until it does that, it is ceding the playing field to China.

A 'Yellow Peril' Revival Fueling Western Fears of China's Rise

Abstract Western concerns about the rise of China are not just the result of cool, hard-headed analysis. As history tells us, they may also come from a subconscious, emotional fear of a non-Caucasian civilization.

Do we arrive at geopolitical judgments from only cool, hard-headed, rational analysis? If emotions influence our judgments, are these conscious emotions, or do they operate at the level of our subterranean subconscious? Any honest answer to these questions would admit that non-rational factors always play a role. This is why it was wrong for Western media to vilify Kiron Skinner, the director of policy planning at the US State Department, for naming racial discomfort as a factor at play in the emerging geopolitical contest between the United States and China.

Skinner was correct in saying that "the Soviet Union and that competition, in a way, it was a fight within the Western family". Referring to the contest with China, she said: "it's the first time that we will have a great power competitor that is not Caucasian". That China is not Caucasian is a factor in the geopolitical contest and it may also explain strong emotional reactions in Western countries to China's rise.

Take the ongoing trade dispute between the United States and China as an example. Critics of China are rational and correct when they state that China has stolen intellectual property and occasionally bullied US firms into sharing their technology. But a calm, rational description of China's behavior would also add that such behavior is normal for an emerging economy.

The United States also stole intellectual property, especially from the British, at a similar stage of its economic development. Equally important, when the United States agreed to admit China into the WTO as a 'developing country', it agreed that 'under the WTO's agreements on intellectual property, developed countries are under "the obligation" to provide incentives to their companies to transfer technology to less developed countries'. This is a point that Yukon Huang, a former World Bank economist, has pointed out.

Most Western portrayals of China's emergence as a great power lack balance. They tend to highlight negative dimensions of China's rise but omit the positive

---

Originally published in East Asia Forum, Jun 5, 2019

K. Mahbubani, *The Asian 21st Century*, China and Globalization,
https://doi.org/10.1007/978-981-16-6811-1_25

129

dimensions. When US Vice President Mike Pence gave a comprehensive speech on China on 4 October 2018, he said: "Over the past 17 years, China's GDP has grown nine-fold; it's become the second largest economy in the world. Much of this success was driven by American investment in China". This is a factually incorrect statement. China's economic success has been primarily driven by the rejuvenation of the Chinese people, not US investment.

Though Washington prides itself as a center of calm and rational strategic thinking, such an unbalanced speech was not attacked in the liberal media. Instead, many cheered the US Vice President for attacking China.

This virulent anti-China atmosphere is reminiscent of the mid-1980s when Western media attacked Japan ferociously. The distrust of yellow-skinned people has resurfaced again. As former US ambassador Chas Freeman has observed: 'In their views of China, many Americans now appear subconsciously to have combined images of the insidious Dr. Fu Manchu, Japan's unnerving 1980s challenge to US industrial and financial primacy, and a sense of existential threat analogous to the Sinophobia that inspired the Anti-Coolie and Chinese Exclusion Acts'.

The people of the United States need to question how much of their reactions to China's rise result from hard-headed rational analysis and how much are a result of deep discomforts with a non-Caucasian civilization. We may never know the real answer as these titanic struggles between reason and emotion are probably playing out in deep subconscious terrains. Still, we should thank Kiron Skinner for alluding to the fact that such subconscious dimensions are at play here. The time has come for an honest discussion of the 'yellow peril' dimension in US-China relations. As Freud taught us, the best way to deal with our subconscious fears is to surface them and deal with them.

Is China Expansionist?

Abstract China's emergence as a great power has prompted many fears that it will start to become aggressive and militaristic. But while European powers have acted this way historically, China's own long history tells us that it wields power in a very different manner.

The Chinese soldier who pushed the Indian Colonel Santosh Babu (who tragically died) and thereby triggered the violent clash between Chinese and Indian soldiers in mid-June 2020 should be court-martialed. Both sides suffered casualties, the worst since 1975. This one push by one Chinese soldier has set back China-India relations severely, undermining all the good work that had been done over several years by Prime Minister Manmohan Singh and Premier Wen Jiabao, as well as by Prime Minister Narendra Modi and President Xi Jinping. Equally importantly, it has reinforced a growing belief, especially in the western world, that as China's economy becomes stronger and stronger, China will abandon its "peaceful rise" and behave as a militarily expansionist power. This could well happen. It would be naive to believe otherwise. However, a deep study of Chinese history and culture would also show that the continuation of a peaceful rise is equally plausible.[1]

One key point needs to be emphasized at the outset. As China becomes more and more powerful, it will flex its muscles and use them more. This is normal great power behavior. Indeed, the term "benevolent great power" is an oxymoron. No great power is altruistic. All great powers will pursue their national interests. So will China. However, while the goals of all great powers are similar, the methods might differ. China has become and will become more assertive. Yet it need not become more aggressive. These two words "assertive" and "aggressive" are often confused with each other. A study of the great power behavior of America and China will illustrate the differences.

Graham Allison has wisely warned his fellow Americans to be careful in what they wish for China. He writes, "Americans enjoy lecturing Chinese to be 'more

Originally published in PRISM, Oct 21, 2020

---

[1] Kishore Mahbubani, is the author of the book, Has China Won? (Public Affairs, 2020). This essay contains excerpts from *Has China Won?*

© The Author(s) 2022
K. Mahbubani, *The Asian 21st Century*, China and Globalization,
https://doi.org/10.1007/978-981-16-6811-1_26

131

like us.' Perhaps they should be more careful what they wish for. Historically how have emerging hegemons behaved? To be more specific, how did Washington act just over a century ago when Theodore Roosevelt led the US into what he was supremely confident would be an American century? […] In the decade that followed his arrival in Washington, the US declared war on Spain, expelling it from the Western Hemisphere and acquiring Puerto Rico, Guam, and the Philippines; threatened Germany and Britain with war unless they agreed to settle the disputes on American terms; supported an insurrection in Colombia to create a new country, Panama, in order to build a canal; and declared itself the policeman of the Western Hemisphere, asserting the right to intervene whenever and wherever it judged necessary—a right it exercised nine times in the seven years of Roosevelt's presidency alone."[2]

If America's behavior during its period of emergence as a great power conforms to the historical norm, China's behavior so far, defies the norm. Of the five permanent members of the UN Security Council (who represent the great powers), only one has not fought a war in 40 years; China. Indeed, China has not even fired a bullet across its borders since a naval skirmish with Vietnam in 1989. The recent fighting between Chinese and Indian soldiers was brutal and savage. However, both sides adhered to their agreement not to use their firearms. Article VI of this agreement, signed in 1996, states, "Neither side shall open fire, cause bio-degradation, use hazardous chemicals, conduct blast operations or hunt with guns or explosives within two kilometers from the line of actual control."[3] The strategic discipline shown by Chinese and Indian soldiers is commendable.

In contrast to China, in the last three decades, America has fought a war or been involved in military actions every year. The Congressional Research Service, an independent body, produced a study entitled, "Instances of Use of United States Armed Forces Abroad, 1798–2018." In theory, there should have been a reduction in American interventions after the Cold War ended in 1989. This study demonstrates that in the 190 years preceding the end of the Cold War, American troops were deployed a total of 216 times, or 1.1 times per year on average. However, in the 25 years after the end of the Cold war, America increased its military interventions sharply and used its armed forces 152 times, or 6.1 times per year.[4]

John Mearsheimer has described what happened in his book, *The Great Delusion*. He writes, "With the end of the Cold War in 1989 and the collapse of the Soviet Union in 1991, the United States emerged as by far the most powerful country on the planet. Unsurprisingly, the Clinton administration embraced liberal hegemony from the start, and the policy remained firmly intact through the Bush and Obama administrations. Not surprisingly, the United States has been involved in numerous wars during this period and has failed to achieve meaningful success in almost all of

---

[2] Allison (2017).

[3] "Agreement Between the Government of the Republic of India and the Government of the People's Republic of China on Confidence-Building Measures in the Military Field Along the Line of Actual Control in the India-China Border Areas," November 29, 1996.

[4] Congressional Research Service, "Instances of Use of United States Armed Forces Abroad, 1798–2018," December 28, 2018, https://www.hsdl.org/?view&did=819747.

those conflicts."[5] Stephen Walt adds, "US military action has led directly or indirectly to the deaths of 250,000 Muslims over the past three decades (and that is a low-end estimate, not counting the deaths resulting from the sanctions against Iraq in the 1990s)."[6]

The big question here, therefore, is thus; why has China refrained from using its military in recent decades? What are the deeper roots of this pattern of behavior? Henry Kissinger has explained well why the Chinese avoid military options. He says, "[The] foundations [of China's distinctive military theory] were laid during a period of upheaval when ruthless struggles between rival kingdoms decimated China's population. Reacting to this slaughter (and seeking to emerge victorious from it), Chinese thinkers developed strategic thought that placed a premium on victory through psychological advantage and preached the avoidance of direct conflict."[7] Kissinger has accurately distilled the essence of the advice given by China's master strategist Sun Tzu, who once said; "All warfare is based on deception... Pretend inferiority and encourage his arrogance... For to win one hundred victories is not the acme of skill. To subdue the enemy without fighting is the acme of skill."[8]

If China were to try to make a case that it is inherently not a militaristic power, it would have many strong arguments to deploy. The first argument is historical. If Chinese civilization is inherently militaristic, this militaristic streak, especially the desire to conquer and subjugate other territories, would have surfaced long ago. Over the past two thousand years, China has often been the single strongest civilization in the Eurasian landmass. If China was inherently militaristic, it would have and should have conquered territories overseas, as the European powers did. Future historians will, for example, marvel at the fact that even though Australia is geographically close to China, it was physically occupied and conquered by far more distant British forces. Indeed, had James Cook sailed directly, it would have taken him at least 90 days to reach Australia's Botany Bay, having departed from Plymouth Dockyard in August of 1768; counterfactually, was he instead to have sailed from China, he would have found himself ashore in Australia in just under 30 days.

This Chinese reluctance to conquer Australia and other overseas territories is not because China always lacked a navy. Before the Portuguese and Spanish began the ruthless European policies of colonizing the world in the sixteenth century, the Chinese had by far the strongest navy in the world. At the start of the fifteenth century, nearly a hundred years before Christopher Columbus tried to find a route to the so-called Spice Islands, China sent out seven naval expeditions, under the remarkable leadership of Admiral Zheng He, a legendary Chinese figure. He traveled as far as Africa on ships that were far larger in size than the Portuguese or Spanish vessels: "The stars of the Chinese fleet were the treasure ships—sweeping junks, several stories high, up to 122 m long and 50 m wide. In fact, they were about four times

---

[5] Mearsheimer (2018).

[6] Walt (2011).

[7] Kissinger (2011).

[8] ibid.

bigger than the 'Santa Maria,' the ship Columbus sailed to America on behalf of the Spanish crown."

Along the way, he did get into military battles. For example, in his voyages between 1409 and 1411, he "captured King Alagak-Konara of Ceylon and chose Yapanaina to be the king instead," and in his voyages between 1413 and 1415, he "captured Sekandar, king of Sumatra (Atcheh) and then installed a new king."[9]

Yet, quite remarkably, China did not conquer or occupy any overseas or distant territories. Singapore's former foreign minister George Yeo remarked that, "throughout Chinese history, the Chinese have been averse to sending military forces far away... In the eighth century, at the peak of China's development during the Tang Dynasty, they had an army near the Fergana Valley in Central Asia, when the Abbasids were moving eastwards. They clashed. In the famous battle of Talas, the Abbasids defeated the Tang army, and the Chinese never crossed the Tianshan Mountains again in their history."[10]

The relatively peaceful streak of the Han Chinese people is brought out when their behavior is compared with some of their neighbors. One of the most powerful and terrifying imperialist expansions in human history was carried out by China's immediate neighbors in the North, the Mongols. Led by the brutal and dynamic Genghis Khan, these relatively small Mongolian tribes (far smaller in population than the Chinese people) conquered not just China but almost all of Asia, becoming, in the thirteenth century, the only East Asian force to threaten an invasion of Europe. Yet the more powerful Chinese empire never emulated this conquering example of its neighbors.

The Mongols conquered and ruled China itself for over a century. In an article for the Asia Society, Jean Johnson writes that, "Genghis Khan moved his troops into the quasi-Chinese Chin-ruled north China in 1211, and in 1215 they destroyed the capital city. His son Ogodei conquered all of North China by 1234 and ruled it from 1229 to 1241. Genghis Khan's grandson, Kublai Khan, defeated the Chinese Southern Song in 1279, and for the first time, all of China was under foreign rule. In 1271 Kublai Khan named his dynasty Yuan which means 'origin of the universe.' The Yuan dynasty in China lasted from 1279 to 1368."[11] As a result, there was massive cross-fertilization between Mongolian and Chinese culture. In this process, the Mongols could have transferred their militaristic culture into the software of Chinese civilization. Instead, the opposite happened. The Chinese progressively civilized their Mongol rulers, and while Kublai Khan fought wars with China's neighbors, he made no effort to conquer the world like his grandfather Genghis Khan tried to do.

What was the powerful anti-military DNA of Chinese civilization that eventually infected Mongol rulers? It probably goes back to Confucius. The Chinese have long had a saying that "just as good iron is not transformed into a nail; a good man is not made into a soldier." At several points in the *Analects*, Confucius cautions against

[9] Lorenz (2005).

[10] Yeo (2019).

[11] Jean Johnson, "The Mongol Dynasty," Asia Society, https://asiasociety.org/education/mongol-dynasty.

people who only have the strength of soldiers. In one dialogue, Zilu said, "Does the *junzi* prize valor?" The Master said, "The *junzi* gives righteousness the topmost place. If a *junzi* had valor but not righteousness, he would create chaos. If a small person has valor and not righteousness, he becomes a bandit." In another dialogue, Zilu said, "Master, if you were put in charge of the three army divisions, then whom would you wish to have with you?" The Master said, "Those who fight tigers with their bare hands, wade across rivers, and are willing to die without regret—I would not want their company. I would certainly want those who approach affairs with fearful caution and who like to lay careful plans for success."[12]

In contrast to American culture, where there is a strong built-in reverence for the man in uniform, Chinese culture has revered scholars more than soldiers, even though there are military figures who are celebrated in folklore and literature for their patriotism and loyalty. Overall, there is an even greater reverence for the man who is skilled in both, encapsulated in the idea of 文武双全 (*wén wǔ shuāng quán*), that is, someone who is both a fine scholar and soldier.

Still, all these arguments from history will not convince many who believe that China's recent behavior has demonstrated that it has a militaristic streak, and also lies about its military intentions and actions. For example, it is widely believed that Xi Jinping reneged on his promise not to militarize the South China Sea islands. In December 2016, the Wall Street Journal reported, "For a man who stood at the White House in September 2015 and promised not to militarize the South China Sea, Xi Jinping is sure doing a lot of militarizing."[13] In two articles for the *Washington Post*, John Pomfret wrote that, "China routinely makes commitments that it does not keep. Just remember Xi's 2015 promise to then-President Barack Obama not to militarize the islands it created in the South China Sea,"[14] and again that Xi "broke his promises to President Barack Obama not to militarize the seven Chinese-made islands in the South China Sea."[15] The *Economist* was perhaps the most forthright in its accusation of Xi's broken promise, declaring in April 2018, "Less than three years ago, Xi Jinping stood with Barack Obama in the Rose Garden at the White House and lied through his teeth. [...] China absolutely did not, Mr. Xi purred, 'intend to pursue militarization' on its islands."[16]

If Xi had indeed made such a promise and reneged, it would only go to confirm a widespread belief in the West that China has become aggressive and expansionist. It would also confirm a belief that the Chinese are being perfidious and deceptive when they claim that China will rise peacefully. So what is true?

[12] Confucius, "The Analects of Confucius," trans. Robert Eno, 2015, https://chinatxt.sitehost.iu.edu/Resources.html.

[13] Shugart (2016).

[14] Pomfret (2018a).

[15] Pomfret (2018b).

[16] "China Has Militarised the South China Sea and Got Away with It," The Economist, June 21, 2018, https://www.economist.com/asia/2018/06/21/china-has-militarised-the-south-china-sea-and-got-away-with-it.

Few Americans can claim to know China as well as Ambassador Stapleton Roy. Born in China, a fluent Mandarin speaker, Roy also served as the American ambassador to China from 1991 to 1995 and has stayed exceptionally well informed on US-China relations. He explained what happened: In a joint press conference with President Obama on September 25, 2015, Xi Jinping had proposed a more reasonable approach on the South China Sea. Xi had supported full and effective implementation of the 2002 Declaration on the Conduct of Parties in the South China Sea, signed by China and all ten ASEAN members; had called for early conclusion of the China-ASEAN consultations on a Code of Conduct for the South China Sea; and had added that China had no intention of militarizing the Spratlys, where it had engaged in massive reclamation work on the reefs and shoals it occupied. Roy said that Obama missed an opportunity to capitalize on this reasonable proposal. Instead, the US Navy stepped up its naval patrols. China responded by proceeding with militarization. In short, Xi did not renege on a promise. His offer was effectively spurned by the US Navy.

While there is no question that China has restrained itself from militarily "aggressive" behavior, it is also clear that China has become more "assertive" as it emerges as a new great power, using non-military means to project its power. When Norway conferred the Nobel Peace Prize to Chinese dissident Liu Xiaobo in 2010, Norway was put in diplomatic cold storage. Ties were cut. When the Australian Prime Minister called for an independent inquiry into the causes of Covid-19 in April 2020, China froze the imports of Australian barley. The use of economic means to pressure smaller countries is normal great power behavior. The United States cut off World Bank loans to poor Ethiopia when it made the mistake of repaying high-interest loans to American banks. France punishes its former colonies in Africa when they fail to heed the wisdom of Paris.

It's also true that Chinese diplomacy has become assertive with the younger "wolf warrior" diplomats issuing sharper statements and rebuttals. This has triggered a backlash. Yet, they are only shooting off sharp words, not bullets. As the old English proverb says, "sticks and stones may break my bones but words will never break me." A world where pointed words replace bullets is a safer world.

Like other great powers, China is selective when it comes to conforming to international law. It respects the UN Convention on the Law of the Sea but walked away from the decision of the Law of the Sea Tribunal on the South China Sea. The United States also walked away from the World Court in 1986 when it decreed that the US support for the Sandinistas in Nicaragua violated international law, including "not to use force against another State," "not to intervene in its affairs," "not to violate its sovereignty," and "not to interrupt peaceful maritime commerce."[17] The US Ambassador to the UN then called the court a "semi-legal, semi-juridical, semi-political body, which nations sometimes accept and sometimes don't."[18]

---

[17] "Case Concerning Military and Paramilitary Activities in and Against Nicaragua," International Court of Justice, 27 June 1986, https://www.icj-cij.org/files/case-related/70/070-19860627-JUD-01-00-EN.pdf.

[18] Allison (2016).

There is one area where China takes a fierce stand: It will not brook any interference in its internal affairs. Hence, it will reject all foreign criticisms of its treatment of Uighurs or Hong Kong. So far, China has restrained its military responses to Hong Kong, unlike Prime Minister Jawaharlal Nehru of India, who reacted to personal appeals from President John F. Kennedy and Prime Minister Harold MacMillan by invading Goa. On the Uighurs, China's position is technically correct under international law. The British government used a similar argument when the UN tried to investigate British crimes in Northern Ireland. The then British Foreign Secretary, Michael Stewart, told the UN that this would amount to interference in the internal affairs of the UK. This also explains why not a single Islamic state supported the western countries when they wrote a letter to the UN criticizing China's treatment of the Uighurs. The record shows that only the West, which represents 12 percent of the world's population, has been critical of China's internal behavior. The remaining 88 percent have not joined this western crusade.

To explain the continued western suspicions of China, let me add a slightly provocative but historically accurate note. There is one deep-seated reason for the strong suspicions that western minds have about China. There has been buried deep in the unconscious of the western psyche an inchoate but real fear of the "yellow peril." Since it is buried deep in the unconscious, it seldom surfaces. When senior American policymakers make their decisions on China, they can say with all sincerity that they are driven by rational, not emotional, considerations. Yet, to an external observer, it is manifestly clear that America's reactions to China's rise are influenced by deep emotional reactions, too. Just as individual human beings have difficulty unearthing the unconscious motives that drive our behavior, countries, and civilizations also have difficulty unearthing their unconscious impulses.

It is a fact that the yellow peril has lain buried in western civilization for centuries. Napoleon famously alluded to it when he said, "Let China sleep; when she awakes she will shake the world." Why did Napoleon refer to China and not to India, an equally large and populous civilization? Because no hordes of Indians had threatened or ravaged European capitals. By contrast, hordes of Mongols, a "yellow race," had appeared at Europe's doorstep in the thirteenth century. As Noreen Giffney recounts, "in 1235, Mongol armies invaded Eastern Europe and the Rus' principalities between 1236 and 1242. [...] The Mongol onslaught was followed by a swift and mysterious withdrawal to the surprise and relief of westerners."[19]

The latent fear of the yellow peril surfaces from time to time in literature and art. As a child living in a British colony, I read the popular Fu Manchu novels. They left a deep impression on me. Subconsciously, I began to believe that the personification of evil in human society came in the form of a slant-eyed yellow man devoid of moral scruples. If I, as a non-westerner, could internalize this ethnic caricature, I suspect that these subconscious fears have also affected the reactions of American policymakers to the rise of China.

The strong anti-China mood that has swept through Washington, DC, may in part be the result of rational dissatisfaction with some of China's policies, probably as a

---

[19] Giffney (2012).

result of the fear of China's unfamiliar culture, but also in part from deeper emotional undercurrents. As the former US ambassador Chas Freeman has observed, "in their views of China, many Americans now appear subconsciously to have combined images of the insidious Dr. Fu Manchu, Japan's unnerving 1980s challenge to US industrial and financial primacy, and a sense of existential threat analogous to the Sinophobia that inspired the Anti-Coolie and Chinese Exclusion Acts."[20]

Given the psychological reality of this yellow peril undercurrent, American people need to question how much their reactions to China's rise result from hard-headed rational analysis and how much is a result of deep discomfort with the success of a non-Caucasian civilization. We may never know the real answer, as these struggles between reason and emotion are playing out in subconscious terrains. Still, we should thank Kiron Skinner, a former Director of Policy Planning in the State Department of the Trump Administration, for alluding to the fact that such subconscious dimensions are at play here. As she said in her testimony before Congress, "It's the first time that we will have a great power competitor that is not Caucasian." The time has come for an honest discussion of the "yellow peril" dimension in US-China relations. The best way to deal with our subconscious fears is to surface them and deal with them.

China's reemergence as a great power should not have come as a surprise. From the years 1 to 1820, the two largest economies were always those of China and India. Their return to great power status was perfectly natural. However, the speed of China's return has been unnatural. Its speed of return is off the charts. In 1980, its economy, in purchasing power parity (PPP) terms was one-tenth the size of America. By 2014, it had become larger.

As its economy grew, so too did its defense budget. China today is a much stronger military power. The balance of power vis-à-vis America has shifted drastically. It has also spent its defense budget relatively wisely. China is focused on using the strategies adopted by a weaker military power engaged in asymmetric warfare. China spends its budget on sophisticated land-based missiles that could make US aircraft carrier battle groups utterly ineffective. An aircraft carrier may cost USD 13 billion to build. China's DF-26 ballistic missile, which the Chinese media claims are capable of sinking an aircraft carrier, costs a few hundred thousand dollars. New technology is also helping China to defend itself against aircraft carriers. Professor Timothy Colton of Harvard University told me that aircraft carriers become "sitting ducks" when they face the threat of hypersonic missiles, which are maneuverable and fly at tremendous speed, at varying altitudes.

The discomfort about China's reemergence as a major military power is perfectly understandable. China has clearly emerged as a more formidable military competitor. However, the long history of China suggests that China will be very careful about using its military capabilities. The recent tragic episode on the China-India border would have only reinforced the Chinese belief that the use of military force as a first option is unwise. The real competition between America and China will be in the economic and social fields. The main reason why America successfully

---

[20] Freeman Jr. (2019).

defeated the mighty Soviet Union without fighting a war with it is that the American economy outperformed the Soviet economy. The threat by President Ronald Reagan to outspend the Soviet Union in military expenditures eventually convinced Soviet Premier Mikhail Gorbachev to sue for peace. Could the same happen between America and China? Or could the opposite happen? Most projections show that within a decade or two, China will have a larger economy in nominal market terms. Should America change its strategy when it becomes the number two economy in the world? Or should it do so beforehand? Equally, should it heed this famous advice of President Dwight Eisenhower? As he told the American Society of Newspaper Editors, "every gun that is made, every warship launched, every rocket fired signifies, in the final sense, a theft from those who hunger and are not fed, those who are cold and are not clothed."[21]

There is absolutely no doubt that China will emerge as a formidable geopolitical competitor of the United States It would be wise to plan for this outcome. Yet, as George Kennan wisely advised at the beginning of the titanic contest against the Soviet Union, the outcome of the contest would not be determined by the competition in the military realm. Instead, he said that the outcome would be determined by the ability of America to "create among the peoples of the world generally the impression of a country which knows what it wants, which is coping successfully with the problems of its internal life and with the responsibilities of a world power, and what has a spiritual vitality capable of holding its own among the major ideological currents of the time."[22]

Kennan's emphasis on "spiritual vitality" is even more relevant in the ongoing geopolitical contest with China. It is this dimension that will determine the outcome of the contest against China, not the military dimension. Since China has the world's oldest civilization, the only civilization to have recovered from four major shocks in its history, it would be a serious mistake for an American policymaker to underestimate the strength and resilience of Chinese civilization in the peaceful contest that will take place between the two powers.

References

Allison G (2016) Heresy to say great powers don't bow to tribunals on Law of the Sea? The Straits Times, 16 July 2016. https://www.straitstimes.com/opinion/heresy-to-say-great-powers-dont-bow-to-international-courts

Allison G (2017) Destined for war: can American and China escape Thucydides's trap? Houghton Mifflin Harcourt, New York

Eisenhower DD (1953) The chance for peace. Washington DC, 16 Apr 1953. http://www.edchange.org/multicultural/speeches/ike_chance_for_peace.html

Freeman Jr., CW (2019) On hostile coexistence with China. 3 May 2019. https://chasfreeman.net/on-hostile-coexistence-with-china/

Giffney N (2012) Monstrous Mongols. Postmedieval: J Medieval Cult Stud 3(2):227–245

---

[21] Eisenhower (1953).

[22] Kennan (1947).

John J (2018) Mearsheimer, the great delusion: liberal dreams and international realities. Yale University Press, New Haven

Kennan G(X) (1947) The sources of soviet conduct. Foreign Affairs, July 1947

Kissinger H (2011) On China. Penguin, New York, 25

Lorenz A (2005) Hero of the high seas. Der Spiegel, 29 Aug 2005. https://www.spiegel.de/intern ational/spiegel/china-s-christopher-columbus-hero-of-the-high-seas-a-372474-2.html

Pomfret J (2018a) A China-US truce on trade only scratches the surface of a broader conflict. Washington Post, 3 Dec 2018. https://www.washingtonpost.com/opinions/2018/12/03/china-us-truce-trade-only-scratches-surface-broader-conflict/?utm_term=.0e6e9a186448

Pomfret J (2018b) How the world's resistance to China caught Xi Jinping off guard. Washington Post, 21 Dec 2018. https://www.washingtonpost.com/opinions/2018/12/21/how-worlds-resistance-china-caught-xi-jinping-off-guard/?utm_term=.105ab7ca5227

Shugart T (2016) China arms its great wall of sand. Wall Street J, 15 Dec 2016. https://www.wsj.com/articles/china-arms-its-great-wall-of-sand-1481848109

Walt SM (2011) The myth of American exceptionalism. Foreign Policy, 11 Oct 2011. https://foreig npolicy.com/2011/10/11/the-myth-of-american-exceptionalism/

Yeo G (2019) A continuing rise of China. Business Times (Singapore), 30 Oct 2019. https://www.businesstimes.com.sg/opinion/thinkchina/a-continuing-rise-of-china

How Dangerous Is China?

Abstract The peaceful reemergence of China is one of the greatest success stories of contemporary human history.

ZEIT Professor Mahbubani, in the past several decades, the West has engaged closely with China, hoping both for mutual benefits and that democracy would take root in China. That's not how things have turned out, however. China's rise has contributed to growing inequality in Western countries, and its authoritarian model has even found admirers in some democracies today. Was it foolish for the West to build close ties with China?

Kishore Mahbubani Absolutely not. The surprising thing about the West's disappointment is that it has actually succeeded in many of its critical goals with China. When the United States emerged as a great power in the late nineteenth century, guess what? They soon started wars. China is the only permanent member of the UN Security Council which hasn't fought a war in 40 years. The peaceful reemergence is one of the greatest success stories of contemporary human history.

Mathias Döpfner Kishore, we agree about the facts and figures of China's rise, but we strongly disagree about the consequences. Western democracies should redefine their relationship with China. China's admission to the World Trade Organization in 2001 was a historic mistake. The desired "change through trade" has happened solely to the advantage of China, which is even more authoritarian today. Its economy grew from representing an 8% share of global GDP to a roughly 19% share, while the US's share went down from 20 to 15% and the European share declined from 24 to 16%. It has never been a symmetrical competition. China has never accepted the rules of free and open markets, guided by the principle of reciprocity. That's why we have to try everything to come to new terms. Not only for business reasons: The future of democracy in Europe is at stake.

Mahbubani Historically, the largest economies in the world were always those of China and India. Europe and North America have taken off only in the last 200 years.

Originally published in Die Zeit, Jun 17, 2020

So the past two centuries of Western domination have been a major historical aberration. In 1960, the United States, with less than 5% of the world's population, had an unnaturally big share of 50% of global GDP. It had to end. You also have to see that China's cheaply manufactured goods enabled Europeans and Americans to maintain their standard of living. Of course, you can frame the debate in terms of a good authoritarian state versus a good democratic state. But I think what you are seeing now is the return of Chinese civilization. And it's been unwise for the US to launch a major geopolitical, irrational and emotional challenge against China.

Döpfner Growing economic dependency on China will lead to more political influence for Beijing. When the CEO of Daimler has to apologize twice to the Chinese government because of a harmless Dalai Lama quote in an advertisement on Instagram, this gives you a hint of what's coming. And when the video conference company Zoom is censoring China-critical accounts, that is the ultimate proof.

Mahbubani I think when future historians look back, they'll be puzzled by the Western expectation that a country like China, with 4,000 years of political history, could be changed by a country like the US, with a history of fewer than 250 years. The assumption that the rest of the world will, over time, become just like the West is arrogant.

Döpfner It isn't arrogant to distinguish between free and unfree societies. It seems that you put democracy and dictatorship on the same moral level.

Mahbubani I would say, let everybody live the way they want to.

Döpfner Really? What does that mean in concrete terms? Let me give you an example: If you google "idiot" in the US, one of the first search results is Donald Trump. In China, the search term "Winnie the Pooh" is censored because Xi Jinping looks similar to that cartoon bear. Isn't that a very telling symbol for the asymmetry between the West and China?

Mahbubani But freedom has grown in China. When I first went to China in 1980, people had to wear Maoist uniforms, they couldn't choose where to live or work. Today they can, and they may even travel freely. If China was a kind of dark, oppressive Gulag system, why should 130 million Chinese tourists return there voluntarily every year? Chinese people respect and support their government system because, in the hundred years of humiliation from 1842 to 1945, the West trampled on their country. And now that China is strong, you come and ask why don't you change your government?

Döpfner Where is the promised change through trade politically? What about the values of freedom, the rule of law, and human rights? Just look at the social credit system in China. Or the fact that people with opposing views are disappearing or being put into jail. Or the camps for members of the Uighur minority. Yes, China's growth is an incredible success story. But the price of authoritarianism that the Chinese society has had to pay is high. One thing is clear to me: That model should not be imported to Europe. I want to live a free life in an open society.

Mahbubani I can assure you, Mathias, that the Chinese will not take away your free lifestyle in an open society.

Döpfner Ask the activist Joshua Wong from Hong Kong: He would say China has taken away his freedom. Chinese encroachment will spread step by step from Hong Kong to other countries.

ZEIT Mr. Döpfner, you argue that Europe should side with the US and decouple from China. How many jobs in Europe are you willing to sacrifice in this process?

Döpfner In 2019, for example, VW delivered 650,000 cars to the US and 4.2 million cars to China. That is not an attractive market, that is dependency. But we have to insist on true reciprocity. And in order to make progress here, we should not exclude decoupling. Roughly 8% of German trade takes place with China. We cannot change that overnight. So sure, decoupling would be tough, but not impossible. Nevertheless, the rules that apply to us in China are also valid for Chinese companies here. If China lives up to that, we can stop arguing over principles.

Mahbubani Out of the 7.5 billion people in the world, 12% live in the West and 88% live outside the West. If any Western country decides to decouple from China, you'll be decoupling yourself from the rest of the world. When it comes to geopolitics, countries do not put values as priority number one, and this is true of every country, certainly of the US. The majority of the countries in the world are still focused on trying to improve the livelihoods of their people, and they're looking for reliable development partners to work with, whether they agree or disagree with what China is doing. Apart from this reality, you're absolutely right that ideally, we must have clear rules and a level playing field for everyone.

ZEIT Mr. Mahbubani, you argue that China historically has always been peaceful and therefore the world shouldn't worry. At this year's National People's Congress in Beijing, however, the Communist Party dropped the word "peaceful" from the phrase "peaceful reunification" with Taiwan. Also, China ignores international rules in the South China Sea. President Xi Jinping appears to be pushing China's rise in a fairly aggressive manner.

Mahbubani If there is one lesson from the history of geopolitics it's that there is no such thing as a benevolent superpower. The day that China will use military means will certainly come. Thus far, however, China has shown extraordinary strategic restraint. Militarily, it could take all the islands in the South China Sea within 24 h. It hasn't done so.

Döpfner China is not using traditional forms of warfare because it understands that modern war is not waged with bombs and soldiers, but with business power and data. In these two fields, China is extremely aggressive.

Mahbubani I strongly disagree with the notion that China is a threat to democracy's global impact.

ZEIT What then would be your advice to countries like Australia? It asked for an independent inquiry into the coronavirus outbreak and is now facing economic sanctions from China. The Netherlands and Sweden have also been threatened by Beijing after voicing criticism of China.

Mahbubani The use of economic might for geopolitical purposes was not started by China. The US has played that game for a long time. In the case of Australia, my advice would be that since Australia is surrounded by 4 billion Asians, it should adjust to new realities. When the United States became very powerful and removed governments all over Central America, Central America had to adjust. The answer for all small and medium-sized countries is: When new superpowers emerge, we have to adapt and adjust.

Döpfner Aren't you in a way advocating the unlimited principle of opportunism? There must be limits. We agree, for example, that companies should not use child labor. So, there is always a framework. But since the principle of unprincipledness is so seductive, more and more business people in Europe are even saying China may be the better ally than America. That is very short-sighted. It's time to decide whether we prefer an alliance with an imperfect democracy or an alliance with a perfect authoritarian state.

Mahbubani You mentioned child labor. Let me tell you a story. A Belgian NGO discovered and shut down a factory in Bangladesh that was using child labor. One year later, those child workers became child prostitutes.

Döpfner Sorry, what does that tell us? We cannot ignore evil because there is a worse one.

ZEIT But since Germany and Europe can afford some degree of political luxury, where should they position themselves in the new rivalry between China and the US?

Mahbubani The best role for Europe is to be an independent actor. If you are big enough, you don't have to become a satellite of anybody. I know that in multilateral institutions like the UN, Europe has actually been reluctant to stand up and explain to the United States that strengthening global rules would be good for the US and for the world. I don't understand why Europe doesn't do that.

ZEIT What makes you hopeful that China would comply with multilateral rules? Reality has shown that it doesn't.

Mahbubani The United States has created exceptions for itself and China will do the same. But if you create multilateral rules that work out for everybody, I predict that China would abide by them 95% of the time.

Döpfner In the long run, heterogenous competition is stronger than homogeneous monopolies. So, dictatorships fail. But in the midterm, I'm afraid that an unfair competitive system will continue to advance China's growth. At the same time, domestic control over the Chinese people is limiting the possibility to speak up. These two factors may lead to a situation where unilateral, authoritarian leadership becomes even stronger.

Mahbubani I agree with you that authoritarian systems will fail. Hence, if China keeps succeeding in the next few decades, its system may be flexible, not authoritarian.

Döpfner Kishore, I find this fundamentally important, because I'm not so sure the principles of freedom and fair competition are going to prevail over the next decades. Take the example of artificial intelligence, AI: Unfortunately, China is in a much better position here than America or Europe. Why? Because the speed of AI progress is very much driven by a regulatory framework. In China, you have no restrictions regarding privacy or data ownership, because the only principle of regulation is the well-being of the state. How should we deal with this unfair advantage?

Mahbubani I think Europe is sophisticated enough to tell both the US and China that if you want to develop AI, you must do so on the basis of certain rules. The rest of the world would trust Europe—and this is important—because you've got no authoritarian agenda.

ZEIT One final question to both of you: If you look back 100 years into history when the rivals Germany and Britain were competing for dominance, it marked the end of what some call the first globalization. With China and the US engaged in a trade war including punitive tariffs, are you afraid that we might be witnessing the end of the second era of globalization?

Mahbubani I'm optimistic that globalization will continue. Asia is now home to the world's largest middle class, and I know their aspirations: They want to have the same kind of comfortable lives that many in the West enjoy. So once Covid-19 is over, once everybody can start traveling again, I assure you, globalization will come back with a vengeance. In fact, I would say: Watch out, phase three of globalization is coming!

Döpfner We are seeing a renationalization, a crisis of Europe and globalization, for two reasons. One is the corona pandemic, which should be solved on an international level. Instead, though, it has led most countries to focus on their self-interest. The second reason is the rise of China as a non-democratic superpower. In the long run, though, I'm 100% optimistic that globalization will prevail. There is simply no alternative. All big problems can only be solved in a global context, like climate change. If we increase the constructive pressure of an US/EU alliance—combined with dialogue—on Beijing, we might be able to strike a new trade deal. Then freedom and globalization will prevail.

What China Threat? How the United States and China Can Avoid War

Abstract Instead of trying to contain and prevent the risk of China, which is on track to becoming the world's largest economic power, the US should develop a strategy for engaging with China to respond to global challenges.

Within about 15 years, China's economy will surpass America's and become the largest in the world. As this moment approaches, meanwhile, a consensus has formed in Washington that China poses a significant threat to American interests and well-being. General Joseph Dunford, the chairman of the Joint Chiefs of Staff (JCS), has said that "China probably poses the greatest threat to our nation by about 2025." The summary of America's 2018 National Defense Strategy claims that China and Russia are "revisionist powers" seeking to "shape a world consistent with their authoritarian model—gaining veto authority over other nations' economic, diplomatic, and security decisions." Christopher Wray, the FBI director, has said, "One of the things we're trying to do is view the China threat as not just a whole-of-government threat, but a whole-ofsociety threat… and I think it's going to take a whole-of-society response by us." So widespread is this notion that when Donald Trump launched his trade war against China, in January 2018, he received support even from moderate figures such as Democratic senator Chuck Schumer.

Two main currents are driving these concerns. One is economic: that China has undermined the US economy by pursuing unfair trade practices, demanding technology transfers, stealing intellectual property, and imposing non-tariff barriers that impede access to Chinese markets. The other current is political: that China's successful economic development has not been accompanied by the liberal democratic reform Western governments, and particularly the United States, had expected; and that China has become too aggressive in its dealing with other nations.

Reading about the imminent threat American officials believe China poses, it is not hard to see why Graham Allison, in his book *Destined for War*, reaches the depressing conclusion that armed conflict between the two countries is more likely than not. Yet since China is not mounting a military force to threaten or invade the United States, not trying to intervene in America's domestic politics, and not engaged

---

Originally published in Harper's, Feb 2019

© The Author(s) 2022
K. Mahbubani, *The Asian 21st Century*, China and Globalization,
https://doi.org/10.1007/978-981-16-6811-1_28

147

in a deliberate campaign to destroy the American economy, we must consider that, in spite of the increasing clamor about the threat China poses to the United States, it is still possible for America to find a way to deal peaceably with a China that will become the number one economic, and possibly geopolitical, power within a decade—and to do so in a way that advances its own interests, even as it constrains China's.

America must first reconsider a long-held belief about China's political system. Since the collapse of the Soviet Union, American policymakers have been convinced that it would only be a matter of time before the Chinese Communist Party (CCP) followed the Soviet Communist Party into the political grave. Politicians and policy-makers on both ends of the political spectrum accepted, implicitly or explicitly, the famous thesis of Francis Fukuyama that there was only one historical road to follow.

When Bill Clinton explained in March 2000 why he supported China's admission to the World Trade Organization, he stressed that political liberation would inevitably flow from economic liberalization, concluding that "if you believe in a future of greater openness and freedom for the people of China, you ought to be for this agreement." His successor, George W. Bush, shared the same conviction. In his 2002 National Security Strategy, he wrote, "In time, China will find that social and political freedom is the only source of that national greatness." Hillary Clinton was more explicit. According to her, by persisting with Communist Party rule, the Chinese "are trying to stop history, which is a fool's errand. They cannot do it. But they're going to hold it off as long as possible."

It is worth considering the conviction of American policymakers that they could so confidently dispense political prescriptions to China. No other empire, of course, has accumulated as much economic, political, and military power as the United States has. Yet, it has still been less than 250 years since the Declaration of Independence was signed, in 1776. China, by contrast, is considerably older, and the Chinese people have learned from several thousand years of history that they suffer most when the central government is weak and divided, as it was for almost a century after the Opium War of 1842 when the country was ravaged by foreign invasions, civil wars, famines, and much else besides. Since 1978, however, China has lifted 800 million people out of poverty and created the largest middle class in the world. As Graham Allison wrote in an op-ed for *China Daily*, an Englishlanguage newspaper owned by the Chinese government, "it could be argued that 40 years of miracle growth have created a greater increase in human wellbeing for more individuals than occurred in the previous more than 4,000 years of China's history." All this has happened while the CCP has been in power. And the Chinese did not fail to notice that the collapse of the Soviet Communist party led to a decline in Russian life expectancy, increase in infant mortality, and plummeting incomes.

In American eyes, the contest between America's and China's political systems is one between a democracy, where the people freely choose their government and enjoy freedom of speech and of religion, and an autocracy, where the people have no such freedoms. To neutral observers, however, it could just as easily be seen as a choice between a plutocracy in the United States, where major public policy decisions end up favoring the rich over the masses, and a meritocracy in China, where major public policy decisions made by officials chosen by Party elites on the basis of ability and performance have resulted in such a striking alleviation of poverty. One fact cannot be denied. In the past 30 years, the median income of the American worker has not improved: between 1979 and 2013, median hourly wages rose just 6%—less than 0.2 percent per year.

This doesn't mean that the Chinese political system should remain in its current form forever. Human rights violations—such as the detention of hundreds of thousands of Uighurs—remain a major concern. Within China today, there are many voices calling for reforms. Among them is the prominent liberal scholar Xu Jilin. And in *Rethinking China's Rise: A Liberal Critique*, David Ownby has produced an excellent English translation of eight essays Xu has written over the past decade. Xu lodges his sharpest criticisms against his fellow Chinese scholars, and especially against what he sees as their excessive focus on the nationstate and insistence on China's essential cultural and historical difference from Western political models. He argues that this overemphasis on particularism, in fact, marks a departure from traditional Chinese culture, which, as exemplified by its historical *tianxia* model of foreign relations, was a universal and open system. Criticizing the blanket rejection by "extreme nationalists" among his Chinese academic peers of "anything created by Westerners," Xu argues instead that China has historically succeeded because it was open. However, not even a liberal like Xu would call for China to replicate the American political system. Instead, he argues that China should "employ her own cultural traditions," through promoting a "new *tianxia*": on the domestic front, "Han people and the various national minorities will enjoy mutual equality in legal and status terms, and the cultural uniqueness and pluralism of the different nationalities will be respected and protected," while its relations with other countries "will be defined by the principles of respect for each other's sovereign independence, equality in their treatment of each other, and peaceful coexistence."

China's political system will have to evolve with its social and economic conditions. And, in many respects, it has evolved significantly, becoming much more open than it once was. When I first went to China, in 1980, for instance, no Chinese were allowed to travel overseas as private tourists. Last year, roughly 134 million traveled overseas. And roughly 134 million Chinese returned home freely. Similarly, millions of the best young Chinese minds have experienced the academic freedom of American universities. Yet, in 2017, eight in ten Chinese students chose to return home. Though the question remains: If things have been going well, why is Xi imposing tighter political discipline on Communist Party members and removing term limits? His predecessor, Hu Jintao, delivered spectacular economic growth, but this period was also marked by a spike in corruption and party factionalism led by Bo Xilai, the Chongqing party secretary who tried to challenge Xi's rise to power, and Zhou Yongkang, the powerful domestic security chief under Xi's predecessor. Xi believed these trends would delegitimize the CCP and end China's successful rejuvenation. Against these dire challenges, he saw no realistic alternative to reimposing strong central leadership. Despite doing this (or, because he did this), Xi remains hugely popular.

Many in the West have been alarmed by the enormous power Xi has accumulated, taking it as a harbinger of armed conflict. Xi's accumulation of power, however, has not fundamentally changed China's longterm geopolitical strategy. The Chinese have, for instance, avoided unnecessary wars. Unlike the United States, which is blessed with two nonthreatening neighbors in Canada and Mexico, China has difficult relations with a number of strong, nationalistic neighbors, including India, Japan, South Korea, and Vietnam. Quite remarkably, of the five permanent members of the UN Security Council (China, France, Russia, the United States, and the United Kingdom), China is the only one among them that has not fired a single military shot across its border in 30 years, since a brief naval battle between China and Vietnam in 1988. By contrast, even during the relatively peaceful Obama Administration, the American military dropped 26 thousand bombs on seven countries in a single year. Evidently, the Chinese understand well the art of strategic restraint.

There have, of course, been moments when China seemed close to war. Richard McGregor's book, *Asia's Reckoning*, which focuses on the strategic relationship between the United States, China, and Japan since the postwar period, vividly documents the precarious moments between China and Japan since 2012. After Japanese Prime Minister Yoshihiko Noda "nationalized" the disputed Senkaku Islands in September 2012, Chinese and Japanese naval vessels came perilously close to each other. Yet while many seasoned observers predicted a military clash between the two countries in 2014, none came to pass.

Much has been made of the possibility of conflict in the South China Sea, through which roughly one-fifth of all global shipping passes each year, and where the Chinese have converted isolated reefs and shoals into military installations as part of larger, contested claims to sovereignty over portions of the waters. But contrary to Western analyses, China, while undeniably more politically assertive in the region, has not become more aggressive militarily. The smaller, rival claimants to sovereignty in the South China Sea, including Malaysia, the Philippines, and Vietnam, control a number of islands in the waters. China could easily dislodge them. It has not done so.

When considering the familiar narrative of Chinese aggression in the South China Sea, it must be remembered that the United States itself has missed opportunities to defuse tensions there. A former US ambassador to China, J. Stapleton Roy, told me that in a joint press conference with President Obama on September 25, 2015, Xi Jinping not only proposed an approach to the South China Sea that included the endorsement of declarations supported by all ten members of the Association of Southeast Asian Nations but, more significantly, added that China had no intention of militarizing the Spratly Islands, where it had engaged in massive reclamation work on the reefs and shoals it occupied. Yet the Obama Administration made no effort to pursue China's reasonable proposal. Instead, the US Navy stepped up its patrols. In response, China increased the pace of its construction of defensive installations on the islands.

Just as careful diplomacy is required in military matters, it is also integral to America's economic relations with China. Virtually no well-known mainstream economist agreed with Trump, or his top trade adviser Peter Navarro and trade representative Robert Lighthizer, that America's trade deficits were the result of unfair practices by other countries. Martin Feldstein, the former chairman of Ronald Reagan's Council of Economic Advisers, has pointed out that America's global trade deficit is due to the fact that its consumption outweighs its domestic production. Imposing tariffs on low-cost Chinese goods will not rectify this structural feature but will serve only to make many essential goods less affordable to ordinary Americans.

Trump's trade war against China nevertheless won him broad mainstream support, which was the result of a major mistake that China has made. It ignored growing perceptions and complaints, including by leading American figures, that China has been fundamentally unfair in many of its economic policies. "The US has a strong case" against China in "alleg[ing] that China persists with discriminatory policies that favor local companies and penalize foreign firms," as George Magnus notes in *Red Flags*, recommending that the United States engage China in a dialogue to encourage the latter to open up "market access in nonpolitically sensitive commercial and service-producing sectors" through avenues such as the US-China Comprehensive Economic Dialogue.

Magnus's suggestion of dialogue through existing institutions is a far wiser route for America to take than Trump's trade war. If the Trump Administration had focused its economic campaign against China on the areas of these unfair practices, it would generate a great deal of global support for this campaign. Indeed, the WTO provides many avenues to do so. Conceivably, China may also privately acknowledge mistakes made in these areas and alter its policies. However, the growing perception in China and beyond was that the real goal of the Trump Administration was not just to eliminate unfair trade practices, but to undermine or thwart China's longterm plan to become a technological leader in its own right. Although the United States has the right to implement policies to prevent the theft of its technology, as Martin Feldstein has indicated, this should not be conflated with its efforts to thwart China's long-term, stateled industrial plan, Made in China 2025, designed to make China a global competitor in advanced manufacturing, focusing on industries like electric cars, advanced robotics, and artificial intelligence.

Both Feldstein and Magnus agree that in order to maintain supremacy in high-tech industries like aerospace and robotics, the US government, rather than pursuing tariffs, should invest in areas such as higher education and research and development. In short, America needs to develop its own long-term economic strategy to match that of China. In both policy and rhetoric, it is clear to see that China's leadership has a vision for its economy and people. Plans like Made in China 2025 and the infrastructure projects are undertaken in the Belt and Road Initiative (BRI), such as the construction of high-speed railways, demonstrate China's efforts to become a global competitor in new, advanced industries. At the same time, China's leaders have emphasized that the country can no longer pursue GDP growth at the expense of social costs such as inequality and environmental pollution. This Xi made clear when he declared in 2017 that the principal contradiction facing Chinese society is now "between unbalanced and inadequate development and the people's ever-growing needs for a better life." As Magnus sums it up, this means a shift in focus to "improving the environment and pollution, lowering income and regional inequality, and strengthening the social safety net." Although, as Magnus writes, China's economy faces several important challenges, China's leaders have, at the very least, taken steps to address them. It is time for the United States to do the same.

However, to work out a longterm strategy, America needs to resolve a fundamental contradiction in its economic assumptions. Most sophisticated American economists believe that government-led industrial policies do not work, arguing instead for free-market capitalism. If this American belief is correct, Trump's main trade negotiator, Robert Lighthizer, should not have opposed China's 2025 government-led plan to upgrade its technological capabilities. Lighthizer should have sat back and allowed this Chinese industrial initiative to fail, as the Soviet Union's economic plans did.

However, if Lighthizer believed that the 2025 plan could succeed, he should have considered the possibility that America should revisit its ideological assumptions and, like China, formulate a long-term comprehensive economic strategy to match the Chinese plan. Even Germany, arguably the world's leading industrial power, has such a strategy, called Industry 4.0. It's obviously less intrusive than the Chinese version of industrial policy, which, as Scott Kennedy of the Center for Strategic and International Studies has described, involves the state playing "a significant role... in providing an overall framework, utilizing financial and fiscal tools, and supporting the creation of manufacturing innovation centers." Why couldn't the United States formulate a plan to match?

Ironically, the best country that the United States could work within formulating such a longterm economic strategy might well be China. China is keen to deploy its USD 3 trillion reserves to invest more in the United States. Adam Posen, the head of the influential Peterson Institute for International Economics, has already noted that Trump's trade war with China and the rest of the world has led to net foreign invest-ment in the United States to fall to nearly zero in 2018. America should also consider participating in China's Belt and Road Initiative, the Chinese governmental program launched in 2013 to strengthen regional economic cooperation in Asia, Europe, and Africa through massive investments in infrastructure. The countries currently partic-ipating in BRI would welcome US participation, as it would help balance China's influence. In short, there are many economic opportunities America could take advan-tage of. Just as Boeing and GE, two major American corporations, have benefited from the explosion in the Chinese aviation market, firms like Caterpillar and Bechtel could benefit from the massive construction undertaken in the BRI region. Unfortu-nately, America's ideological aversion to stateled economic initiatives will prevent both mutually beneficial longterm economic cooperation with China and needed industrial strategies in the United States.

As China rises, America faces two stark choices. First, should it continue with its current mixed bag of policies toward China, with some seeking to enhance bilateral relations and others effectively undermining them? On the economic front, with the exception of Trump's latest trade war with China, American policies have consis-tently treated China as a partner, while America's political and especially military policies have most often treated China as an adversary. Second, can the United States match China and develop an equally effective longterm strategic plan to manage the latter's rise? The simple answer is yes. However, if China is to be America's number one strategic priority, as it should be, the obvious question is whether America can be as strategically disciplined as China and give up its futile wars in the Islamic world and its unnecessary vilification of Russia.

It was rational for the United States to have the world's largest defense budget when its economy dwarfed every other in the world. Would it be rational for the world's numbertwo economy to have the world's largest defense budget? And if America refuses to give this up, isn't it a strategic gift to China? China learned one major lesson from the collapse of the Soviet Union. Economic growth must come before military expenditure. Hence, it would actually serve China's long-term interests for the United States to burn money away on unnecessary military expenses.

If America finally changes its strategic thinking about China, it will also discover that it is possible to develop a strategy that will both constrain China and advance US interests. Bill Clinton provided the wisdom for this strategy in a speech at Yale University in 2003, when he said, in short, that the only way to manage the next superpower is to create multilateral rules and partnerships that would tie it down. For example, though China lays claim to reefs and shoals in the South China Sea, the UN Law of the Sea Convention has prevented it from declaring the entire South China Sea an internal Chinese lake. China has also been obliged to implement WTO judgments that have gone against it. International rules do have a bite. Fortunately, under Xi Jinping, China is still in favor of strengthening the global multilateral architecture the United States created, including the International Monetary Fund, the World Bank, the United Nations, and the WTO. China has contributed more UN peacekeepers than the four other Permanent Members of the UN Security Council combined. Hence, there is a window of opportunity for cooperation between America and China in multilateral forums.

To seize the opportunity, American policymakers have to accept the undeniable reality that the return of China (and India) is unstoppable. Why not? From the year 1 to 1820, China and India had the world's two largest economies. The past two hundred years of Western domination of global commerce have been an aberration. As PricewaterhouseCoopers has predicted, China and India will resume their number one and two positions by 2050 or earlier.

The leaders of both China and India understand that we now live in a small, interdependent global village, threatened by many new challenges, including global warming. Both China and India could have walked away from the Paris Agreement after Trump did so. Both chose not to. Despite their very different political systems, both have decided that they can be responsible global citizens. Perhaps this may be the best route to find out if China will emerge as a threat to the United States and the world. If it agrees to be constrained by multiple global rules and partnerships, China could very well remain a different polity—that is, not a liberal democracy—and still not be a threatening one. This is the alternative scenario that the "China threat" industry in the United States should consider and work toward.

The Great Paradox of Donald Trump's Plan to Combat China

Abstract The Trump Administration overestimates the threat that China poses to American livelihoods and values. Yet, in launching a geopolitical contest with China without first working out a comprehensive long-term strategy, it also underestimates the popularity and resilience that the Chinese Communist Party is demonstrating.

The great paradox about the Trump administration's response to the challenge from China is that it is both overestimating and underestimating this challenge. The overestimation is clear; the underestimation, which is more dangerous, less so.

Secretary of State Mike Pompeo spelled out clearly his case for overestimation in his speech of the Nixon Library on July 23, 2020. "We're seeing staggering statistics of China trade abuses that cost American jobs and strike enormous blows to the economies all across America, including here in Southern California," Pompeo said. "And we're watching a Chinese military that grows stronger and stronger and indeed more menacing." One could be forgiven for believing that China is about to mount a military invasion of the United States. Yet, there is no doubt that in the military field, the United States is much stronger than China. In his speech, Pompeo said, "We've called on China to conform its nuclear capabilities to the strategic realities of our time." If China heeded his call, then it would have to add over 55 hundred nuclear weapons to its stockpile since it only has over three hundred weapons, compared to almost six thousand for the United States.

Pompeo also declared that the Chinese Communist Party (CCP) was exploiting America's "free and open society" and "sent propagandists into our press conferences, our research centers, our high-schools, our colleges, and even into our PTA meetings." In short, Chinese agents of influence have infiltrated all segments of American society and could undermine it. The most telling word Pompeo used to describe the CCP was "Frankenstein." This word implies that a monster was now threatening America. It would be reasonable for an American to feel scared after hearing the speech.

Yet, even though the recent speeches on China by Trump administration officials have been strident, they ultimately underestimate the challenge posed by China

Originally published in The National Interest, Jul 29, 2020

because they fail to realistically explain its nature. Pompeo makes it clear that it is the communist ideology of the CCP that is threatening America: As he said, "General Security Xi Jinping is a true believer in a bankrupt totalitarian ideology. It's this ideology that informs his decades-long desire for the global hegemony of China communism." If global hegemony was indeed China's goal, then Americans can relax. Any such ambition of global hegemony will fail. The world will reject it.

The CCP is actually a far more formidable competitor to America because its primary goal is not global hegemony. It is to revive the world's oldest and most resilient civilization and restore its natural place as the most successful civilization for most of human history. And the CCP is doing a very good job at this process of revitalization. One little known fact about the CCP is that since its creation in 1949, 71 years ago, this is the strongest it has ever been.

A Harvard Kennedy School Ash Center study titled "Understanding CCP Resilience," published in July 2020 explains why the CCP is so popular in China. "Regime theory has long argued that authoritarian systems are inherently unstable because of their dependence on coercion, over-centralization of decision making, and the privileging of personal over institutional power," according to the report. "Over time, these inefficiencies tend to weaken the legitimacy of the ruling government, leading to generalized unrest and citizen dissatisfaction." This is what should have happened in China. Instead, as this report says that "the Party appears to be as strong as ever. A deeper resilience is founded on popular support for regime policy." This is why the report concludes that "there is little evidence to support the idea that the CCP is losing legitimacy in the eyes of its people."

Pompeo was also underestimating and misunderstanding the Chinese challenge when he spoke of the distinction between the CCP and the Chinese people. He said, "We must also engage and empower the Chinese people—a dynamic freedom-loving people who are completely distinct from the CCP." Here are some important statistics. Each year over 20 million Chinese apply to join the CCP. About 12% of them get in, making it as difficult to join the CCP as it is to get into leading universities in America. In short, the CCP is not a party about to crack up under American pressure: it is floating on an ocean of legitimacy among 1.4 billion Chinese people, who are now happy as they are experiencing a new high tide in the history of Chinese civilization. The 2020 Edelman Trust Barometer reports that 90% of the Chinese people support the Chinese government.

All this explains a key weakness of the American strategy toward China. No country, with the possible unwise exception of the current Australian government, has jumped onto the American bandwagon as it rushes to confront China. Not even close allies like the UK. One influential British figure noted in Davos in January that the UK would proceed to install 5G technology from Huawei as British Intelligence agencies had thoroughly scrubbed the Huawei software. He confidently asserted that the United States could not arm-twist the UK as the United States needed the UK as much as the UK needed the United States. By July, the UK had capitulated. One can only imagine the arm-twisting that took place. What a contrast to the Cold War when the UK and the United States were complete comrades-in-arms.

The Trump administration is right on one point. There are rising levels of concern around the world on the new assertiveness displayed by China from the "wolf warrior" diplomats in Europe to the killings of the Indian soldiers in the Himalayas. An intelligent and thoughtful American strategy that tried to balance Chinese assertiveness by developing a wide network of friends across the globe could work. Instead, as Richard Haas says, "under this administration, we treat the European Union as an economic foe, bash South Korea and Japan... it is not realistic to expect allies to stand up to a powerful neighbor if they cannot count on us."

If the Trump administration or the United States is serious about taking on the Chinese challenge, it needs to do a complete reboot and work out a thoughtful long-term strategy. It should also heed the advice of its previous strategic thinkers in trying to understand the real nature of the CCP. As George Kennan said, "Our first step must be to apprehend and recognize for what it is, the nature of the movement with which we are dealing. We must study it with the same courage, detachment, objectivity, and same determination not to be emotionally provoked or unseated by it."

Kennan also advised that the United States should adopt the virtues of "modesty and humility." These virtues are absolutely critical if the United States is to develop a deep and realistic understanding of the enormous challenge posed by China.

HK People Must Understand They've Become a Pawn

Abstract While the protests in Hong Kong are widely seen as a fight for democracy and freedom, they must also be understood in the context of the growing US-China geopolitical contest.

Editor's Note

Why have the US and China, the world's two biggest powers, increasingly turned hostile against each other? How should Hong Kong affairs be understood in the context of China-US rivalry? The US and other Western countries are in a deep internal crisis. Is it time for them to reform their political systems? In a world of profound change, international affairs observers nowadays are working to find answers to these questions. Global Times reporters Yu Jincui and Bai Yunyi solicited the insights of Kishore Mahbubani, distinguished fellow at the Asia Research Institute, National University of Singapore, and a veteran diplomat, in a written interview recently.

GT: Does the deterioration in China-US relations in recent months go beyond your expectation? Will this trend continue after the US November election? How will different election results influence bilateral relations?

Mahbubani: The recent deterioration of China-US relations was not a surprise. It could have been predicted. As I argue in my book, Has China Won?, the US decision to launch a geopolitical contest against China was driven by a few major structural forces. Here are a few. Firstly, as Harvard Professor Graham Allison has observed, such a geopolitical contest inevitably breaks out when the No. 2 power (today China) becomes stronger relative to the No. 1 power (today the US). Secondly, the US resents the growing international influence of China, through initiatives like AIIB and the Belt and Road Initiative. Thirdly, as former assistant secretary of state Kurt Campbell has documented, Washington expected that "US power and hegemony could readily mold China to United States' liking." In short, the US expected China to become

---

Originally published in Global Times, Jun 18, 2020

K. Mahbubani, *The Asian 21st Century*, China and Globalization,
https://doi.org/10.1007/978-981-16-6811-1_30

like the US, a liberal democracy. The US is disappointed that this expectation (even if misplaced) didn't happen. In addition, the Western psyche has long had a fear of the "yellow peril." As a result of such structural forces, there is bipartisan support in the US for the current US policy of launching a contest against China.

This US-China geopolitical contest will continue after November, regardless of who wins. Nonetheless, there is also no doubt that a Biden administration (if it emerges) will be more courteous toward China. The public insults will cease. Despite this, the US could also become a formidable competitor for China under Biden as his administration will be able to rally more effectively the friends and allies of the US, like the Europeans, who have become disenchanted with the Trump administration. Nonetheless, there is also greater hope that a more rational Biden administration could accept my book's recommendation that the US and China should work together, instead of against each other, to handle common challenges, like Covid-19 and global warming.

GT: China and the US have seen increasing competition and conflicts in terms of economy, technology, political systems, and global leadership. In which areas do you think the conflicts can be alleviated and in which areas are conflicts likely to intensify?

Mahbubani: It is difficult to anticipate the future course of the US-China geopolitical contest because the US has not worked out a comprehensive and thoughtful long-term strategy for managing China. It was Dr. Henry Kissinger who shared this insight with me. As a result of a lack of strategy, many of the actions taken by the US against China, like the trade war, are also hurting the interests of the American people, especially after Covid-19.

The fundamental question that the US needs to answer before formulating a strategy on China is whether the key strategic goal of the US should be to protect the primacy of the US in the global system or to enhance the well-being of the people. The choice is clear: primacy or people.

So far, many in the administration believe that the US should protect its primacy. Sadly, this impulse has also resulted in the US fighting unnecessary wars, wasting, for example, US$ 5 trillion in unnecessary post-9/11 wars. However, the average income of Americans in the bottom 50% has gone down over the past 30 years. If this US$ 5 trillion had been given instead to the bottom 50%, each American in this group would have received a check for US$ 30,000.

In short, if the US focuses its efforts on improving the well-being of its people and dealing with climate change, many areas of competition can be avoided, like the trade wars. However, if the US focuses on primacy, the US competition with China will step up in many areas, resulting in many actions like blocking Huawei from selling its 5G technology and resisting Chinese initiatives, like the Belt and Road Initiative.

The world hopes that the US will take the wiser course of enhancing the well-being of its people.

GT: Some scholars in China and the US think that China-US relations have been at their worst point over the past four decades and that it will take decades to resolve the estrangement. If this is the case, how will the China-US confrontation influence world patterns in the next few decades? Will countries have to take sides?

Mahbubani: There are 330 million people living in the US and 1.4 billion in China. Six billion people live outside these two countries. It is clear that these six billion people, who live in 191 countries, are deeply troubled by the US-China geopolitical contest as they believe both countries should come together with the rest of the world to deal with pressing global challenges, like Covid-19 and global warming. Hence, few countries, if any, are rushing to take sides. The vast majority of humanity would be relieved and happy if both US and China could set aside their geopolitical contest and focus on restarting the global economy, which has deeply stalled since Covid-19, and retooling it to address climate change. One of the key goals of my book, Has China Won?, is to persuade both countries to pay greater attention to the views of the rest of the world.

One clear indication of the views of the rest of the world was provided by the refusal of any country to follow the US when it left the World Health Organization (WHO). Hence, one way to send signals of the views of the 7.8 billion of our world is to revitalize and work with key multilateral organizations, like the UN. Both Chancellor Angela Merkel and President Emmanuel Macron have spoken out about the importance of multilateralism. The world should encourage the European Union to provide leadership in revitalizing multilateral institutions. They could help to stabilize a world disrupted by the US-China geopolitical contest.

GT: You recently said Hong Kong has become a "pawn" in the escalating rivalry between the US and China, can you elaborate on your views?

Mahbubani: In the geopolitical contest that the US has launched against China, the US will naturally look for opportunities to embarrass China. This is natural super-power behavior. The US also believes that both the recent unrest in Hong Kong and the proposed enactment of a national security law provide a convenient propaganda weapon to use against China, especially in the Western world. It's therefore important for the people of Hong Kong to realize that it has become a political football that will be kicked around in the geopolitical contest. In any football match, the players enjoy kicking the ball and using it to score goals, especially propaganda goals. Sadly, the football gets damaged. If the people of Hong Kong do not understand that they have become a pawn in a geopolitical contest, they may come to grief.

Many of the Western countries who have been supporting the demonstrations and disruptions in Hong Kong believe that their interests are best served by instability in Hong Kong as it is seen as an embarrassment for China. Actually, if the Western countries, including the US and the UK, did a sober calculation of their real long-term interests, especially their primary interest in revitalizing the global economy, they would come to the realization that stability in Hong Kong and its continuation as a vibrant commercial and financial center could enable Western companies to get full benefit from China's growth.

GT: Hong Kong under the British colonial rule was one of the frontlines of the West in Asia before 1997, but now China has resumed sovereignty over Hong Kong. Beijing is enacting a national security law for the city but is strongly opposed by the West. What's behind such a clash?

Mahbubani: Every country has national security laws. Article 23 of the Basic Law states explicitly that, "The Hong Kong Special Administrative Region shall enact laws on its own to prohibit any act of treason, secession, sedition, subversion against the Central People's Government, or theft of state secrets, to prohibit foreign political organizations or bodies from conducting political activities in the Region, and to prohibit political organizations or bodies of the Region from establishing ties with foreign political organizations or bodies." This failure of the Hong Kong authorities to exercise their responsibilities has led to the central government enacting such legislation.

Every country has national security laws. These laws are designed to protect countries from foreign interference in their societies, especially in their domestic politics. For example, the US has the freest press in the world but, until recently, no foreigner could own a TV station in the US. Rupert Murdoch had to give up his Australian citizenship and become a US citizen before he could own a TV station in the US. From 2017 onwards, the US has allowed 100% foreign ownership. Nonetheless, the State Department has used alternative legislation, the Foreign Agents Registration Act (FARA), to regulate foreign-owned TV stations. The American people were outraged when reports surfaced that Russian money may have helped the election of Trump, even though these reports were not confirmed. Curiously, as the New York Times has documented, the US has a history of intervening in other countries' elections. Dov Levin, assistant professor of International Relations at Carnegie Mellon University, found 81 instances of overt and covert interventions in other countries' elections by the US, as compared to 36 by the Soviet Union/ Russia, between 1946 and 2000. On 17 February 2018, Scott Shane wrote in the New York Times, "The United States' departure from democratic ideals sometimes went much further. The C.I.A. helped overthrow elected leaders in Iran and Guatemala in the 1950s and backed violent coups in several other countries in the 1960s. It plotted assassinations and supported brutal anti-Communist governments in Latin America, Africa and Asia."

Since every country in the world has national security laws, the new laws to be adopted in Hong Kong can follow best international practices in countries that have civil and personal rights comparable to Hong Kong's. There is no need to reinvent the wheel here.

I am confident that Hong Kong can remain a vibrant commercial and financial hub and an open cosmopolitan city if the national security legislation conforms to well-established international norms and is implemented by the independent courts of Hong Kong. However, to achieve this goal, the leaders of Hong Kong must make a massive effort in public education to explain these new laws to the people of Hong Kong.

GT: The death of George Floyd has led to massive protests in the US. Not long after the protests began, US politicians have threatened to use the army to quell protests. Why did they take a totally different attitude toward Hong Kong's violent protesters?

Mahbubani: In most societies (but not all), peaceful protests are legal. In no society are violent demonstrations legal. Hence, it was legitimate for both the Hong Kong police and US police officers to clamp down on violent demonstrations, although wise police forces do it with careful restraint. The Hong Kong Police have done a truly admirable job as they have been able to respond effectively to violent demonstrations without any loss of life. By contrast, some American citizens have lost their lives.

It was a huge mistake for some Hong Kong demonstrators to turn violent. In all healthy societies, there is one cardinal unbreakable rule. The state authorities must have a monopoly on violent methods to preserve law and order. This is why police officers have the authority to legally arrest citizens. Citizens don't have the authority to arrest police officers. The violent demonstrators have done enormous damage to their cause by using stones and metal rods as weapons to attack policemen in Hong Kong.

History teaches us that the most successful demonstrations have been peaceful ones. Great leaders, like Mahatma Gandhi and Martin Luther King have led peaceful protests. At the same time, most protests arise out of underlying socio-economic conditions. It is a tragedy that the living standards of the bottom 50% in Hong Kong, like the bottom 50% in the US, have not gone up in recent times. This is the root cause of the demonstrations in Hong Kong and the US. Fortunately, Hong Kong is in a good position to take care of its bottom 50%. Hence, I remain optimistic for Hong Kong.

GT: The US response to the Covid-19 pandemic is disappointing. Why has the world's only superpower performed so poorly amid the epidemic? Is the Trump administration to blame or is it a result of the accumulated problems in US society and its political system?

Mahbubani: The US response to Covid-19 is particularly surprising and disappointing because for many decades American society was the source of envy and inspiration for the world. When Mr. Deng Xiaoping made his famous visit to the US in January–February 1979, the Chinese people could see how well off the American working classes were then. Sadly, since then, as I document in Has China Won?, the The US has become the only major developed society where the average income of the bottom 50% decreased over the 30-year period to 2010. Two Princeton University economists, Anne Case and Angus Deaton, have documented how this has led to a "sea of despair" among working class white people. They also document how poor economic prospects "compounds over time through family dysfunction, social isolation, addiction, obesity, and other pathologies".

It is therefore a mistake to only blame the Trump administration for the current problems in American society. They have been accumulating over time. The major contributor to the problems of American society was the Reagan-Thatcher revolution. President Ronald Reagan famously said, "Government is not the solution to our problem, government is the problem." As a result, key government institutions, including internationally respected expert bodies like the FAA and FDA, have been seriously weakened. When institutions of government weaken, the ability of the government to handle social crises, like inequality in the US or health crises, like Covid-19, is also severely hampered.

GT: In your opinion, after the Covid-19 pandemic, will the West gradually begin an era of "big government?" Since the eighteenth century, the West has barely reformed its political system. Do they need to make a reflection or reforms?

Mahbubani: In speaking about the "West" and "big government," one has to make a major distinction between the European Union (EU) member states and the US. It's true that both the EU members and the US performed badly in response to Covid-19 as their fatality rates per million (Spain 580, Italy 562, UK 610, USA 339) are higher than East Asian rates (for example, Japan 7, China 3, Singapore 4 and Vietnam 0).

Yet, on balance, many EU member states have developed a healthy balance between the roles of government and markets in developed societies. Their experience mirrors the wise advice of the Nobel Laureate Amartya Sen who said that the countries who succeed are those who combine the "invisible hand" of free markets and "visible hand" of good governance. This is why some of the Scandinavian states, like Denmark and Finland, are viewed as models for the rest of the world to follow.

By contrast, after President Ronald Reagan, the US has abandoned the "visible hand" of good governance. The US needs to develop a new consensus on rebuilding key government institutions to take care of the significant socio-economic problems that the US has built up. William J. Burns, the president of Carnegie Endowment for International Peace and a former deputy secretary of state has written that he watched "the slow and painful desiccation of government—political leaders far more interested in demeaning institutions than modernizing them, bureaucracies sinking beneath too many layers and procedures, and a public that saw a yawning gap between its interests and those of policy elites." He further stated, "First, it is long past time to end the war on government." If the American people were to heed the advice of Ambassador William Burns and end their war on government, they would be better off.

GT: The unrest in the US is worrying. Will it trigger similar disorder or chaos in more countries? Will the world see more collapses of governments, widening wealth gaps, and turmoil in more countries in the post-pandemic era?

Mahbubani: The US remains the world's largest economy. If its growth falters, or if it continues to slide backward, this will be bad for the world, not just for the US. It is in the interest of the global community to see the US economy grow again.

However, if the US economy, as well as the economies of the rest of the world, are to grow again, we must go back to the global consensus that existed in the world before President Trump was elected. Firstly, we must agree that the world is better off when we refrain from trade wars and instead work together to lower tariff and non-tariff barriers to trade. Second, we must work to strengthen, rather than weaken, the World Trade Organization. Indeed, as I explain in my book, The Great Convergence (which has been translated into Chinese), we must strengthen all UN affiliated multilateral organizations, including the World Health Organization. Third, we must also continue to push for Free Trade Agreements like the RCEP (Regional Comprehensive Economic Partnership) and the CPTPP (Comprehensive and Progressive Agreement for Trans-Pacific Partnership). It's truly encouraging that Premier Li Keqiang said on May 28, 2020, "China has a positive and open attitude toward joining the CPTPP".

In short, even though the economic slowdown in the US will be a drag on the global economy, it is still possible for East Asia, including both Northeast Asia and Southeast Asia, to keep growing if we retain our faith in open economies and free trade. Just as the US and Europe were able to keep their economies growing strongly in the 1950s and 1960s by progressively liberalizing their economies more and more, today East Asia can set the pace. As a result, many of the developing economies in the rest of Asia, Africa and Latin America will be drawn to integrate their economies more closely with East Asia.

It's fortunate that the 1945 rules-based order, gifted by the West to the world, has not collapsed, even though the Trump administration has walked away from it. Even though many Europeans feel as insecure about the future as many Americans do, Europe, led by Germany and France, have not walked away from global multilateral institutions. Using the platform of the Asia-Europe Meeting (ASEM), pioneered by former Singapore Prime Minister Mr Goh Chok Tong, East Asia and Europe should work together to stabilize the global rules-based order.

Covid-19 'Enhanced China's Position in the World Order'

Abstract Even though China was the first country to have to deal with the outbreak of Covid-19, its handling of the virus has actually served to enhance China's position vis-a-vis traditional powers like the US and Western Europe.

The world economy came to a screeching halt in 2020 following the outbreak of Covid-19, a respiratory illness caused by the novel coronavirus, officially called SARS-CoV-2. To curb the rapid spread of the virus, many countries have implemented lockdowns and other unprecedented physical distancing measures, restricting huge swathes of the global population to their homes.

As the world scrambles to invent a vaccine amid rising numbers of deaths, there is intense speculation regarding the origin of the virus. While some blame China for the start of the pandemic, the origin of the virus is yet to be determined. Despite challenges, China has managed to keep its casualty figures from the virus relatively low compared to some Western countries.

In an interview with DW, Kishore Mahbubani, a former Singaporean diplomat and distinguished academic, spoke about the response of China and East Asian nations to the pandemic and how it compared to that of Western nations.

DW: The Covid-19 pandemic appears to have changed the world order drastically. How has the health emergency shaped China's position in global affairs?

Kishore Mahbubani: Before the pandemic broke out, China was slowly heading toward becoming the world's number one economic power. China initially stumbled into tackling the health crisis and made some crucial mistakes. The muzzling of the whistleblower, Li Wenliang, was an unfortunate event.

But once China recovered, it took care of Covid-19. The world was amazed at how effectively China put a stop to a very dangerous virus. All of this enhanced China's position in the global world order.

Originally published in DW, April 30, 2020

167

How did China manage to keep a low death rate from the Coronavirus?

China's low death rate is in line with other East Asian countries—Singapore, Japan, South Korea—and territories like Taiwan and Hong Kong. China controlled the pandemic by locking down the country quickly and decisively. That was the secret in keeping the death rate so low.

China has very strong institutions of administration which have strengthened over the years. In comparison, the US has weakened its public service agencies, defunded, demoralized, and delegitimized them. That's another reason China has done better in the management of the crisis.

The US has accused the World Health Organization (WHO) of being "China-centric" in its policy. How will the WHO's role shape up in light of growing political discontentment in the US?

I was Singapore's ambassador to the US for over 10 years. During my time there, I keenly observed how countries tried to cut funding for the UN. In the case of the WHO, even though it's such a critical organization for the world, the West, which includes both the US and the EU, have weakened the WHO by reducing mandatory contributions.

The WHO can't make long-term plans or recruit long-term health inspectors from voluntary contributions. Now that China is emerging as a great power, it will be good for China to bring back mandatory funding for the WHO to its previous levels. If China does that, it will find a lot of support for its campaign. China has made a good start by pledging an additional $30 million (€27.5 million) as a voluntary contribution to the WHO. But I think Beijing can do more to strengthen the long-term capabilities of the WHO.

There are several conspiracy theories on the origin of the novel coronavirus. Why do you think there's more focus on this than on handling the outbreak, particularly in Western societies?

When Covid-19 broke out, China and the US could have left their differences aside and fought a common enemy together, which was a rational and sensible thing to do. Sadly, the pandemic has enhanced the geopolitical contest between the US and China. This geopolitical contest was enhanced by US President Donald Trump's trade war against China.

The US and some Western countries are using Covid-19 as a means to embarrass China. They are making some allegations that this virus was secretly manufactured in a Chinese laboratory. However, in the West, the good thing is that you have both sets of voices—voices condemning China and voices praising China.

Respectable, credible Western journals like The Lancet and Nature have studied these allegations and come to the conclusion that the information provided by China is correct, and that the virus arose from natural causes. As soon as China decoded the genome of the virus, it was shared with the world.

Will the coronavirus pandemic make the West more wary of China and Chinese businesses?

The American wariness of China isn't just due to Covid-19. It's a result of the geopolitical contest between the US and China. The only issue on which President Trump gets bipartisan support is when he beats up China. This type of anti-China sentiment is due to a long-term structural geopolitical contest between the US and China, not because of Covid-19.

Even if President Trump doesn't win in November, I can sadly and confidently predict that the US-China geopolitical contest will continue. The US will definitely make use of the mistakes China made in Covid-19 to enhance its criticism of China.

In your book, *Has China Won?*, you praised Xi Jinping's governance and said that, "There is a very strong potential that Xi Jinping could provide to China the beneficent kind of rule provided by a philosopher king." Does that statement stand true after the way China has handled the coronavirus pandemic?

When you run a country of 1.4 billion people—it's one of the toughest jobs in the world. Every day that China hangs together as a country is a miracle. If you want to judge any leader of China, you should not judge them by their statements, but by the results of their rule.

In the last three to four decades, the Chinese have experienced the greatest improvement in their standard of living. Clearly, the Chinese people have benefited a lot from this rule. If this record continues, and my guess is that it will, it will show that China has achieved a certain level of competence in leadership and government administration.

China has been criticized by many countries in the West for capitalizing on the pandemic, by sending masks and kits. How much truth is there in this statement?

It's very difficult to find out what is true and not true. I would listen to the governments of countries like Italy, Greece, Serbia. They still seem to be relatively happy with the help they have received from China.

Whereas, if you look at the governments of France and Germany—they seem to be upset with what China has said or done. China is not perfect. It can make mistakes. Maybe when China sent masks, it sent them too quickly without checking them for quality.

At the end of the day, we have to wait and see what the outcome of this entire situation will be. I predict that more and more countries will reach out to China for assistance as Covid-19 hits harder.

A significant portion of Singapore's coronavirus cases are from dormitories housing foreign workers. How did the Singaporean government tackle the outbreak in these dormitories?

Singapore's management of Covid-19 has been greatly admired by the rest of the world. However, we were slow to spot what was happening in the foreign worker dormitories. We could have acted faster to stop it from growing. Once Singapore recognized the problem, I think Singapore did a very effective job in managing it.

Singapore was remarkably generous in trying to help the foreign workers. The prime minister of Singapore sent a message to the families of these foreign workers in countries like India and Bangladesh, telling them to not worry as Singapore is taking care of their family members. Foreign workers in Singapore also have the same access to world class health facilities that citizens do.

If you look at the overall number of deaths in Singapore from the virus — it's just 14. It's a remarkable track record, as compared to countries like the US, where the death toll is over 55,000.

How did Asian countries like Singapore, China, and South Korea handle misinformation related to Covid-19, as compared to countries like the US?

East Asian countries learned the validity of good science from the West. Even today, East Asia relies on the West for major breakthroughs in areas like medicine. All of us in East Asia are genuinely puzzled that the Trump administration has walked away from science and prescriptions during this pandemic. This is not completely true of the West as New Zealand and Germany are paying attention to science as carefully as East Asia.

How China Could Win Over
the Post-coronavirus World and Leave
the US Behind

Abstract As the US-China geopolitical contest gains momentum, the US has to ask itself if it can truly improve the lives of the people in the 191 remaining countries around the world.

To understand the post-Covid-19 world that is coming, there is one important human statistic we must bear in mind: 330 million people live in the US; 1.4 billion in China, and approximately 6 billion in the rest of the world. These 6 billion, who live in 191 countries, have begun preparing themselves for the US-China geopolitical contest. Their choices will determine who will win.

For most Americans, the contest is a no-brainer. Given a choice between a freedom-loving democratic US and an oppressive Communist China, the 6 billion would choose the US. Indeed many aspects of the US remain more appealing: great universities (for example, Harvard and Yale); Broadway, and Hollywood. Yet declining powers can also retain their cultural attractions. Witness the UK with Cambridge and Oxford, Shakespeare and Jane Austen.

The elites who run these 191 countries have been mostly educated in Western-style universities. They have learned to apply the cold calculus of reason to work out cost–benefit analyses of what both the US and China have to offer them. Sentiments won't play a role here. They have to decide at the end of the day which country, the US or China, will improve their citizens' living conditions.

Africa is a prime example. African leaders have studied East Asian economic success stories and learned from them. Trade, not aid, spurs economic growth. China is now the world's largest trading power; its total trade is USD 4.43 trillion compared to USD 3.89 trillion for the US To boost trade within Africa, first-rate infrastructure is needed. China is now the world's infrastructure superpower, building badly needed ports, railways, roads, and power stations in Africa. These projects include the megaport at Bagamoyo, Tanzaniya and the Addis Ababa-Djibouti Railway, which is the first fully-electrified cross-border railway in Africa. Paul Kagame, president of Rwanda, has said: "The Chinese bring what Africa needs: investment and money for

Originally published in MarketWatch, April 18, 2020

governments and companies." Here's one leading indicator. When China convenes China-Africa summit meetings, all African leaders turn up.

It's commonly believed that China is sucking all these poor countries into a debt trap. A peer-reviewed academic study found this perception to be untrue. In a 2019 research paper, Johns Hopkins professor Deborah Brautigam concluded that most of these countries voluntarily signed on to these loans and had positive experiences working with China. Brautigam writes, "The evidence so far, including the Sri Lankan case, shows that the drumbeat of alarm about Chinese banks' funding of infrastructure across the BRI and beyond is overblown." She continues, "…a large number of people have favorable opinions of China as an economic model and consider China an attractive partner for their development.

For example, in 2014, 65% in Kenya, 67% in Ghana, and 85% in Africa's most populous country, Nigeria, held favorable views of China." Hence, when China launched its Belt and Road Initiative (BRI), to build infrastructure from Central Asia to Africa (and even to Latin America), most countries signed on. Yes, China has made mistakes with BRI. Mahathir bin Mohamad protested against its terms when he became Prime Minister of Malaysia in 2018. However the deal was quietly renegotiated, and Mahathir became one of the key opening speakers of the BRI Summit in Beijing in 2019.

Italy is another leading indicator of how the world is turning. It's a member of the G-7, the core group of the Western club. Its economy is ailing. China has stepped up to offer new investment in Italy. Former Italian Minister of Economy and Finance Giovanni Tria has called Chinese investments "a circle virtuous, satisfying and diffuse growth" and referred to them as "a train that Italy cannot afford to miss." Now, Covid-19 has given China-Italy relations a major boost. While its fellow EU members initially balked at helping Italy, China responded almost immediately, sending 31 tons of much-needed medical equipment, pulmonary ventilators, face masks, and protective suits.

In previous disasters, such as the 2004 Boxing Day Tsunami that hit Indonesia, the US was the first to arrive with aid. China offered little. With Covid-19, the roles have reversed. The 6 billion people outside the US and China are genuinely shocked to see the sharp contrast between the competent responses of China and the incompetent responses of the US They would agree with the assessment of the World Health Organization: "China's bold approach to contain the rapid spread of this new respiratory pathogen has changed the course of a rapidly escalating and deadly epidemic".

Equally importantly, a leading Western medical journal, The Lancet, published an open letter from leading medical and public health professionals also praising China's response, noting that efforts made by "scientists, public health professionals, and medical professionals of China… [were] remarkable."

Winning friends and influencing people

Yet all of this doesn't mean that the vast majority of countries will abandon the US and join China's camp. Far from it. Most countries want to maintain good ties with both powers, they just don't want to be forced to choose. If China offers good and cheap

5G technology from Huawei, for example, most countries (including US allies such as the UK, Germany and France) want the freedom to choose the best technology or their telecommunications infrastructure. So when the US imposes sanctions on countries buying from Huawei, it's causing problems with friends.

Freedom to choose what is best for one's own country is a demand that many friends of the US are calling for. India and Turkey want to be free to choose S-400 missiles from Russia; Indonesia wants to buy Sukhoi jet fighters. Similarly, the UK, France and Germany want the freedom to trade with Iran through INSTEX, a special clearing mechanism they set up to facilitate trade with Iran.

The US can still recover a lot of influence it enjoyed in the world. Vast reservoirs of goodwill toward the US remain, for example, among the 10 ASEAN nations of Southeast Asia. Indeed, two of them, Philippines and Thailand, are "technically" treaty allies with the US. Yet there is no doubt that both of these countries are now closer to China than to the US. All 10 ASEAN countries do more trade with China than with the US. To balance this, the stock of US investment in ASEAN countries is far greater. Indeed, America's total investment in ASEAN of USD 328 billion is far more than what it has invested in India, China, Japan and Korea combined. By contrast, the Chinese investment in ASEAN is about USD 150 billion.

The 10 ASEAN countries, like the 181 other countries, don't want to be caught in a zero-sum geopolitical contest between the US and China. Quite reasonably, they want to keep their options open. With skillful diplomacy, the US can still win the game. Sadly, the art of diplomacy has been lost in Washington DC This has created a massive opening that China has taken full advantage of, on its way to victory over the post-Covid-19 world.

Why Attempts to Build a New Anti-China Alliance Will Fail

Abstract The biggest problem with the "Quad" is that the big strategic game in Asia isn't military but economic. The countries that make up the Quad are far too diverse in their economic interests and historical vulnerabilities to make it a tenable long-term alliance.

Australia, India, Japan, and the United States have perfectly legitimate concerns about China. It will be uncomfortable living with a more powerful China. And it's equally legitimate for them to hedge by cooperating in the Quadrilateral Security Dialogue, informally known as the Quad. Unfortunately, the Quad will not alter the course of Asian history for two simple reasons: First, the four countries have different geopolitical interests and vulnerabilities. Second, and more fundamentally, they are in the wrong game. The big strategic game in Asia isn't military but economic.

Australia is the most vulnerable. Its economy is highly dependent on China. Australians have been proud of their remarkable three decades of recession-free growth. That happened only because Australia became, functionally, an economic province of China: In 2018–2019, 33% of its exports went to China, whereas only 5 percent went to the United States.

This is why it was unwise for Australia to slap China in the face publicly by calling for an international inquiry on China and Covid-19. It would have been wiser and more prudent to make such a call privately. Now Australia has dug itself into a hole. All of Asia is watching intently to see who will blink in the current Australia-China standoff. In many ways, the outcome is pre-determined. If Beijing blinks, other countries may follow Australia in humiliating China. Hence, effectively, Australia has blocked it into a corner.

And China can afford to wait. As the Australian scholar, Hugh White said: "The problem for Canberra is that China holds most of the cards. Power in international relations lies with the country that can impose high costs on another country at a low cost to itself. This is what China can do to Australia, but [Australian Prime Minister] Scott Morrison and his colleagues do not seem to understand that." Significantly, in November 2019, former Prime Minister Paul Keating warned his fellow Australians

---

Originally published in Foreign Policy, Jan 27, 2021

K. Mahbubani, *The Asian 21st Century*, China and Globalization, https://doi.org/10.1007/978-981-16-6811-1_33

that the Quad would not work. "More broadly, the so-called 'Quadrilateral' is not taking off," he told the Australian Strategic Forum. "India remains ambivalent about the US agenda on China and will hedge in any activism against China. A rapprochement between Japan and China is also in evidence … so Japan is not signing up to any program of containment of China." While India has clearly hardened its position on China since Keating spoke in 2019, it is unlikely to become a clear US ally.

Japan is also vulnerable but in a different way. Australia is fortunate to have friendly neighbors in the Association of Southeast Asian Nations. Japan only has unfriendly neighbors: China, Russia, and South Korea. It has difficult, even tense, relations with all three. It can manage difficult relations with Russia and South Korea; both have smaller economies. But the Japanese are acutely aware that they now have to adjust to a much more powerful China again. Yet this is not a new phenomenon. With the exception of the first half of the twentieth century, Japan has almost always lived in peace with its more powerful neighbor, China.

As the East Asia scholar Ezra Vogel wrote in 2019, "No countries can compare with China and Japan in terms of the length of their historical contact: 1500 years." As he observed in his book China and Japan, the two countries maintained deep cultural ties throughout much of their past, but China, with its great civilization and resources, had the upper hand. If for most of 1500 years, Japan could live in peace with China, it can revert to that pattern again for the next 1000 years. However, as in the famously slow Kabuki plays in Japan, the changes in the relationship will be very slight and incremental, with both sides moving gradually and subtly into a new *modus vivendi*. They will not become friends anytime soon, but Japan will signal subtly that it understands China's core interests. Yes, there will be bumps along the way, but China and Japan will adjust slowly and steadily.

India and China have the opposite problem. As two old civilizations, they have also lived side by side over millennia. However, they had few direct contacts, effectively kept apart by the Himalayas. Unfortunately, modern technology has no longer made the Himalayas insurmountable. Hence, the increasing number of face-to-face encounters between Chinese and Indian soldiers. Such encounters always lead to accidents, one of which happened in June 2020. Since then, a tsunami of anti-China sentiment has swept across India. Over the next few years, relations will go downhill. The avalanche has been triggered.

Yet China will be patient because time is working in its favor. In 1980, the economies of China and India were the same size. By 2020, China's had grown five times larger. The longer-term relationship between two powers always depends, in the long run, on the relative size of the two economies. The Soviet Union lost the Cold War because the US economy could vastly outspend it. Similarly, just as the United States presented China with a major geopolitical gift by withdrawing from the Trans-Pacific Partnership (TPP) trade agreement in 2017, India did China a major geopolitical favor by not joining the Regional Comprehensive Economic Partnership (RCEP). Economics is where the big game is playing. With the United States staying out of TPP and India out of RCEP, a massive economic ecosystem centered on China is evolving in the region. Here's one statistic to ponder on: In 2009, the size of the retail goods market in China was USD 1.8 trillion compared with USD 4 trillion for that market in the United States. Ten years later, the respective numbers were USD 6 trillion and USD 5.5 trillion. China's total imports in the coming decade will likely exceed USD 22 trillion. Just as the massive US consumer market in the 1970s and 1980s defeated the Soviet Union, the massive and growing Chinese consumer market will be the ultimate decider of the big geopolitical game.

This is why the Quad's naval exercises in the Indian Ocean will not move the needle of Asian history. Over time, the different economic interests and historical vulnerabilities of the four countries will make the rationale for the Quad less and less tenable. Here's one leading indicator: No other Asian country—not even the staunchest US ally, South Korea—is rushing to join the Quad. The future of Asia will be written in four letters, RCEP, and not the four letters in Quad.

Biden Should Appear 'Tough & Fierce' on China, but Cooperate 'Below the Radar'

Abstract The main preoccupation for the Biden Administration will be to solve its domestic issues and prevent the future reelection of Donald Trump. While this may mean that Biden has to appear tough on China, he should quietly work with allies in Asia to cooperate with China.

A diplomat for 33 years, he served as Singapore's Ambassador to the United Nations from 1984 to 1989, and subsequently 1998 to 2004. In between, he held the position of Permanent Secretary at Singapore's Foreign Ministry from 1993 to 1998.

Sitting down with Mothership for an interview a few days before President-elect Joseph Biden is set to be inaugurated on Jan. 20, he gave his thoughts on what a Biden presidency would mean for Singapore and the region, his cabinet picks so far, as well as the future of American democracy, especially in the wake of recent events like the Capitol Hill siege.

Here is the transcript of the interview Mothership did with Mahbubani:

The inauguration of Joe Biden is next week. Do you think he's the right man for the moment?

Absolutely. Because the United States has never been as divided and as polarized as it is today. It's a deeply fractured society. And it's shown by the fact that 74 million Americans voted for Donald Trump, even though most people in the world think that Donald Trump is not fit to be the president of the United States of America, but that's an indication of how divided and polarized American societies have become.

So what you need in America, is some kind of grandfatherly figure, who's a very nice guy who speaks softly, whom you sort of fall in love with immediately. And that's Joe Biden.

Actually, America is very lucky that it is Biden that is becoming the President on Jan. 20, because just imagine, if he has a heart attack, and Kamala Harris becomes the Vice President. She's very competent, but she cannot bring the country together in a way that Biden can. And therefore, it's very important that Biden succeeds.

Originally published in Mothership, Jan 17, 2021

What do you think will be his priorities in his first 100 days?

I suspect for his priorities in the first 100 days, he would clearly want to focus, number one, on fighting Covid-19.

I mean, it's actually quite shocking in terms of number of deaths, in terms of the spread of Covid-19, the Trump administration has been completely incompetent in its management of Covid-19. So I think clearly he's got to find ways and means of stopping it.

And then, of course, it's always the economy. I think he's aware that the one reason why 74 million Americans voted for Donald Trump is because many of them in the working classes, lower middle classes, haven't seen their incomes improve in 30 years. And this is documented in my book *"Has China Won?"*.

And so this creates what the Nobel laureate Angus Deaton has called "a sea of despair" among the white working classes. So he's got to address that. He's got to find ways and means of improving the living standards of these angry white working classes. And if he succeeds, then America will become less polarized.

Have you met Biden personally? Can you share with our audience about your personal interactions with him? Or what you've heard from some of your American friends?

Well, I have not had the pleasure of meeting Biden personally, but at least two of my good friends are among his close advisers, and they've been with him for decades.

From them, I get a firsthand feel of how Biden is doing.

Let's say we were having this interview exactly a year ago, on Jan. 15, 2020. If you had asked me then, does Biden have a chance of becoming president? I would have said no, he's too far behind!

But when I spoke to his advisers, they said "Kishore, we know he'll do bad in New Hampshire, he'll do bad in Iowa, we know that. But we just got to keep going till we get to North Carolina, and then we'll take off."

And that's exactly what happened.

Who is winning? Trump or Biden? Biden has more routes to 270 than Trump.

Because you heard about him already from your friends, were you surprised by the election results?

I was surprised by how well Donald Trump did.

I bought the conventional wisdom, as you know, before the elections that there will be a blue wave. There was a lot of support for the Democrats. Democrats will increase the number of seats in the House, they failed, would maybe take back the Senate, but they barely got that. And that they would win more seats in the legislature and they didn't.

And they thought Biden would win handsomely. But actually, it is quite amazing how many people voted for Donald Trump, including, by the way, some of the minorities, some of the blacks, some Latinos. So it shows that there are a lot of people in America who are still very, very angry.

But at the end of the day, we should be grateful that Biden has won because just as he will calm America down, I think he will also calm the world down.

Turning to China, do you think the Chinese government was surprised? Do you think the Chinese would prefer to deal with Trump or Biden?

I think the Chinese always take a long view.

And the Chinese realize that they cannot control the outcome of the US elections, and they just have to live with whoever gets elected. Either Donald Trump or Biden.

But the paradox about Biden being elected for China is that on the one hand, everything will change. Because for a start, Biden and his cabinet will be very polite. They'll be very civil. They won't insult China. They will make policies slowly and carefully. No more tweets or tantrums. That's what Donald Trump did, right?

It'd be very, very different. His style would be the exact opposite of Donald Trump.

But on the other hand, nothing will change because Biden's hands are tied. There is a very strong anti-China consensus in Washington DC.

And there is a very strong feeling that this time around the US must stand up to China. So if Biden is seen to be soft on China, he'll be attacked in Washington DC.

So on the one hand, it looks as though everything is changing. On the other hand, nothing is changing.

Do you think relations between China and the US would improve under the Biden administration?

Well, the answer to that question is very, very complicated. I'll give a three-part answer if you don't mind. Part one, this is what Biden should do. As I mentioned earlier, he should focus on fighting Covid-19, he should focus on improving the economy, on improving the livelihood of the Americans. These should be his three priorities.

But to do that, he should therefore press the pause button on the geopolitical contest with China and say, okay, first, let me fix my mothership, the United States of America before I come to deal with China. We should be the logical, rational, sensible thing to do. And we all think that the US is a logical, sensible, rational society. Sadly, it's not.

Because the US, especially key members of the establishment, have become very emotional about China, they see China as a real threat, and they are really frightened that America would become the number two power. So because of the rock solid consensus in Washington, DC, that the US must stand up to China, he cannot press the pause button. He has to be seen to be tough on China.

So for example, one thing he could do is to just get rid of the tariffs that Trump has imposed on China. But if he does that, he'd be attacked on all fronts, right? So he can't do it, his hands again, tied. But this is why that's all.

So that was what he cannot do. The final part is what can he do, and I would say what he can do is to be very cunning. He should pretend that he's beating up China every day. So in his rhetoric, he should be very strongly anti-China.

But behind the scenes, he should quietly work to see where he can cooperate with China on issues where they have a common interest, like climate change, like

Covid-19, and also in growing the economy. So there are many areas of common interests—which actually I documented in my book *Has China Won?*—where he should work under the radar screen.

So above the radar screen, he should be very, very tough and fierce on China. Below the radar screen, he should cooperate with China. But that requires a certain degree of political dexterity on his part, but clearly, outside of the US, China is his number one challenge.

It was just announced that Kurt Campbell is going to be the top US diplomat for this region. What do you think this signifies?

Well, I think very highly of Kurt Campbell. In fact, during the Covid-19 shutdown, Kurt Campbell and I were on the same debating team, and we debated two other Americans, Minxin Pei and Susan Thornton on a channel called Intelligence Squared Debates (US).

So you can watch that video, you'll see how Kurt and I were on the same side, arguing for a more rational approach toward China. And so in the course of that, I also had a long conversation with him when we were preparing for this debate. So I think very highly of Kurt Campbell, I think he's a very good choice because he's a calm, stable and rational actor. And I also did, by the way, a podcast with him once. So I've had lots of interactions with Kurt Campbell.

So someone like him, I believe, would be a calming influence on US-China relations. But at the same time, I've also no doubt that Kurt Campbell will be very tough on China.

And his background, by the way, he's more of a Japanologist. And I'm told that he's a very good friend of the current Japanese Prime Minister, Mr. Suga. So all that will, I guess, play in the equation also.

And what do you think of Biden's Cabinet picks so far?

From working at Tsukiji fish market to being Prime Minister of Japan: Self-made man Yoshihide Suga.

I think they've been very good. I think the choice of Secretary of State, I don't know him, Tony Blinken. But I have friends who have worked with him, worked for him. And he's a very calm, stable, rational person. I think in many ways, history will see that Trump's Secretary of State Mike Pompeo will be regarded as one of the worst American secretaries of state, because he's very erratic, and he makes decisions emotionally.

So for example, almost the last two weeks of the Trump administration, he suddenly lifted all restrictions on Taiwan.

Hang on a second, these agreements on Taiwan were negotiated over years, and they maintain a very careful balance between American interests and Chinese interests. They were negotiated by some of the top negotiators like Henry Kissinger. Then you just throw them away! That's amazing! How can you do that?

And in future, why should any country sign an agreement with the US if the Secretary of State can just tear it up unilaterally?

I mean, that's exactly the wrong sort of behavior that you should get from the Secretary of State. But of course, Mike Pompeo was not stupid. He was doing it for a reason. He wants to become the next President of the United States of America. And he wants to become the next Donald Trump. So he's going to behave like Donald Trump.

So you have a lot of confidence in Biden's team. What do you think would be their impact on our region here?

I think we cannot tell now, because a lot depends on the capacity of the incoming Biden administration to listen to what Southeast Asia wants. And it's very clear, if the Biden administration sent anybody to Southeast Asia, and talk privately to all the countries, Indonesia, Malaysia, Thailand, Singapore, and all that, they'll get a very clear message.

And the message is in two parts. Yes, we want to see a strong US presence in Southeast Asia. We want to see more US investment in Southeast Asia, we want to see a US military presence in Southeast Asia.

Part two, don't make us choose between the US and China. We want to be friends with the US We want to be friends with China. In fact, that's also what DPM Heng Swee Keat said recently, that's also what PM Lee Hsien Loong said in his article in the magazine, Foreign Affairs.

So that will take some adjustment. So it's very important for the people in the Biden administration who used to work in the Obama administration, they mustn't think they can go back to the world of the Obama administration, because Southeast Asia has moved on in the last few years. There's a new Southeast Asia.

Storming of Capitol Hill shows division in US society, but also strength of its institutions: DPM Heng.

So it's very important that the new Biden team make an extraordinary effort to come to Southeast Asia and listen carefully to what Southeast Asians want.

And of course, the Biden administration is more likely to listen than the Trump administration, which had lost completely the art of listening.

We'll like to get your views on the future of US democracy. We have seen very sad footage of what has happened in the Capitol Hill siege. What do you think caused the violent outbreak to happen?

Yes, I think it's an absolute mistake for the liberals in America just to blame Donald Trump. Donald Trump, of course, aggravated the problem. But the problem is a deep structural problem in American society, which I mentioned earlier, that the living conditions of the bottom 50 percent have not improved over 30 years.

So there's a very angry white working class in America. And at the same time – is why I devote an entire chapter of my book to explaining what has gone wrong in American society – it's a deep rooted structural problem, which is explained in chapter seven of my book, "America has become a plutocracy".

You must spend some time trying to understand how dangerous a plutocracy is. And the difference is very clear. In a democracy, you have a government of the 100%, by the 100%, for the 100%. In a plutocracy you have the government of the 1%, by the 1%, for the 1%.

So in the past, in the US, which had a lot of social mobility, the playing field was tilted in favor of the poor, is easier for the poor. So if you're playing football, right, and you're running downhill, you're more likely to score goals. And the rich have to run up here. And that's fair, you must give more chances to the poor to score goals so that they can compete with the rich.

But in the last 30 years, the playing field has shifted. Now the poor in America have to run uphill to score goals. And the rich can just run downhill. So the whole playing field is tilted in favor of the rich in America.

As a consequence of this, the US, which was known for its social mobility in the past, has lost its social mobility. And if you look at the magazine, Foreign Affairs, there's a very famous economist, Branko Milanović, who came out with an article and just read the last line.

The last line says: the only way to save America is to get politics out of the grip of the rich, because the rich control, not just the economy, but also the political system. And the people at the bottom suffer.

So this is a very deep structural problem. And trying to change the playing field to make it either even level or balance it in favor of the poor, is going to be very difficult.

The sad part is that many Americans have not accepted the reality that America has become a plutocracy, even though very important people in the world like the late Paul Volcker, who was a friend of mine, told me America has become a plutocracy.

Martin Wolf of The Financial Times says America has become a plutocracy. The Nobel laureate, Joseph Stiglitz, says America has become a plutocracy.

So the first thing that America needs to do is to accept the reality that it is a plutocracy. And when it accepts that reality, then you can solve that problem.

Recently, with social media companies censoring Trump, there have been criticisms from some world leaders, including German Chancellor Angela Merkel, who think that this is against the spirit of democracy. What do you think of this view?

This is an issue on which opinion is very, very sharply divided. And the answers given by different societies reflect their own historical experiences.

So for example, in Europe, they went through tyrannical leaders like Hitler. That's why Chancellor Merkel has criticized Twitter for censoring Donald Trump. They say no, you must always allow everyone to speak out. So that's one point of view, which may be right or which may not be right.

But I think it is important for each country to understand its own circumstances. And I think in the case of Singapore, for example, I am actually very grateful that Singapore is very tough, and cuts off anybody who might inflame opinions in Singapore because, at the end of the day, we are still a new society, we are a multiracial society.

So it's important for us to have much tougher safeguards. And so for example, in Europe, Macron will support the drawing of cartoons of Prophet Muhammad. We Singapore will not allow that at all. No way, right?

So it's important to understand the national context of different countries that influences these decisions.

But at the end of the day, I truly believe that anybody who talks about rights, tell him you must never just talk about rights, you must talk about rights and responsibilities. There are two sides to the same coin.

What advice would you give your American friends, with regards to the future of American democracy? Do you have any advice for the American leaders?

I think my advice for the American leaders is that they should realize that the US has had an exceptionally good run for over 100 years.

But right now, America is going through a very difficult patch. So it's got to ask itself a very basic question. Do I keep going on autopilot? Or do I make U-turns and change my policies?

And one thing that heartens me, by the way, on the positive side, is that if you give Americans strong rational arguments, they will accept it.

So like Fareed Zakaria chose my book as one of the books of 2020. And, you know, Larry Summers, the former treasury secretary, former president of Harvard, chose my book as one of the three books of 2020.

That is what I consider the strength of the United States of America. At the end of the day, they're trying very hard to listen and to learn. So I hope that the Americans should go through a period of deep reflection now because that's what America needs today.

And frankly, I want to emphasize that we want to see a strong United States of America. We don't want to see a weak and divided United States of America. So it's in our interest to see the country spend some time healing itself, taking care of its tremendous internal problems, emerge stronger, and that will be better for the world.

We're also keen to ask you a question with regards to China and of course, its influence. This is something that some of our readers are concerned about with the recent case of Dickson Yeospying on the US for China. So, how real do you think is the trend of influence operations from China is, especially in Singapore?

Well, I'm going to give away a big secret. Every country, every serious country in the world, carries out influence operations and looks for spies. So this is normal behavior on the part of countries.

And one of the strengths of Singapore, going back to our founding fathers, Lee Kuan Yew, Goh Keng Swee, S. Rajaratnam, is that they were all very suspicious of all the great powers.

So Singapore has become a very vigilant place. And we've always been looking out for such operations. And as you know, we have expelled American diplomats, and then we have also taken actions against other countries, sometimes quietly.

So I think we have to accept that as a reality. So it's very important that ordinary Singaporeans understand very well, to be very careful, to ensure that they're not used in any way by any foreign power.

How do you think young Singaporeans can continue to stay vigilant? Do you have any advice for them?

The simple advice I have is not to become pro-China or pro-America or pro-India or pro-Malaysia. Just remain pro- Singapore.

And we must always defend Singapore's national interests and that's our responsibility as a citizen of Singapore. So we should be very careful and not be caught on one side or another when other countries have problems.

Biden Should Summon the Courage to Reverse Course on China

Abstract If Biden were to follow the geopolitical wisdom of George Kennan, he would reverse the Trump Administration's disastrous trade war with China, which has only served to harm the American people and strengthen the Chinese Communist Party.

In Alaska last month Antony Blinken, US secretary of state, and Jake Sullivan, national security adviser, gave a public dressing down on democracy and human rights to Yang Jiechi and Wang Yi, China's top foreign policy officials. They did so in the confident belief that the US knows how to triumph slowly and patiently over a communist adversary.

Yet even though the US won the cold war, China may understand better why Soviet communism failed. It is determined not to make the same mistakes.

China's analysis would match that of George Kennan, the US master strategist. Kennan wisely predicted that the cold war would be determined by Washington's ability "to create among the peoples of the world generally the impression of a country that knows what it wants, which is coping successfully with the problem of its internal life and with the responsibilities of a world power". Here's the shocking comparison. Vis-à-vis the Soviet Union, the US was ahead on all three counts. Vis-à-vis China, it is not.

The first indicator of the Soviet collapse came from negative trends in indicators of social well-being: life expectancy, infant mortality, suicides, opioid (or alcohol) addiction. Today it's the US that is doing badly. In contrast to other developed societies, US life expectancy is declining. The educational standards of US teenagers lag behind those of many advanced industrial countries.

If Kennan were alive today, he would be shocked to see the US spending USD 5 trillion on unnecessary wars, while the bottom 50% of Americans have seen their incomes stagnate for decades. There is a "sea of despair" among white working classes.

China is doing the opposite of the former Soviet Union. China believes the Soviet leaders failed because they lost touch with their own people, ignoring their welfare

---

Originally published in Financial Times, Apr 7, 2021

© The Author(s) 2022
K. Mahbubani, *The Asian 21st Century*, China and Globalization,
https://doi.org/10.1007/978-981-16-6811-1_35

while engaged in foreign wars. China hasn't fought a major war in 40 years. Unlike the Soviet Union, it controls military expenditures.

No country has improved its people's well-being as much as China. In terms of human development, the past 40 years have been the best four decades in 4000 years of Chinese history.

China still faces many internal problems. Success is not guaranteed. Yet against the backdrop of a century or more of humiliation and suffering, the lives of the Chinese people have never been better. Hence, the US cold war strategy will not work.

The Biden administration is making a strategic mistake in carrying on with Donald Trump's policies toward China. Curiously, Biden himself declared in 2019 that Trump's trade war had failed to help US workers. The data backs Biden's assessment. In 2009, the size of China's retail goods market was USD 1.4 trillion, compared with USD 4 trillion for the US. By 2019, after three years of Trump's trade war, China's market was approaching USD 6 trillion, bigger than that of the US at USD 5.5 trillion.

Even if Biden's administration wished to change course on China, it is constrained by a rising anti-Chinese mood in the US body politic. Unwise steps taken under Trump remain in place: the closure of China's consulate in Houston, restrictions on Chinese journalists, ending the Peace Corps and Fulbright Scholarship programs in China.

Biden administration officials are clearly afraid to be seen as "soft" on China. However, if they wanted, they could construct a strong case for reversing Trump's policies. They could point to the reality that the Trump administration actually strengthened China and Xi Jinping, its president. How?

The Chinese people can see that their government has protected them well in the Covid-19 emergency. Meanwhile, the Trump administration floundered, resulting in the deaths of more than half a million Americans. When US vice president Mike Pence and secretary of state Mike Pompeo hurled insults at China, they only strengthened the standing of the Chinese government. Similarly, most Chinese thought that their policymakers won the public argument in Alaska. So too, did many other Asians.

All this points to a wiser course available to the Biden administration. It should declare, as Biden did earlier, that Trump was wrong on China. It should then press the pause button on the US- Chinese geopolitical contest, while assessing whether Washington can formulate a better strategy against such a formidable competitor.

Ending the trade war with China would boost economic growth in the US, helping Biden in the 2022 midterm elections. And most of the world would cheer if the Biden administration pressed the pause button, especially while Covid-19 is still raging.

The West Should Heed Napoleon's Advice and Let China Sleep

Abstract The 21st century will see the return of China to the centre stage of world history. The time has come for the West to do a complete reboot and reconsider all its fundamental premises on China.

Two decades into the 21st century, the main challenge it holds for the west has become clear: the return of China to center stage. After managing phase 1 of China's reform well from 1980 to 2020—a period in which China fought no wars—the west is setting itself up for failure in Phase 2.

It is a failure resulting from three flawed assumptions. The first—and most deeply embedded in western minds—is that China cannot possibly be a good partner as long as it is ruled by the Chinese Communist party. Communism was supposed to have been swept into the dustbin of history after the collapse of the Soviet Union in the late 1980s. So, the argument goes, how can the world work with an oppressive party that rules against the wisdom of the Chinese people?

Yet there is plenty of evidence to suggest most Chinese people do not perceive the CCP to be oppressive. In fact, the latest Edelman Trust Barometer report suggests that support for the Chinese government is among the highest in the world. A Chinese-American psychology researcher from Stanford University, Jean Fan, observed after visiting the country in 2019 that "China is changing... fast, in a way that is almost incomprehensible without seeing it in person. In contrast to America's stagnation, China's culture, self-concept, and morale are being transformed at a rapid pace—mostly for the better."

Despite all this, few western minds can escape from the second flawed assumption: even if most Chinese people are happy with the Communist party, they and the rest of the world would be better off were they to switch immediately to a democratic system.

Until the collapse of the Soviet Union and the subsequent implosion of the living standards of the Russian people, some Chinese may have believed in an instant transformation to democracy. Now, many have no doubt that a weak central government will result in massive chaos and suffering for the Chinese people. For evidence, they

---

Originally published in Financial Times, Sep 20, 2020

191
K. Mahbubani, *The Asian 21st Century*, China and Globalization,
https://doi.org/10.1007/978-981-16-6811-1_36

look to 4000 years of Chinese history and, particularly, the so-called "century of humiliation" China suffered from 1842 to 1949.

Moreover, a democratically elected government is not necessarily a liberal one. The democratically elected Indian prime minister Jawaharlal Nehru seized back the Portuguese colony of Goa in 1961, against the protests of then US president John F Kennedy and British prime minister Harold Macmillan. A democratic China would probably be even less patient in dealing with Hong Kong and Taiwan.

A democratically elected Chinese government would also be loath to be seen as weak in dealing with separatist movements in Xinjiang—look at the Indian government's crackdown in Kashmir. Indeed none of China's neighbors, not even the biggest democracies in Asia, are pushing for regime change in Beijing. A stable, predictable China, even as it becomes more assertive, is preferable to the alternative.

The third flawed assumption may be the most dangerous: that a democratic China would inevitably accept western norms and practices, and happily become a member of the western-plus club, as Japan has done.

That is not the cultural dynamic that is sweeping through Asia. Both Turkey and India are friends of the west. Yet Turkey has shifted from the secular ideology of Mustafa Kemal Ataturk to the Islamic one of Recep Tayyip Erdogan—and India has moved from the Anglophilic Nehru to the Hindu devotee Narendra Modi.

We must acknowledge that a tsunami of de-westernization is under way. Even more significantly, when Mr. Erdogan announces the conversion of the Hagia Sophia to a mosque and Mr. Modi resurrects a long-lost Hindu temple on a contested religious site, they are signaling a desire to return to pre-western cultural roots.

Napoleon was right when he warned western nations to "let China sleep, for when she wakes, she will shake the world". Even more than in Turkey and India, there is a potential volcano of anti-western sentiment waiting to explode in China. Currently, the only political force strong enough to hold down these forces of Chinese nationalism is the Chinese Communist party.

The successor to the party could well be far less rational. Keep that in mind, instead of proceeding on autopilot with current policies toward China. The time has come for the west to do a complete reboot and reconsider all its fundamental premises on China. Western governments should learn to live and work with the Chinese leadership, instead of wishing for its transformation or early demise.

Asian Inheritors of a Western Legacy?

Abstract While we must recognize the incredible contributions the West has made to global institutions, especially the United States, the increased influence of Asian nations, in particular China, gives them the opportunity to inherit and reform classic institutions of the current world order for a new era.

Q: The world has suffered from the Covid-19 pandemic in the past year. Against this backdrop, how do you see international relations in the present and in the future?

Covid-19 has had a massive impact on humanity. It spread rapidly to every corner of the world. It has also paralyzed globalization in significant ways. Equally importantly, Covid-19 is posing a question to humanity: is the human species still the smartest species on planet earth?

If it was, the human species should quickly learn the main lesson from Covid-19: all of humanity is now on the same boat. As I documented in "The Great Convergence" (translated into Chinese) before modern globalization, when humanity lived in 193 separate countries, it was also living in 193 separate boats. Covid-19 has reinforced the message that we no longer live in 193 separate boats. Instead, we live in 193 separate cabins on the same boat.

Even though all of humanity now lives on the same boat, contemporary international relations, both in theory and practice, continue to pretend that we live in separate boats. This has, in turn, prevented humanity from cooperating effectively to deal with Covid-19, global warming, and other pressing global challenges.

The time has therefore come for Western scholars to significantly revise their theories and practices of international relations. They should understand and accept the main message of Covid-19: all of humanity now belongs to one community with a shared future.

Originally published in People's Daily, April 6, 2021

K. Mahbubani, *The Asian 21st Century*, China and Globalization,
https://doi.org/10.1007/978-981-16-6811-1_37

Q: You stated several times that the world was a "global village" and "we are all in the same boat". In this "global village", how do you evaluate the significance of multilateralism and free trade?

Since all of humanity now lives in the same boat, it would be suicidal for us to only take care of our cabins only. We also have to take care of the boat as a whole because if the boat sinks, our cabins will sink.

Covid-19 reinforced this message. When the global economy shrank as a result of Covid-19, all economies around the world suffered, proving again that we are on the same boat.

Against this backdrop, we should be truly grateful that the Western countries, led by the US and Europe, established the UN multilateral system in 1945. It's not a perfect system. However, despite all its defects, it has worked well. It has prevented World War III. This is why it was a huge mistake for the US (with the compliant support of some European countries) to progressively weaken the UN multilateral system, especially by depriving it of funding.

Fortunately, some wise American leaders, including Bill Clinton, have advised their fellow Americans to strengthen, not weaken, the UN multilateral system. In 2003, Bill Clinton said that the US "should be trying to create a world with rules and partnerships and habits of behavior that we would like to live in when we're no longer the military, political, economic superpower in the world."

Since President Joe Biden comes from the same party as Bill Clinton, he should heed this wise advice and strengthen multilateralism. President Biden has made a good start by returning to the WHO and the Paris Climate Accords.

Q: You said in a Público interview that China has no aspirations for world leadership. How do you view China's acts and its role on the world stage?

It is wise for China not to aspire for world leadership at this stage of its development. It is no secret that the Western world, especially the US, has become deeply troubled by the rapid return of China. Hence, as I document in my book, Has China Won? (which will soon be published in China), the US will try very hard to maintain its number one position in the world. This is normal behavior for all great powers, as documented by Graham Allison, the Harvard Professor. Nonetheless, despite the opposition of the West, China should continue its policies of opening up its economy and integrating it with the rest of the world. It took great courage for China to plunge into the "choppy waters of globalization". As President Xi said in Davos in January 2017, "we have had our fair share of choking in the water and encountered whirlpools and choppy waves but we have learned how to swim in the process. It has proved to be a right strategic choice".

It is also no secret that many Western populations, including the US, have turned against globalization. This is why the US withdrew from the Trans-Pacific Partnership. By contrast, China has continued to join the Free Trade Agreements, like the Regional Comprehensive Economic Partnership. It has also indicated that it may join the Comprehensive and Progressive Agreement for Trans-Pacific Partnership (CPTPP). This is the best contribution that China can make to uplifting and improving the human condition: to keep its economy open and continue integrating with the world.

Q: You once praised China's resilience and executive ability. Could you please explain it more specifically, especially regarding China's fight against the pandemic?

When Covid-19 surfaced and spread around the world, it would have been more natural for the advanced and developed countries of the West, especially the US and EU members, to handle this pandemic well and competently and for the less developed countries of East Asia, including China, to handle it less well and competently. Instead, to the shock of the world, the opposite happened. The Western countries handled it incompetently, as shown their death rates per million (US: 1430, UK: 1651, Belgium: 1841, France: 1208) and East Asian countries handled it more competently, as shown in the death rates per million (Singapore: 5, Vietnam: 0.4, China: 3, South Korea: 29). Why did China handle the pandemic better than the US? The answer is complicated. However, one important reason is that the US, since the days of Ronald Reagan, has defunded, delegitimized, and demoralized key government offices (including the CDC). This happened because Ronald Reagan famously said, "Government is not the solution to our problem. Government is the problem." By contrast, China, learning from its East Asian neighbors, regenerated a culture and system of meritocracy in its government agencies. Hence, the quality of mind of government administrators in China has been going up. When I was Dean of the Lee Kuan Yew School of Public Policy, NUS from 2004 to 2017, I told the students that the best formula for any country to apply to improve its governance was to implement meritocracy, pragmatism and honesty (MPH). This MPH formula explains Singapore's extraordinary success. It is also being implemented in China. Hence, I am optimistic that the quality of governance in China will continue to improve.

Q: You pointed out in a recent interview that the US now has a "government of the 1%, by the 1%, for the 1%", while the Communist Party of China (CPC) wins the support of the Chinese people. Could you please share more about your understanding of CPC's style of leadership and governance?

There is no question that the US has been one of the successful nations in human history. It is the only country to send a man to the moon. In the same period, America's middle classes prospered. Sadly, in recent years, the US has become the only major developed country where the average income of the bottom 50% has declined over a 30 year period. In part, this is a result of the US becoming a plutocracy, where the interests of the top 1% take priority over the bottom 50%. The late Paul Volcker, former head of the Fed, Joseph Stiglitz and Martin Wolf have called the US a plutocracy. In turn, as the Nobel Laureate Angus Deaton has documented, a "sea of despair" has been created among the working classes in the US.

By contrast, in terms of human, social, and economic development, the bottom 50% in China have had their best 40 years in five thousand years of Chinese history. A Stanford University Professor says "in contrast to America's stagnation, China's culture, self-concept, and morale are being transformed at a rapid pace—mostly for the better". Consequently, support for the Chinese government has grown in China. A rigorous academic study of the Harvard Kennedy School of Government has documented how support for the Chinese government has gone up from 86% in 2003 to 93% in 2016. Similarly, a study by the Edelman Trust Barometer showed that of 11 countries surveyed, the country with the highest level of trust in government was China's government of 90%.

Q: Your latest book raised a question: Has China won? Nearly one year has passed since the book was published. What would your answer be now?

The title of my book, *Has China Won?* has a question mark. It does not say that China has won. However, even though the outcome is far from certain, it does suggest that China is winning because it appears to have a comprehensive long-term strategy to manage the US-China geopolitical contest while the US, sadly, doesn't have a similar strategy, as confirmed to me personally by Henry Kissinger, America's greatest living strategic thinker (who made a historic visit to China 50 years ago)

The main goal of this book is to prevent a major tragedy from emerging in the form of an unchecked, uncontrolled geopolitical contest because the US and China. The book concludes by saying that even though a strong consensus has built up in the Washington DC establishment that the time has come for the US to stand up to China, a rational and objective analysis of the core interests of the US and China will show that there are at least five non-contradictions between the US and China. For example, if the core goal of the US government is to improve the well-being of the American people, and if the core goal of the Chinese government is to improve the well-being of the Chinese people (as it should be), there is no contradiction between American and Chinese interests here. Similarly, both US and China share common interests in dealing with common global challenges like Covid-19 and global warming. It is my sincere hope that my book, *Has China Won?,* will help to improve mutual understanding between the US and China.

Q: You said in a recent article that "the future of Asia will be written in four letters, RCEP, and not the four letters in Quad." How will the RCEP spell the future of Asia? What role will China play?

The reason why the future of Asia will be written in these four letters, RCEP, and not the four letters in QUAD is because the real competition will take place in the economic, not military, spheres. Indeed, it was one of the greatest strategic thinkers of the US, George Kennan, who advised his fellow Americans that they should pay greatest attention to the strength of American society, not the American military. He said: "It is rather a question of the degree to which the United States can create among the peoples of the world generally the impression of a country which knows what it wants, which is coping successfully with the problems of its internal life and with the responsibilities of a world power, and which has a spiritual vitality capable of holding its own among the major ideological currents of the time."

When Kennan spoke about the "spiritual vitality" of American society, he was not talking about the degree of religiosity of Americans, Instead, he was talking about the social and psychological health of American society. Hence, if George Kennan were alive today, he would heartily disapprove of the $5 trillion the US has spent fighting unnecessary wars since 2001 while allowing a "sea of despair" to emerge among the working classes of America. He would also advise his fellow Americans to cut down the military budget, stop fighting wars (and Kennan opposed the invasion of Iraq), and spend money on improving the civilian society of the US. He would have disapproved of Trump's withdrawal from the Trans-Pacific Partnership (TPP).

The best thing both the Biden Administration can do is to find a way of improving its economic engagement with East Asia, though rejoining TPP or cooperating with RCEP, and reducing its military engagements in the region, like in QUAD. China is wise to focus on economic cooperation, through joining RCEP and thinking of joining CPTPP.

Q: China is the first major economy to recover from the pandemic. How would China's economic recovery contribute to the world?

Covid-19 did real damage to the global economy. The IMF estimates that the global economy shrank by 3.5% in 2020. It estimates that it will grow by 5.5% in 2021. However, for it to grow, it needs strong engines of growth.

In this regard, the world should send a thank you note to China for succeeding in achieving positive economic growth in 2020 (1.9%) when the US and EU shrank by (3.4%) and (7.2%) respectively. China saved the world economy in 2020.

It will play an important role in the coming decade. One little known fact about the US and Chinese economies is that while the US economy (USD 21 trillion) is still larger than the Chinese economy (USD 14 trillion), the size of the retail goods market in China has become bigger than that of the US. In 2009 China's market was USD 1.8 trillion, while that of the US was more than twice as large at $4 trillion. However, by 2019, China's market had grown to USD 6 trillion while that of the US only grew to USD 5.5 trillion. In the next ten years, there is no question that the retail goods market in China will grow faster than that of the US.

Countries all over the world, especially in the poor developing countries, will be looking for export markets to boost their economic growth. This is where China can play an important role. It can improve its markets faster, especially for poor developing countries. History has taught us that trade is more effective than aid in promoting economic growth and reducing poverty. The world will be truly grateful to China if it can import more from the rest of the world.

Globalization, Multilateralism and Cooperation

Many of the world's pressing issues, such as COVID-19 and climate change, are global issues, and will require global cooperation to deal with. In short, we now live in a global village. The world needs a world order that enables and facilitates states to work with each other in our global village.

Globalization Is Dead! Long Live Globalization!

Abstract The central paradox of our times is that even though globalization has dramatically improved the human condition over the past few decades, many are now predicting its imminent demise. How did this happen? Because of three key strategic mistakes made by the West in its management of globalization.

We have all heard the refrain: "The King is dead; Long live the King!" The newest version of this is "Globalization is dead; Long live globalization!" This new refrain captures well the central paradox about our times. Globalization has done more to improve the human condition over the past few decades than any other force in human history. Yet, instead of celebrating globalization, many in the world are predicting its imminent demise, especially in the West, even though it was the West that launched our foray into globalization.

How do we explain this paradox? Why has the West turned against its most benevolent contribution to humanity? The simple explanation is that the West has made three strategic mistakes in its management of globalization. More accurately, the mistakes have been by the largest Western power, the United States. Nonetheless, these American mistakes have been compounded by the failure of the second most powerful Western economic force, the European Union, to help and guide the US when the US was making these three strategic mistakes. The passivity of the Europeans contributed significantly to the problem.

Three Mistakes the US Made

So what were the three strategic mistakes made by the US? The first mistake was made by the elites, the top 1% in the US. They reaped huge rewards from globalization, but they failed to help the lower half of Americans who suffered from the inevitable disruptions (or, more accurately, "creative destruction") caused by globalization. The second mistake was to weaken government and governmental institutions when they

Originally published in Dec 1, 2020

should have been strengthened instead. This mistake was made during the famous Reagan-Thatcher revolution when Ronald Reagan famously said, "Government is not the solution to our problem, government is the problem." The consequences of this belief were disastrous. Three decades of defunding, delegitimization, and demoralization of key public service agencies followed it. The third mistake was for the top 1% to create a functional plutocracy in America. What is the essential difference between a democracy and a plutocracy? In a democracy, you have a government of the people, by the people, and for the people. In a plutocracy, you have a government of the 1%, by the 1%, and for the 1%. Most Americans react with disbelief to the claim that their society has functionally become a plutocracy. Yet eminent figures like Paul Volcker, Joseph Stiglitz and Martin Wolf has confirmed this development.

Another paradox surrounds these three strategic mistakes made by the US. The country with the largest strategic thinking industry in the world (embedded in the universities, think tanks, consultancies, non-governmental organizations) is the US. Yet, even though these are three major strategic mistakes, there is no public acknowledgment in the American body politic that these mistakes have been made. Nor has there been much discussion of it in the very influential op-ed pages of leading newspapers like the New York Times and Washington Post, the Wall Street Journal and The Economist. Future historians will have to investigate and explain this curious phenomenon of massive self-ignorance in the American body politic.

Since many Americans would vehemently deny that these strategic mistakes have been made, it is necessary to explain in greater detail how each of these mistakes was made This is what this essay will try to accomplish, while also suggesting some solutions to the problems and mistakes that are identified. This essay will also end with the optimistic conclusion that all three strategic mistakes can be rectified and the US can emerge again as the number one champion of globalization, as it once was. After that, Tom Friedman, Jagdish Bhagwati and Martin Wolf can come out with new editions of *The World is Flat*, *In Defense of Globalization* and *Why Globalization Works* in 2021.

Strategic Mistake One

The first strategic mistake was the failure of the elites in the US to protect the working classes from the inevitable disruptions caused by globalization. Why did this happen? Was it a result of the greed and callousness of the elites in America? Or were there larger historical trends that also contributed to this final strategic mistake?

As usual, the answers to these questions are complicated. Yet, it is also clear that larger historical trends contributed to this mistake. Future historians will see more clearly than we do that the working classes in America suffered because of an unfortunate coincidence of two major moments of history. The first moment was "The End of History" moment captured in the famous essay by Francis Fukuyama. The second moment was "The Return of History" moment, also in the early 1990s, when China and India decided to wake up. The unfortunate result of the coincidence of these two moments is that the West chose to go sleep at precisely the moment when China and India (and the rest of Asia) decided to wake up.

How and why this happened has been documented in my book, *Has the West Lost It?* Here's a brief summary. Francis Fukuyama didn't intend to put the West to sleep. However, when he suggested that Western civilization had reached the end of the road of political and economic evolution, he certainly created the impression among many Western minds, including some leading minds, that Western societies no longer needed to make any serious structural or strategic adjustments to a new world. Only non-western societies had to adjust and adapt. This message inevitably created arrogance, hubris, and complacency in Western societies. As a result, almost no one in the West noticed that the moment the West chose to go to sleep was the moment when it should have woken up instead.

Wake up to what? The West should have seen in the early 1990s that after having essentially gone to sleep for almost two hundred years, China and India decided to wake up. Why was their awakening significant? From the year 1 to 1820, the two largest economies in the world were China and India (see Fig. 1). Hence, when China and India decided to once again wake up, it was inevitable that they would shake the world. As China emerged as a manufacturing superpower, producing better quality goods at lower prices, it was inevitable that some industries in the US would shut down and American workers would lose their jobs. None of this should have been surprising. It is called "creative destruction" in Western economic theory.

Let me acknowledge here that there is some debate among economists whether the emergence of the new industries in China caused job losses in the US. Some economists reject this claim. Yet there are at least two strong and credible economists who have documented how American workers lost jobs as a result of new competition from China. They are Daron Acemoglu of Massachusetts Institute of Technology and Robert Scott of the Economic Policy Institute. Scott and Mokhiber (2018) state that 3.4 million jobs were lost in the US post 2001, while Acemoglu et al. (2016) estimate

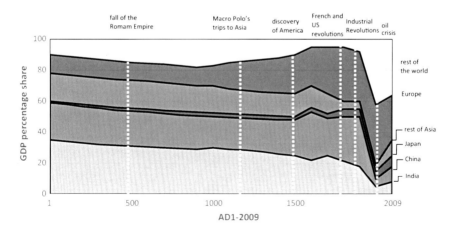

Fig. 1 Share of total world GDP (Mahbubani 2018)

a 2–2.4 million job loss from 1999 to 2011 due to Chinese import competition (Scott and Mokhiber 2018; Acemoglu et al. 2016)

Significantly, while all this was happening, the Clinton Administration made no effort to launch programs to help workers who lost jobs. After the Clinton Administration left office in January 2001, there was once again an unfortunate coincidence of two historical events. The big event that the Bush Administration paid attention to was the attack on the US by Osama bin Laden on September 11, 2001 (remembered as 9/11). Quite naturally, this caused a lot of anger in the American body politic. Consequently, the Bush Administration became involved in two major wars in Afghanistan starting October 7, 2001, and in Iraq starting March 20, 2003. In their anger over the 9/11 attacks, the American people and policymakers didn't notice that something more significant and earth-changing happened in 2001: China's entry into the World Trade Organization (WTO) on December 11, 2001.

As more Chinese exports to the US and the rest of the world obtained duty-free access, it was inevitable that Chinese exports would surge following their entry into the WTO. Indeed, Fig. 2 shows clearly how China's trade with the rest of the world, including the US and Europe, increased significantly after 2001. Clearly, if US policymakers had been more vigilant, they would have paid attention to the increasing plight of American workers. Sadly, they didn't. So this was strategic mistake number one: ignoring the needs and interests of the working classes as they experienced "creative destruction" caused by the return of China, India, and the rest of Asia.

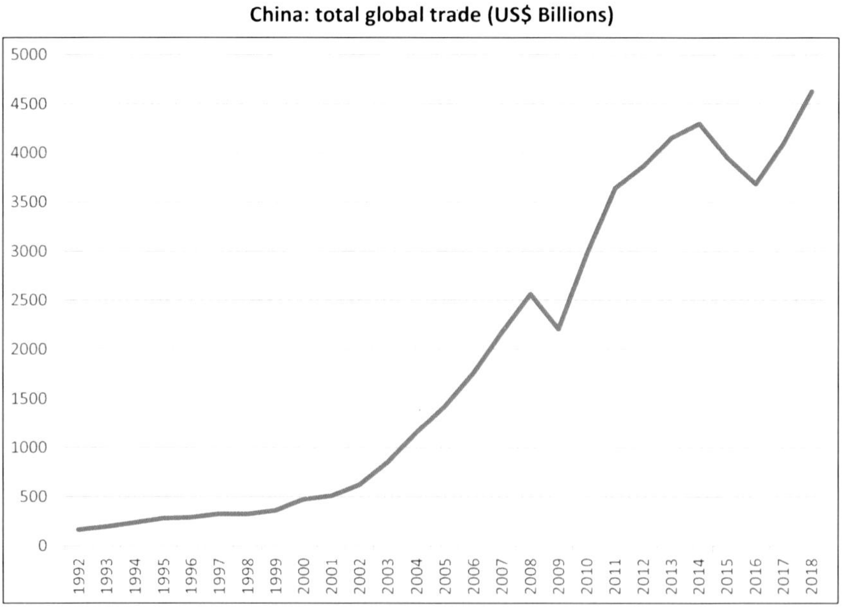

China: total global trade (US$ Billions)

Fig. 2 China: increase in global trade, 1992–2018 (World Bank. https://wits.worldbank.org/Default.aspx?lang=en)

Strategic Mistake Two

Strategic mistake one was clearly compounded by strategic mistake two: the weakening of government institutions, especially in the US. The Reagan-Thatcher revolution of the 1980s left behind two intellectual legacies. The first was the belief that markets knew best. Hence, if an economic problem emerged, the markets would find a solution to it. The second was the belief, as indicated earlier, that "Government is not the solution to our problem, government is the problem." Hence, the idea that governments should play a role in helping workers hurt by economic competition was considered taboo. The markets would create and provide new jobs to workers.

Curiously, even though in theory the Reagan Administration was not in favor of government interventions against market forces, the Reagan Administration intervened at least twice when it believed that free-market forces would hurt American companies. When American automobile companies complained that they could not compete against Japanese automobile manufacturers, the American government arm-twisted the Japanese government into accepting "Voluntary Export Restraints" (VERs) on Japanese car exports to the US. The VERs were implemented in 1981. In addition to VERs, the Reagan Administration also took a second step to protect American companies from Japanese competition: it arm-twisted the Japanese government into accepting a significant upward revaluation of the yen from 240 to the dollar in 1985 to 120 to the dollar in 1988. Clearly, this made Japanese exports uncompetitive. As an aside, let me mention that one unintended positive outcome of the forced revaluation of the yen was that the Japanese companies began to manufacture more in the US and in third countries, including ASEAN countries.

The Reagan Administration, therefore, left behind a contradictory legacy in the US. In theory, it opposed government interventions in markets. In practice, as demonstrated in its actions against Japanese industries, the Reagan Administration actually supported government interventions. Unfortunately, the government intervention it favored was "negative" intervention: using strong-arm tactics to stop Japanese competition. It did not carry out any "positive" intervention, like retraining workers who lost jobs in the face of economic competition.

In this regard, the American attitude of letting market forces take care of creating new jobs is different from both European and Asian approaches. Indeed, the governments of the European Union and several East Asian governments (including Japan, South Korea, Taiwan, and Singapore) invest in worker-training programs. This American antipathy to have government intervention in worker-training programs also extends to opposition to trade unions to protect worker interests. Singapore discovered this when it laid out the red carpet for American MNCs to invest in Singapore in the 1960s and 1970s. These American MNCs insisted that they would only invest in Singapore if the Singapore government prevented Singaporean workers from joining trade unions because, in their eyes, trade unions interfered with market forces. It took some persuasion but, in the end, the American MNCs accepted the Singapore government's argument that the Singapore trade unions could help to create better relations between workers and management in the factories.

This American disdain for setting up schemes and institutions to help workers was also part of a larger philosophical outlook which was captured in a famous statement made by Milton Friedman: "the business of business is business." In short, the only thing that mattered was the bottom line of the companies. If workers had to be fired to improve the profitability of the companies, so be it. Profits were more important than people.

It would be unfair to blame only Milton Friedman for this ethos. One of America's most august institutions is the Harvard Business School (HBS). For several generations, HBS also spread the philosophy that the primary responsibility of firms was to generate greater profits. Hence, only one stakeholder mattered: the shareholders. All the other stakeholders, including the workers and the community, were deemed to be less important. By contrast, the World Economic forum advises firms to pay attention to multiple stakeholders, including "employees, customers, suppliers, local communities and society at large." World Economic Forum (2019).

Strategic Mistake Three

This antipathy of the American business elites to paying attention to larger societal concerns may also be a contributing factor to the third strategic mistake made by the US: the creation of a functional plutocracy that has effectively undermined the American democratic system. In short, the US has gone from having a government of the people, by the people, and for the people toward having a government of the 1%, by the 1%, and for the 1%. What is truly lacking is that even though there is overwhelming evidence that the US has become a plutocracy, there is a powerful resistance to calling the US a plutocracy, even though eminent voices like the late Paul Volcker, Joseph Stiglitz and Martin Wolf have done so. Since there is a lot of political and intellectual resistance to "calling a spade a spade" on this issue, I devoted a whole chapter in my book, *Has China Won?* to explain in careful detail how the US has evolved toward becoming a plutocracy.

Significantly, some of the most wealthy Americans have begun to acknowledge this. Ray Dalio runs the largest, most successful hedge fund in the world, which has succeeded through rigorous empirical research. Dalio has now applied this research to understanding poverty and inequality in America. On his LinkedIn page, Dalio spells out the dramatic decline in the living standards of the majority of Americans and points out that "most people in the bottom 60% are poor" and cites "a recent Federal Reserve study [that showed that] 40% of all Americans would struggle to raise $400 in the event of an emergency (Dalio 2019). Worse, Dalio notes that "they are increasingly getting stuck being poor... the odds of someone in the bottom quintile moving up to the middle quintile or higher in a 10-year period... declined from about 23% in 1990 to only 14% as of 2011." The data on social deterioration in America is undeniable. It undercuts the claims that America is a society where hard work brings rewards. For most people, the rewards have dried up. The platitude "virtue is its own reward" turns out to be grimly and limitingly true.

America's Road to Plutocracy

Why has America performed so badly? The simple explanation is that it demonstrates that a fundamental change has taken place in America's political arrangements, without the American people noticing it. Every two to four years Americans go to the polls to elect their congressmen, senators, governors, and state legislative assembly representatives. And yet, under the surface guise of a functioning democracy, with all the rituals of voting, America has become a society run by a moneyed aristocracy that uses its money to make major political and social decisions. As a result, this class has been able to enact the greatest transfer of wealth that has ever taken place in American society.

The great American philosopher, John Rawls, warned of this danger. He said, "The liberties protected by the principle of participation lose much of their value whenever those who have greater private means are permitted to use their advantages to control the course of public debate." Almost 50 years ago, he warned that if those with "greater private means" are allowed to control the course of public debate, American democracy would be subverted.

This is exactly what happened when the US Supreme Court overturned, in a landmark ruling in *Citizens United v. Federal Election Commission (FEC)* (2010) and in other decisions, many of the legislative restraints on the use of money to influence the political process. The impact of this and other Supreme Court decisions was monumental. Effectively, they helped to transform the American political system. Martin Wolf says that "the Supreme Court's perverse 2010 'Citizens United' decision held that companies are persons and money is speech. That has proved a big step on the journey of the US toward becoming a plutocracy."

Two Princeton University professors have documented how ordinary American citizens have lost their political power and influence. Martin Gilens and Benjamin Page studied the relative influence that the views of average Americans and mass-based interest groups have on policy outcomes versus the views of the economic elite in 1779 cases. They found that,

> economic elites and organized groups representing business interests have substantial independent impacts on US government policy, while average citizens and mass-based interest groups have little or no independent influence. [. . .] When the references of economic elites and the stands of organized interest groups are controlled for, the preferences of the average American appear to have only a minuscule, near-zero, statistically non-significant impact upon public policy. [. . .] Furthermore, the preferences of economic elites (as measured by our proxy, the preferences of "affluent" citizens) have far more independent impact upon policy change than the preferences of average citizens do. [. . .] In the United States, our findings indicate, the majority does not rule—at least not in the causal sense of actually determining policy outcomes. (Gilens and Page 2014)

They reach the following alarming conclusion:

> Americans do enjoy many features central to democratic governance, such as regular elections, freedom of speech and association, and a widespread (if still contested) franchise. But we believe that if policymaking is dominated by powerful business organizations and a

small number of affluent Americans, then America's claims to being a democratic society are seriously threatened.

In the past, the broad middle classes of America had a strong say in determining the fundamental directions of American society. Today, they no longer do. The decisions of the US Congress are not determined by the voters; they are determined by the funders. As a result, America is becoming functionally less and less of a democracy, where all citizens have an equal voice. Instead, it looks more and more like a plutocracy, where a few rich people are disproportionately powerful.

A 2018 study by scholars Alexander Hertel-Fernandez, Theda Skocpol and Jason Sclar of the School of International and Public Affairs, Columbia University, further argued that

> since the mid-2000s, newly formed conservative and progressive Donor consortia—above all the Koch seminars [founded by brothers Charles and David Koch] and the DA [Democracy Alliance]—have magnified the impact of wealthy donors by raising and channeling ever more money not just into elections but also into full arrays of cooperating political organizations. . . . The Koch seminars... allowed donations to be channeled into building a virtual third political party organized around AFP [Americans for Prosperity], an overarching political network able not only to electorally support the Republican Party but also to push and pull its candidates and office holders in preferred ultra-free-market policy directions... To the degree that wealthy donor consortia have succeeded in building organizational infrastructures, they have shifted the resources available for developing policy proposals, pressing demands on lawmakers, and mobilizing ordinary Americans into politics... When plutocratic collectives impose new agendas on political organizations seeking to attract financial resources, the funders reshape routines, goals, and centers of power in US politics well beyond the budgetary impact of particular grants. (Hertel-Fernandez et al. 2018)

The authors thus conclude:

> Our analysis of the Koch and DA consortia highlights that a great deal of big-money influence flows through mechanisms other than individual or business donations to the electoral and lobbying operations...To understand how the wealthy are reshaping US politics, we need to look not just at their election and lobbying expenditures but also at their concerted investments in many kinds of political organizations operating across a variety of fields and functions. Only in this way can we account for the stark inequalities in government responsiveness documented by researchers such as Martin Gilens, Larry Bartels and Benjamin Page.

In theory, the American people would revolt if their votes were taken away from them. Yet, their votes have effectively been hijacked by the rich—but most Americans haven't noticed it yet. Anand Giridharadas, a former *New York Times* columnist, has documented in great detail in *Winners Take All* how the dream of the American middle class has effectively evaporated. As he says:

> A successful society is a progress machine. It takes in the raw material of innovations and produces broad human advancement. America's machine is broken. When the fruits of change have fallen on the United States in recent decades, the very fortunate have basketed almost all of them. For instance, the average pretax income of the top tenth of Americans has doubled since 1980, that of the top 1 percent has more than tripled, and that of the top 0.001 percent has risen more than seven fold—even as the average pretax income of the bottom half of Americans has stayed almost precisely the same. These familiar figures amount to three and a half decades' worth of wondrous, head-spinning change with zero impact on the average pay of 117 million Americans. (Giridharadas 2018)

American scholars on political systems are fond of quoting Lord Acton's famous quip: "Power corrupts. Absolute power corrupts absolutely." After quoting him, they probably whisper under their breaths, "Thank God, we are a democracy with separation of powers. This couldn't happen to us." All those scholars should consider this variation on Lord Acton instead: "Money corrupts. Absolute money corrupts absolutely."

The corrupting effect of money on political processes should be more prominently highlighted in American political discourse. In most societies, when individuals or corporations use money to influence public policy decisions, it is called out corruption. Even people in third world countries that suffer from widespread corruption know it is illegal, though they often do not have the means to oppose it. But in America, it is not considered corruption to use money to influence public policy decisions because the Supreme Court legalized it.

In legalizing the use of massive amounts of money to influence public policy decisions, the Supreme Court had clearly ignored the advice of John Rawls, who warned that if "those who have greater private means are permitted to use their advantages to control the course of public debate," this would be the corrupting result:

> Eventually, these inequalities will enable those better situated to exercise a larger influence over the development of legislation. In due time they are likely to acquire a preponderant weight in settling social questions, at least in regard to those matters upon which they normally agree, which is to say in regard to those things that support their favored circumstances. (Rawls 1999)

This is precisely what has happened over the past few decades: the affluent have gained "preponderant weight... in regard of those things that support their favored circumstances." There has been a relative transfer of wealth and political power from the vast majority of America's population to a privileged superminority. Hence, there is no doubt that America has become a plutocracy.

Simple Solutions and Hard Decisions

So to quote Lenin, "What is to be done?" in response to these three strategic mistakes. The good news is that they can be fixed. Here are three simple steps that can be taken. The first step is for the West, especially the US, to acknowledge that the wounds it has suffered from globalization are self-inflicted, as documented in the three mistakes made. The second step, a natural consequence of the first, is to take remedial measures against the self-inflicted wounds. The third step would be for the West and the East, especially the US and China, to reach a new comprehensive understanding of how to cooperate in managing the common challenges faced in globalization.

Sadly, even though these steps are "simple" in theory, in practice they will be difficult to implement. The first step may be the hardest to take. Most societies, including the US, would prefer to believe that other societies are responsible for their problems. Hence, when Donald Trump launched his trade war against China, few American voices spoke up to say the undeniable truth: America's trade deficits were a result of domestic, not external, factors. The imbalance between consumption and savings was the main reason for the trade deficit. Indeed, even if the trade deficit of the US with China went down, its trade deficit with the rest of the world would not go down. This is exactly what happened between 2017 and 2019, the years of the Trump trade war. In 2019, the US deficit with China dropped from USD 375 billion in 2017 to USD 345 billion in 2019, but its overall trade deficit with the world went up from USD 792 billion in 2017 to USD 854 billion.

Therefore, unless the US acknowledges that its problems with globalization are the result of self-inflicted wounds, it will be difficult for it to take the necessary remedial steps, especially the rebuilding of strong and effective institutions to manage the inevitable challenges of globalization and the reversal of the moves (including the Supreme Court decision legitimizing the unlimited amount of corporate funding for political donations) that have led to the development of plutocracy in the US. In short, the first step and second step are connected. Just as we cannot cure a medical ailment until we acknowledge that we have an ailment, the US cannot reverse the problems it has developed with globalization until it acknowledges that its problems are the result of self-inflicted wounds.

While it is working on a difficult first two steps, the US can begin taking action on the third: reaching a new understanding with China on how to manage the challenges of globalization together. Here too, in theory, the interests of the US and China in this area may appear irreconcilable. However, as I have documented in great length in the final chapter of *Has China Won?*, there are no fundamental conflicts of interest between the long-term interests of the US and China.

Indeed, there are five "non-contradictions" between the US and China, and here's the first non-contradiction. If the primary goal of the US government is to improve the well-being of the American people (as it should be) and if the primary goal of the Chinese government is to improve the well-being of the Chinese people (as it should be), there is no fundamental contradiction between these two goals. Indeed, both governments are more likely to succeed in achieving their respective goals, if they cooperate, rather than engage in a zero-sum game of geopolitical competition. The main obstacle to such win–win cooperation is a belief among many influential voices in Washington DC that the primary goal of the US should be to preserve "primacy" in the global system. However, between "primacy" and "people", clearly the interests of the American people are more important. Sheer common sense makes this clear.

The election of Joe Biden as President provides a tremendous opportunity to reset the US-China relationship. In theory, Biden's hands are tied since a rock solid anti-China consensus has gripped the Washington elite. However, if Biden is politically shrewd, he can navigate this difficult domestic environment in the US by appearing publicly critical of China while privately enhancing cooperation in the areas of mutual benefit between the US and China. He could use the excuse of COVID-19 to remove some trade sanctions against China. This would encourage China to buy more from America, especially in agricultural products. If the farmers in the mid-West swing toward supporting Biden, he would have undercut a significant base from the Republicans before the 2022 and 2024 elections. Hence, paradoxically, economic cooperation with China could help Biden win votes domestically.

In short, even though it appears inconceivable in today's political context that the US and China can cooperate for mutual benefit, the reality is that they can and should do so, especially after the election of Joe Biden. Both sides, especially both governments, should not lose sight of the fact that their primary responsibility is to improve the well-being of their people. They can achieve this by working with each other, not against each other.

References

Mahbubani K (2018) Has the West lost it? A provocation. Penguin UK, London, p 5

Scott RE, Mokhiber Z (2018) The China toll deepens. Economic Policy Institute, Washington, DC. https://epi.org/156645

Acemoglu D, Autor D, Dorn D, Hanson GH, Price B (2016) Import competition and the great US employment sag of the 2000s. J Labor Econ 34(S1):S141–S198

World Bank. World Integrated Trade Solution. https://wits.worldbank.org/Default.aspx?lang=en

World Economic Forum (2019) Davos Manifesto 2020: The Universal Purpose of a Company in the Fourth Industrial Revolution, 2 December 2019. https://www.weforum.org/agenda/2019/12/davos-manifesto-2020-the-universal-purpose-of-a-company-in-the-fourth-industrial-revolution/

Dalio R (2019) Why and how capitalism needs to be reformed (Part 1), LinkedIn, April 4, 2019. https://www.linkedin.com/pulse/why-how-capitalism-needs-reformed-ray-dalio/. See also Board of Governors of the Federal Reserve System, Report on the Economic Well-Being of U.S. Household in 2017, May 2018. https://www.federalreserve.gov/publications/files/2017-report-economic-well-being-us-households-201805.pdf, quoted in Dalio

Gilens M, Page BI (2014) Testing theories of american politics: elites, interest groups, and average citizens. Perspect Polit 12(30:564–581. https://scholar.princeton.edu/sites/default/files/mgilens/files/gilens_and_page_2014_-testing_theories_of_american_politics.doc.pdf

Hertel-Fernandez A, Skocpol T, Sclar J (2018) When political mega- donors join forces: how the Koch network and the democracy alliance influence organized U.S. politics on the right and left. Stud Am Polit Dev 32(2)

Giridharadas A (2018) Prologue. In: Winners take all: the elite charade of changing the world. Alfred A. Knopf, New York

Rawls J (1999) A theory of justice, rev. Belknap Press, Cambridge, MA, p 225

Can the World Order Catch Up with the World?

Abstract The international order has lagged dangerously behind shifting global power dynamics. If leaders do not start addressing the contradictions soon, the most likely result is a crisis—or even conflict—and even more dangerous contradictions.

The international order has lagged dangerously behind shifting global power dynamics. If leaders do not start addressing the contradictions soon, the most likely result is a crisis—or even conflict—and even more dangerous contradictions.

The world turned a corner in 2019. The problem is that the world order didn't turn with it. This disconnect could have disastrous consequences.

The biggest global change has been the start of the "Asian century." Today, Asia is home to three of the world's top four economic powers (in purchasing power parity terms): China, India, and Japan. The region's combined GDP exceeds that of the United States and of the European Union.

The US is no longer even the most globalized power; that title now goes to China. Already a larger trading partner to more countries than the US, China is signing on to more free trade agreements as well, including potentially the largest in history, the Regional Comprehensive Economic Partnership. The US, by contrast, is abandoning FTAs such as the Trans-Pacific Partnership, which Japanese Prime Minister Shinzo Abe has kept alive without the Americans. The US share of global trade continues to shrink.

The world order has not kept pace with these shifting economic dynamics. On the contrary, the US dollar remains the predominant currency for settling international trade. The US and Europe retain control of the two leading global economic organizations: the International Monetary Fund and the World Bank. And the United Nations Security Council—the only body that can issue binding decisions for the UN's 193 member states—is dominated by just a few, largely declining powers.

In theory, the easiest of these incongruities to address should be the inadequate influence of emerging powers like China in the IMF and the World Bank. After all, the US and Europe have already acknowledged—including in the 2006 and 2007 G20

Originally published in Project Syndicate, Dec 26, 2019

communiqués—that "the selection of senior management of the IMF and World Bank should be based on merit," ensuring "broad representation of all member countries."

Yet the anachronistic "gentlemen's agreement" that has kept an American at the head of the World Bank and a European leading the IMF has proved stubbornly resilient. In 2007, Dominique Strauss-Kahn became IMF managing director, succeeded by another French citizen, Christine Lagarde, in 2011.

Six years later, Lagarde declared that the IMF could be based in Beijing by 2027, if growth trends continue and are reflected in the Fund's voting structure. After all, she noted, the IMF's bylaws call for the institution's head office to be located in the largest member economy.

Yet, when Lagarde resigned from her post this year to become president of the European Central Bank, it was yet another European who took her place: the Bulgarian economist Kristalina Georgieva. Likewise, the World Bank presidency passed from Robert Zoellick to Jim Yong Kim in 2012, and then to David Malpass this year. Future historians will marvel at the imprudence of the old powers' shameless refusal to share control of global institutions.

And yet the US and the EU are not the only ones working to safeguard their clout. In the UN Security Council, the five permanent members (P5)—China, France, Russia, the United Kingdom, and the US—also pay lip service to the need for reform, but consistently obstruct progress. Complicating matters further, additional countries attempting to get a permanent seat on the Council are facing resistance from their neighbors: Pakistan is blocking India's bid; Argentina is blocking Brazil; and Nigeria is blocking South Africa. Given these dynamics, the UN Security Council will be even more difficult to reform than the IMF or World Bank.

But, again, failure could be disastrous. If the Security Council's composition is not updated, the body could lose its credibility and moral authority. If the African Union or India (each with over a billion people) refused to abide by Security Council decisions—essentially the decisions of the P5—the international community's most important body wouldn't have much recourse.

To avert such an outcome, the Security Council should adopt a 7-7-7 formula. The first seven would be permanent members—Brazil, China, the European Union (represented by France and Germany), India, Nigeria, Russia, and the US—each of which represents a different region. The second seven would be semi-permanent members, a rotating selection of 28 countries, based on population and GNP. The remaining 160 countries would rotate into the remaining seven seats.

The most difficult incongruity to resolve will be that between America's declining leadership and its currency's role as the leading international reserve currency. Today, more than 40% of cross-border payments and 90% of foreign-exchange trading are settled in US dollars. This reflects decades of trust: the US had deep markets, strong institutions—including efficient courts and an independent central bank—and it did not use the dollar as a tool to advance its own interests.

But, from 2017 through the end of his presidency, US President Donald Trump aggressively undermined the international community's trust in the dollar. He pressured the US Federal Reserve to lower interest rates in order to deliver short-term economic growth as he campaigned for reelection. While weaponizing the dollar, he also labeled China a "currency manipulator" and instructed the US Treasury to put more countries—including close Asian and European allies—under surveillance.

Trump's behavior raised the hackles not only of adversaries (Russia saw a de-dollarization trend) but also of key allies. Jean-Claude Juncker, the outgoing European Commission president, had pledged that the euro would become an "active instrument" of EU sovereignty. It is also telling that France, Germany, and the UK–in collaboration with China and Russia—created an Instrument in Support of Trade Exchanges (INSTEX) to bypass US sanctions on Iran.

But, in a sense, Trump did the world a favor by making undeniable what was already obvious. If world leaders do not start addressing the contradictions plaguing the world order soon, the likely result is a crisis—and even more dangerous contradictions.

Diplomacy: Power or Persuasion

Abstract The revival of diplomacy, based on deploying the art of persuasion, will help to create a more harmonious and cooperative global community. After years of the United States, especially under Donald Trump, retreating from multilateralism, it will require active reasoning, listening, and adjusting for Western powers.

The unusual two-hundred-year period of Western domination of world history is coming to an end. Today we are seeing the return of the rest, especially in Asia. So far, the United States is retreating into unilateralism. The EU is confused, occasionally supporting the United States, occasionally demurring. One great gift of Western civilization to the world has been the art of reasoning. From the days of Plato and Aristotle, we know that good cogent arguments eventually triumph. Sadly, as I discovered in my ten years as Singapore's Ambassador to the UN, the Western powers preferred arm-twisting smaller countries as it was more efficient. This era of arm-twisting is coming to an end as well. But the West should not despair; logical and reasonable arguments can carry more sway. Since the United States, especially under Donald Trump, remains allergic to multilateralism, the EU, an inherently multilateral body, should step in and champion multilateralism. It should revive the UN General Assembly and deploy its full powers of persuasion. As a student of Western philosophy, I deployed Western logical reasoning often in the UN. And it often worked. And I was puzzled that so few Western Ambassadors dived into their own philosophical heritage to use it. I suppose there is only one caveat to using reason. Reasoning is a double-edged sword. If the rest deploy better arguments, the West must relearn the art of listening and adjusting its behavior. In short, the revival of diplomacy based on deploying the art of persuasion will help to create a more harmonious and cooperative global community, but it will require the active reasoning, listening, and adjusting of Western powers.

Modern diplomacy, at least most of it, is essentially a Western creation. In theory, then, the advanced Western countries should be its best practitioners. In practice, as I observed at first hand in my ten years as Singapore's Ambassador to the UN (1984–89 and 1998–2004), major Western powers, including both the United States

Originally published in SAIS Review, Sep 1, 2020

and the European Union (EU), preferred to bully other countries into submission instead of trying to persuade them through respectful diplomatic engagement. A former UN Secretary-General, Boutros Boutros-Ghali, who served only one term, made the same observation: "It would be some time before I fully realized that the United States sees little need for diplomacy; power is enough... the Roman Empire had no need for diplomacy. Nor does the United States. Diplomacy is perceived... as a waste of time and prestige and a sign of weakness."[1]

This bullying strategy has never been wise. However, it was a feasible approach to take when the West was overwhelmingly dominant. Now, this artificial era of Western domination of world history is coming to an end. As I document in "Has the West Lost it?", from AD 1 to 1820, the two largest economies were always those of China and India.[2] Only after that period did Europe take off, followed by the United States. Viewed against the backdrop of the past two thousand years, the recent period of Western relative over-performance against other civilizations is a historical aberration. All such aberrations come to a natural end. This is happening now.

Fortunately, all is not lost for the West. If the West, especially the United States and EU, were to recover the lost virtues of good persuasive diplomacy, it may still retain significant influence in the world. As the ambassador of a small country in the UN, I used to tell my staff that the only weapons we could deploy in multilateral institutions were reason, logic, and charm. Fortunately, they were and remain powerful weapons. As a life-long student of Western philosophy, I have discovered that reasonable and logical arguments travel well across the different cultures and languages in the large UN family of 193 nations. Hence, I was puzzled that Western diplomats rarely tried to persuade. To be fair, I should mention here that Western powers were not the only ones to try and bully smaller countries. Other great and middle powers, such as Australia, Brazil, China, India, Nigeria, Russia, and South Africa would also try to flex their political and economic muscles.

Yet, the Western powers could bully a lot more since Western power was so overwhelming. Recently, that Western power has begun to recede. Here are two key statistics. In 1980, the size of the American economy, in Purchasing Power Parity (PPP) terms was ten times larger than China's. By 2014, it had become smaller.[3] Similarly, in PPP terms, the top four largest economies today are China, the United States, India and Japan. Not one European country is in the top four.

Since the relative power of the European states is going to slide further downwards in the coming decades, it would be wise for the EU countries to take the lead in steering a new course toward practicing more diplomacy in the twenty-first century, which will be an Asian century. There are five concrete steps that the EU can undertake. Firstly, the EU should abandon its policy of silently supporting the current efforts of the United States to weaken or cripple global multilateral institutions.

---

[1] Patomaki (2002).

[2] Mahbubani (2018).

[3] The World Bank, DataBank: World Development Indicators, https://databank.worldbank.org/home.aspx.

Secondly, it should opt out of the recent Western practice of unilaterally intervening in conflict or crisis situations, without the legitimizing authority of the UN. Thirdly, it should remind the United States that diplomacy was invented to talk to enemies, not friends. The United States has reversed two thousand years of diplomatic practice by insisting that the "establishment of diplomatic relations" is a gesture of friendship. Friends don't need diplomatic channels to talk to each other. Only enemies do. This is why diplomats need diplomatic immunity. Fourthly, the EU should take the lead in establishing equitable and mutually beneficial relations between regional multilateral organizations. A first step would be to establish stronger relations between the world's most successful regional organization, the EU, and the world's second most successful organization, ASEAN. This would be a concrete way of demonstrating that Eastern and Western societies can cooperate in the diplomatic arena. Fifthly, and perhaps most importantly, the EU should rejuvenate the UN General Assembly and enable it to serve as the "Parliament of Man." This essay will spell out how the EU can take the lead in these five areas. Fortunately, most of the rest of the world will respond positively if the EU were to undertake these five initiatives.

References

Mahbubani K (2018) Has the west lost it? A provocation. Allen Lane Penguin, London, p 1
Patomaki H (2002) Kosovo and the end of the united nations? In: Van Ham P, Medvedev S (eds) Mapping European security after Kosovo. Manchester University Press, Manchester, p 84

UN: A Sunrise Organization?

Abstract As the UN commemorates its 75th anniversary, few today see it as a beacon of hope. To revive the fortunes of the UN, greater financial support and more inclusive reforms to the General Assembly and the Security Council will make it truly indispensable to solving the common challenges facing humanity today.

In 2000, I was the Singapore Ambassador to the United Nations when the UN General Assembly (UNGA) unveiled its Millennium Development Goals (MDGs). Kofi Annan was UN Secretary-General. Bill Clinton was the US president. It was a time of great hope. Everyone believed that the UN represented the only vehicle for humanity to come together and cooperate. By contrast, even though many world leaders, including Chinese President Xi Jinping and US President Donald Trump, addressed the UNGA by video at the special commemoration of the 75th Anniversary, the air of doom and gloom surrounding the UN was clear and palpable. Few believe today that the UN still functions as a beacon of hope.

This conventional wisdom of pessimism on the UN is dead wrong. If there is one global organization that has become indispensable for humanity, it is the UN! Why so? Covid-19 has sent humanity a clear metaphysical message. All of humanity is now in the same boat. In the past, when 7.7 billion people lived in 193 separate countries, it was as though they were living in 193 separate boats. Now they live in 193 separate cabins on the same boat. This is why Covid-19 could spread from one end of planet Earth to another in a matter of months.

There is only one problem with our global boat. We have governments taking care of each cabin. We have no strong institutions of global governance to manage our global boat as a whole. The only organization which enjoys the universal representation of humanity and can provide such global leadership is the UN. In a small, shrinking, interdependent planet Earth, the UN has become an indispensable organization. Hence it will grow as a sunrise organization in the twenty-first century.

Originally published in China Daily, Sep 23, 2020

K. Mahbubani, *The Asian 21st Century*, China and Globalization,
https://doi.org/10.1007/978-981-16-6811-1_41

Still, it faces real challenges. The most powerful country, the United States, has become disillusioned with the UN. At the height of Covid-19, when humanity needed to cooperate to fight it, the US left WHO (after leaving UNESCO earlier). It has paralyzed the WTO.

Can we persuade the US to support the UN again? Yes, we can. In 2003, President Bill Clinton gave a powerful speech in Yale University. He said that if the US was going to be the number one country forever, it could continue behaving unilaterally. Yet, if the US could conceive of becoming number two, it would be in the long-term national interest of the US to "create a world with rules, partnerships, and habits of behavior" that the US would like to live in if and when it becomes number two. In due course, American pundits and policymakers will come to accept the wisdom contained in Bill Clinton's advice.

Yet, the UN cannot rest on its laurels. It needs to constantly reinvent and reform itself. As the new rising power, China can help to provide some quiet leadership in UN reform, especially since China believes in a "community of shared future". Every community needs a parliament where members can share their views, discuss, compromise and reach a consensus. The only functioning global parliament is the UNGA. Working with other key stakeholders, like the EU, the African Union, Latin America, India, and ASEAN, China can help to quietly revive the UNGA.

Similarly, the UN Security Council (UNSC) needs reform. It was wise of the founding fathers of the UN to give the great powers a veto in the UNSC as it gave them a powerful stake in the UN. This is why the US has not left the UN, even though it left the League of Nations. However, the veto power was intended for the great powers of today and tomorrow, not the great powers of yesterday. UNSC reform is difficult. The biggest obstacle is the lack of agreement on who should be the new permanent members.

This is why, in my book, *The Great Convergence*, I proposed a new formula of seven permanent members, seven semi-permanent members, and seven elected members. This 7-7-7 formula will bring in India, Brazil and an African state (to be chosen by Africa) as permanent members. Getting India in is key. As Martin Wolf of the *Financial Times* wisely said, "Exhausted by the burden of its pretensions, the UK should soon offer its seat on the security council of the United Nations to its former colony."

Finally, the finances of the UN need to be fixed. The European Union (EU) members believe in the UN but they have been strangling the necessary funding for the UN because they believe they pay too much. Unwisely, the EU led the charge to reduce mandatory contributions to the WHO from 62% in 1970–71 to less than 20% today.

To address these grievances of the EU, we must reduce the percentage of Western funding to the UN. The West European and Other States Group represent only 12% of the world's population but they contribute over 50% of the UN Budget. This should stop. Asians, who represent over 50% of the world's population, should pay more.

In his speeches, President Xi has announced generous voluntary contributions to key UN projects. It would be good for other Asian states to follow China's example in announcing their willingness to contribute more to the UN system. This could strengthen the UN and make it once again a beacon of hope. Asians can then feel proud that in the twenty-first century, the Asian Century, they led the way in reviving and rejuvenating the UN.

Can the World Health Organization Be Rejuvenated?

Abstract The Covid-19 pandemic has revealed the importance of multilateral institutions like the WHO to manage global challenges. Rather than weakening them, as has been done for the past 50 years, it should be rejuvenated through a coordinated effort by all nations.

Kofi Annan, the late UN Secretary-General, often said the world was a "global village". He was right. Our world has shrunk. The recent spread of Covid-19 worldwide, affecting both rich and developing countries, confirms that all 7.5 billion people of the world live in a global village.

Wise philosophers, both Eastern and Western, like Confucius and Plato, have taught us that when we live in a small community, we must develop commonly agreed rules and regulations to manage common spaces and everyday challenges.

Kofi Annan has also said, "we need rules of the road and norms to guide relations between individuals and communities. This is as true of the global village as it is of the village each of us may have come from." Therefore, if we have become a global village, we should be strengthening global village councils, like the family of UN organizations, who formulate rules and norms as well as manage our global commons and global challenges. Sadly, in recent decades we have been doing the opposite. We have been weakening the UN organizations, including the World Health Organization (WHO).

Why did we carry out this irrational act? The answer is complicated. It is so complicated that I wrote a book, *The Great Convergence* (which has been translated and published in Chinese), to explain this irrationality. However, one key reason stands out.

The wealthiest countries of the world, especially the affluent Western countries, unwisely decided that their interests would be better served by weakening the UN. Many Western countries deny that they are doing this. However, having served as the Singapore Ambassador to the UN twice (from 1984 to 1989 and from 1998 to 2004), I have seen firsthand how the West has weakened the UN. There is also strong evidence to back up this claim.

Originally published in Global Times, Mar 17, 2020

K. Mahbubani, *The Asian 21st Century*, China and Globalization,
https://doi.org/10.1007/978-981-16-6811-1_42

Take the WHO as an example. The West weakened it in three ways. First, the West starved the WHO of reliable mandatory funding. It used to be 62% in 1970–71. In 2017, it collapsed to 18%. Why is this significant? The WHO can only recruit long-term health inspectors from mandatory funding, not voluntary contributions. The second mistake was to focus on biomedicine, with its focus on individual behavior, instead of social medicine.

Epidemics like Covid-19 spread faster if we don't take care of social conditions. The third mistake was to dilute the role of the WHO and favor institutions like the World Bank controlled by the West. The World Bank lending on health went from roughly half of the WHO budget in 1984 to more than two and a half times bigger by 1996.

Today, as both the US and the European Union are being severely afflicted by Covid-19, they should ask themselves whether it was wise to starve the WHO funding for several decades. They should also re-examine their motives for doing so. Indeed, the US and the EU had different reasons.

The US weakened UN institutions because they constrained the ability of the US to act unilaterally. A former director of the National Intelligence Council told me directly, "Kishore, I can understand why small states like Singapore want stronger multilateral institutions. However, the US finds them constraining."

He was honest. The EU, by contrast, was primarily concerned about spending less money. The EU countries resented the fact that combined together, they contributed more than 30% of the UN budget, yet they had less than 15% of the vote for the spending decisions.

Now that the US and the EU have been severely affected by Covid-19, they should logically conclude that it was unwise for them to weaken the WHO. Indeed, there is no question that the Western countries, which are now the most affected, would benefit from a strong WHO. Sadly, even though Western societies worship reason, they find it difficult to change some of their past irrational policies. Too many vested interests will prevent the West from making a logical U-turn away from the weakening of the WHO.

This provides a tremendous opportunity for China. Unlike the Western countries, China has declared that its goal is to strengthen the family of UN organizations, including the WHO.

As President Xi Jinping said in Geneva in 2017, "pandemic diseases such as bird flu, Ebola and Zika have sounded the alarm for international health security. The WHO should play a leadership role in strengthening epidemic monitoring and sharing of information, practices, and technologies." His words were prophetic.

So, what can China do to strengthen the WHO? The first step is to take the lead in calling for a sharp increase in the share of mandatory funding. This will enable the WHO to make wiser and more strategic long-term plans, including developing long-term capabilities for managing future pandemics. Undoubtedly, more epidemics will come.

However, the question is not just about money. It is also about creating a global ethos that supports President Xi's statement that humanity is now a "community of shared future." The people who understand best that humanity is now a "community with a shared future" are the world's doctors and health administrators.

They know better than anyone else that viruses and bacteria don't respect borders. They carry no passports. They cross borders effortlessly. Hence, we should find ways and means of bringing together all the global health professionals more frequently.

The WHO can and should hold more meetings of global health professionals. At such meetings, we should pre-emptively anticipate the next few global health crises and put in place plans and measures to protect humanity as a whole. Fortunately, as we have discovered with Covid-19, the solution won't necessarily be found in expensive medicines. It also lies in simple improvements in personal hygiene.

One of the key lessons I learned from my 10 years in the UN community is that constant face-to-face meetings raised the level of trust and understanding among representatives coming from all corners of the world. Hence, I am confident that if the WHO, with the strong support of China, could convene regular meetings of the global health professionals in all fields, it would significantly increase the level of trust among them.

With this global sea of trust, humanity would be better able to handle future global health crises: When this happens, the world will thank China for planting the seeds that led to the establishment of communities of trust in our small global village.

Multilateral Diplomacy

Abstract Multilateral diplomacy has been central to the world order since World War II. Understanding how and why institutions and systems were established is essential to understanding where we have been and how to move forward in an increasingly shrinking world.

Multilateral diplomacy is a sunrise industry. The acceleration of globalization and the consequential shrinking of the globe has led to the literal, not metaphorical, creation of a global village. Every village needs its councils. All the processes of multilateral diplomacy serve to fulfill the functions of these global village councils. For the purposes of this chapter, 'multilateral diplomacy' will be defined as the practice of involving more than two nations or parties in achieving diplomatic solutions to supranational problems. As former UN Secretary-General Kofi Annan has said, 'diplomacy has expanded its remit, moving far beyond bilateral political relations between states into a multilateral, multifaceted enterprise encompassing almost every realm of human endeavor'.[1] Several key themes will run through this chapter on multilateral diplomacy. One key theme is the theme of diversity. Since multilateral diplomacy is a rapid growth industry, new forms are emerging constantly, making it difficult to provide a comprehensive description of all types. A second key theme is a constant tension between justice and power in all the multilateral processes. In theory, multilateral diplomacy is guided by some key principles of the international order. Also, in theory, international organizations have been set up, by agreements reached in multilateral diplomacy, to perform certain functions and deliver certain global goods for the benefits of all—in other words, provide global governance in their relevant fields—and not to act as a means to the major powers' ends. In practice, however, power usually trumps principles and ideals. A third key theme is a tension

Originally published in Oxford Handbook of Modern Diplomacy, Apr 2013

[1] 'Address by Secretary-General Kofi Annan to the American Academy of Diplomacy upon receiving the Academy's "Excellence in Diplomacy" Award in Washington, DC, on November 28', United Nations Press Release, 30 November 2001.

© The Author(s) 2022

K. Mahbubani, *The Asian 21st Century*, China and Globalization, https://doi.org/10.1007/978-981-16-6811-1_43

between universal organizations such as the United Nations which represent all of humanity and often enjoy great legitimacy, and several smaller and more informal groups or coalitions (like the G8 and G20) which also try to address key global challenges.

Functions of Multilateral Diplomacy

Multilateral diplomacy serves multiple functions. At the apex, it serves as the 'Parliament of Man'. The only way to find out what the 7 billion people of our planet think on any global challenge is to hear the voices of their national representatives in universal forums, like the UN General Assembly (UNGA) or universal conferences, like the Copenhagen conference on climate change. When disagreements surface, as they did at Copenhagen, they simultaneously reflect, like national parliaments do, the different views of the global population and can provide a safety valve.

A second, related function, especially for the 'Parliament of Man' after discerning the urgent needs of the global village, is to set aspirational goals for humanity. Hence, the UN Millennium Summit of 2000 set the Millennium Development Goals (MDGs) for 2015. Many MDGs will not be met but they have nonetheless inspired action on several fronts to improve the living conditions of the very poor on our planet. Without universal organizations like the UN, such agreements would be more difficult.

A third and also related function is norm creation. The world has essentially become a more civilized place since the Second World War through the steady accretion of civilizing norms. For example, the adoption of the Universal Declaration of Human Rights by UNGA in 1948 represented a great leap forward. It delegitimized heinous practices like slavery and torture. More recently the adoption by UNGA of two significant initiatives of banning landmines and cluster weapons indicate clearly how the norm creation function of multilateral diplomacy can serve to make the world a more civilized place. Similarly, UN conventions on children and women have significantly improved norms in these areas. Another significant breakthrough came when the UN Summit of 2005 endorsed the concept of 'Responsibility to Protect' (R2P).[2] Of course, one central tension remains when creating norms within institutions such as the UN, where there still exists a contradiction between the sovereign members and the need to reach decisions that these sovereign members are compelled to follow. For the moment, the only way to handle this is through 'consensus'.

Multilateral diplomacy is also the means to negotiate international treaties that improve the state of the world. Two examples stand out. The Nuclear Non-Proliferation Treaty (NPT), adopted on 1 July 1968, in force since 5 March 1970, and renewed indefinitely on 11 May 1995, prohibits the development or transfer of nuclear weapons or related technologies by and to non-weapon holding states. The only non-signers today are Israel, India, and Pakistan. It has succeeded (with minor

---

[2] See chapter "Can the World Health Organization Be Rejuvenated?", this volume.

exceptions) in preventing nuclear proliferation and delegitimized nuclear weapons. Sadly, the main violators of the NPT as a group have been the nuclear-weapon states, which have not moved quickly to fulfill their obligations to get rid of their horrific nuclear weapons. Similarly, the UN Convention on the Law of the Sea has created a common set of rules for the use of the world's oceans, which cover 70% of the earth's surface. The Convention, concluded in 1982, came into force in 1994 and 159 countries and the European Union have joined the treaty. The US, despite being one of the bigger beneficiaries of the treaty, has not ratified it, although it has largely adhered to its principles and rules.

All these processes of norm creation and treaty negotiation have served to lay down and strengthen international law. Just as the adherence to the rule of law domestically has generated social and political stability, greater adherence to international law has progressively reduced wars since the Second World War. Indeed the number of people dying from wars has reached historic lows. This one statistic alone should make the skeptics of multilateral diplomacy think twice before rubbishing it. Avoidance of war has improved the human condition.

Against this backdrop, the United States, the most powerful actor on the world stage, made a strategic error when it made a concerted effort to delegitimize UNGA as representing the voice of humanity. This decision was driven in part by the powerful pro-Israel lobby in Washington which was concerned over the anti-Israel resolutions passed by the UNGA. The American decision served neither the long-term interests of Israel nor those of the US. Indeed, the view advocated by the American right for the US to forget about the UN and work with the Community of Democracies was easily refuted by Anne-Marie Slaughter who pointed out that many of the opponents of the US war on Iraq belonged to this Community of Democracies. In short, a new American strategic approach is required if multilateral diplomacy is to serve well its key function as the 'Parliament of Man'.

In theory, UNGA also has a role to play in conflict resolution and peace-building. In practice, especially since the end of the cold war, the UN Security Council (UNSC) has played a key role in this area, but its record on this is chequered. While it solved many long-standing problems in Guatemala, Namibia, Cambodia, and the former Yugoslav Republic of Macedonia, and oversaw the inauguration of new national governments following the resolution of conflicts in El Salvador and Mozambique, the UNSC failed woefully in the Balkans, failed to prevent genocide in Rwanda, and has been remarkably ineffective on the Israel–Palestine issue.

Both problem-solving and furtherance of international cooperation is also carried out by the multilateral diplomacy processes of the many specialized agencies that have emerged since the Second World War (including the World Trade Organization (WTO), World Health Organization (WHO) , International Atomic Energy Agency (IAEA), International Labour Organization (ILO), UN Environment Programme (UNEP), to mention only a few). Overall, the WTO and its predecessor, the General Agreement on Tariffs and Trade, have been spectacularly successful, with world trade growing three times faster than world output growth, from USD 296 billion in 1950 to over USD 8 trillion in 2005, thereby improving human welfare, increasing international interdependence, and creating a powerful vested interest in preserving global stability. Trade now accounts for almost one-fifth of the world's total GDP, up from only five percent in 1950.[3] Even though the latest Doha Development Round is in trouble, all the previous trading rounds succeeded even if the negotiations had been long and protracted. Equally importantly, there has also been no significant backsliding into trade protectionism, even in the world financial crisis of 2007–2009.

On a smaller scale, in terms of the number of countries involved in multilateral diplomacy but not in terms of impact, the G20 Summits of November 2008 and April 2009 played a critical role in saving the world from going over a financial precipice.[4] These institutions and processors of multilateral diplomacy have so far passed the 'critical stress tests' surviving great crises, although of course the G20 could be made more inclusive, transparent, and participatory by periodic issue-wide inclusion of other stakeholders, as espoused by the 'Global Governance Group' in New York.

Kick-started by the global financial crisis, banking regulation will become an increasingly important challenge for ensuring the stability and sustainability of our world economic system; this is yet another area in which the tools of multilateral diplomacy can be put into action. The Basel Committee made up of representatives of all G20 major economies plus a few others,[5] is a good example of multilateralism at work. Advocates of the second and third Basel Accords have called for the strengthening of international standards to reduce the risks faced by financial institutions, and for the creation of 'buffer' funds that will allow financial institutions to better withstand future periods of stress. Multilateral diplomacy enabled Basel to succeed.

The many and multiple functions performed by multilateral diplomacy demonstrate the importance of understanding how multilateral diplomacy works. More recently, this importance has been further demonstrated by how much of it is now done at the leaders' level. Leaders today consider it an essential part of their job description to travel overseas and attend summit meetings. By contrast, Sir Edward Gray never once traveled abroad during his long tenure as Britain's foreign secretary from 1905 to 1916. How times have changed!

Forms of Multilateral Diplomacy

Multilateral meetings that take place in a year have taken on so many forms, and at so many different levels, that it would be difficult to measure all of them. However, even a cursory attempt at counting them will show that since the creation of the UN and

---

[3] 'World exports and world GDP, 1870 < EN> –2005', *World Trade Report 2007*, World Trade Organization, 244. Available at: http://www.wto.org/english/res_e/booksp_e/anrep_e/wtr07-0b_e. pdf.

[4] See chapter "Diplomacy: Power or Persuasion", this volume.

[5] As of October 2010, members include: Argentina, Australia, Belgium, Brazil, Canada, China, France, Germany, Hong Kong SAR, India, Indonesia, Italy, Japan, Korea, Luxembourg, Mexico, the Netherlands, Russia, Saudi Arabia, Singapore, South Africa, Spain, Sweden, Switzerland, Turkey, the United Kingdom, and the United States.

the Bretton Woods Institutions (BWI) in 1945, multilateral meetings have exploded, especially in the last two decades.

Any attempt to classify all the multilateral meetings will also face serious difficulties. Nevertheless, if one were to look for a few conceptual baskets to capture most of them, these conceptual baskets could be entitled as (1) universal, (2) functional/specialized, (3) regional, (4) ad hoc.

The creation of the UN and the BWI spawned the industry of universal gatherings and conferences which tried to get all of humanity represented. These universal gatherings have grown from the regular annual meetings of UNGA, the International Monetary Fund (IMF), and World Bank to now include all kinds of global conferences, from the UN Conference on the Law of the Sea to conferences on population, women, and the global environment.

After the failure of Copenhagen, there is now a new pessimism about the future of such global conferences. The new conventional wisdom is that such universal meetings are unworkable as they try to reconcile too many different interests. Yet, even in a small village, it would be folly to ignore the wishes of even a significant minority. True global solutions in a global village require the 'inclusion' of all members of the village in a solution. A dispassionate analysis of Copenhagen will show that it failed for many reasons, including the incompetence of the Danish chairmanship, the shift of power away from the West, the inability of President Barack Obama to persuade the US Congress to impose limits on American greenhouse gas emissions, and the need for China and India to maintain their economic growth rates to sustain their poverty alleviation efforts. In short, multilateral diplomacy exercises are inherently complex and success in them requires skillful leadership, like the kind provided by Ambassador Tommy Koh of Singapore when he ably steered the UN Convention of the Law of the Sea to a successful conclusion despite the many contradictions between groups like the 'Landlocked and Geographically Disadvantaged States' and the 'Continental Shelf' countries. Hence, when universal conferences fail, we should not blame the format. We should blame the lack of skill of the participants and the inherent contradictions of individual states' interests.

The UN family has also created a variety of specialized agencies with their own intergovernmental annual conferences and governing councils that provide direction and guidance on the basis of decisions reached through multilateral diplomacy. While some of their annual conferences and governing councils have also been derailed by political differences, which hamper the ability to provide good global leadership and governance in the respective fields, their track record shows that whenever a common danger is faced, the global community has been able to come together. This is especially true of the reaction to pandemics that do not respect national borders. Hence, it is useful to observe how multilateral diplomacy works well in specialized organizations like WHO to understand how humanity can come together and work together in universal multilateral conferences.

Multilateral diplomacy is growing very rapidly at the regional level. The most successful example of regional cooperation is provided by the European Union (EU). While most laud the economic achievements of the EU, its most striking achievement is not just that there are no wars, but that there is also zero prospect of war between any two EU member states. This is the gold standard of regional cooperation that all other regions should try to emulate. Sadly, no other region comes close.

Nevertheless, one untold story of the world has been how this European gold standard has gradually infected other regional organizations. I can speak with personal experience on what is possibly the second most successful regional organization, namely the Association of Southeast Asian Nations (ASEAN). When I first attended ASEAN meetings in the early 1970s, you could feel the distrust and suspicion among the five founding members. Yet two decades later, when I led the Singapore senior official delegation to ASEAN meetings, there was a much more relaxed and trusting atmosphere for concluding business. Two decades of regional multilateral diplomacy had changed the chemistry of ASEAN meetings and improved trust.

When people come together and interact frequently, over time, they develop a sense of community. This in turn reduces the prospects for conflict and enhances the prospects for cooperation. This is why after practicing multilateral diplomacy for over three decades in many different forums, universal and regional, I am a strong believer in its value. The fact that no two ASEAN states have gone to war with each other (despite some close shaves) since ASEAN's creation provides clear and powerful proof of the value of multilateral diplomacy.

Multilateral diplomacy at the regional level has also become a major sunrise industry. ASEAN, for example, has succeeded not just in enhancing cooperation between its ten members but also in providing an essential geopolitical platform for other Asian powers to meet and confer on neutral ground. It began with ASEAN inviting China, Japan, and Korea to join them at the famous ASEAN + 3 meetings. These meetings demonstrated their value quickly. When bilateral relations worsened between China and Japan and their leaders could not meet bilaterally, they could meet each other without losing face in the multilateral setting provided by ASEAN + 3 meetings. The meetings have now effectively expanded to ASEAN + 8 with India, Australia, New Zealand, Russia, and the US joining the East Asia Summit meetings.

Relative to the EU, ASEAN is a latecomer. Hence, as the world moves ever more firmly into the Asian century, it would have been natural for the EU to undertake the bold initiative of proposing Asia-Europe cooperation. Instead, the EU remained passive and ASEAN took the lead. Prime Minister Goh Chok Tong of Singapore proposed an Asia-Europe Meeting (ASEM).

Fortunately, the EU embraced his proposal readily. I know this from firsthand experience as I traveled to several EU capitals to promote Prime Minister Goh's idea. The first ASEM Summit in Bangkok in March 1996 was an unqualified success. Unfortunately, the Asian Financial Crisis erupted soon after. This gave EU countries a valuable opportunity to demonstrate that they were not 'fair weather' friends of Asia. Sadly, the EU failed this test, demonstrating once again that European policymakers' judgments are clouded by short-term thinking. With the recovery of Asia, the ASEM process is back on track. Ironically, Europe got into trouble a decade later. Fortunately, the Asian states are showing wiser judgment by not walking away from Europe in its hour of travails.

The success of multilateral diplomacy in Asia has profound implications for the global order as we move into a completely new era of world history marked by the end of Western domination and the return of Asia. It is vital to remember that from the year 1 to 1820, China and India consistently provided the world's largest economies. Hence, by 2050, when they return to their natural places in the global hierarchy of nations, the center of gravity of world history will also shift to Asia.

Therefore, what Asia does will drive world history. It would not have been inconceivable for the rising Asian powers to reject the Western-based principles that provided the foundations for the 1945 rules-based order created by the US and Europe. Fortunately, the rising Asian powers have decided to embrace rather than reject these Western principles. Ironically, the big question the world faces today is whether the Western states will respect their own principles of global order. Under international law, the use of force is justified only if it is an act of self-defense or authorized by the UN Security Council. The invasion of Iraq in March 2003 did not meet either criterion. Hence, as Kofi Annan declared, the Iraq war was illegal.[6] If the Western states would like rising Asian powers to respect the key Western principles that underpin our global order, they must lead by example. This is why American attitudes toward multilateral diplomacy are critical.

The success of multilateral diplomacy is also demonstrated by the creation of various ad hoc diplomatic gatherings. The most famous and most powerful ad hoc group today is the G20. It saved the world from an economic meltdown in early 2009. Unlike established universal and regional groupings, like the UN or EU, the G20 has no headquarters or even rules of procedure. It is still truly ad hoc. But despite this, its ability to deliver results also shows the value of multilateral diplomacy. The success of a club is shown when outsiders clamor to get in and no insiders want to leave it. This is certainly true of the G20.

Other ad hoc forms of multilateral diplomacy have also emerged, with varying degrees of legitimacy and success. The initiatives against landmines and cluster bombs, despite initial opposition from established powers like the US, Russia, and China, found significant international momentum and were subsequently legitimized when both were endorsed by UNGA. A less successful example of ad hoc multilateral diplomacy is provided by the Proliferation Security Initiative (PSI) launched by the US. Its goal is to allow the interdiction of third-country ships suspected of carrying nuclear weapons in the high seas. Even though it has over 90 states supporting it, it is still opposed by several countries, including China which disputes its legality, and has therefore not yet been endorsed by the UN system.

---

[6] See for example, 'Iraq war illegal, says Annan', *BBC News*, 16 September 2004. Available at: http://news.bbc.co.uk/2/hi/3661134.stm.

Inherent Tensions of Multilateral Diplomacy

International negotiations are supposedly conducted by reasonable men and women sitting around a table to arrive at a mutually beneficial agreement. This practice is deemed to be a significant advance in human civilization as we are seen to have moved away from the 'primitive' world when men made decisions by using their clubs and weapons, not reason. There is no doubt that the voice of 'Reason' has played a role in international negotiations and multilateral diplomacy.

My three decades of experience with multilateral diplomacy (in all its forms) have taught me that when I walk into a multilateral setting, I will encounter three voices: reason, power, and charm. The voice of charm has been underestimated. One simple story will illustrate how it works. In 1981 the UNSC was totally deadlocked over the selection of the next secretary-general. Fortunately, a young Ugandan diplomat (representing an extremely weak country just recovering from Idi Amin's excesses) named Olara Otunnu was elected as the president of the UNSC in December 1981. Using his charm and persuasiveness, he found a solution to the deadlock. Similarly, the legendary Singapore diplomat, Tommy Koh, was also able to use his considerable charm to persuade diplomats from over one hundred countries to agree to a solution in the law of the sea negotiations. Charm works in multilateral diplomacy as in other areas of life.

But neither reason nor charm can override the voice of power, which remains the single strongest factor in multilateral diplomacy and international relations. My two years in the UNSC in 2001–2002 taught me that we have not traveled far from the 'primitive' world order when brute strength and power drove human decision-makings. The five permanent members (P5) would use the power of the veto formally and, more often, informally to distort the decision-making procedures of UNSC, with the result that instead of the UNSC fulfilling its charter obligations of 'preserving international peace and security', it was used to further the national interests and positions of the P5.

The biggest distortion has occurred on the Israel–Palestine issue. There is now a near-universal consensus in the international community that we need to have a two-state solution and that the forty-five-year illegal Israeli occupation of Palestinian land has to end. Any kind of global democratic voting will show there are over six billion people who will vote for a two-state solution. However, the views of six billion people are being thwarted by six million Israelis who have managed to dominate American decision making. This global distortion could ultimately lead to a long-term tragedy for Israel when the new correlation of forces begins to constrain American power significantly in the twenty-first century.

To rescue the UN and strengthen multilateral diplomacy, we have to quickly resolve the Israel–Palestinian issue because it has generated more international political poison than any other issue. It has caused the double delegitimization of the UN: delegitimization of the UN in the eyes of the American public because the American media has highlighted its anti-Israel positions in UNGA and delegitimization of the UN in the eyes of 1.6 billion Muslims who notice the pro-Israel positions of the

UNSC. Hence, until the Israel–Palestine issue is resolved, the UN will be effectively crippled and multilateral diplomacy will be consequently constrained.

The insistence of the P5 in putting 'national interests' ahead of 'global interests' has led to many other distortions in UNSC decision making. The Clinton Administration blocked an effective international response to prevent genocide in Rwanda by refusing to allow the word 'genocide' in a UNSC resolution. Similarly, the Bush Administration distorted the role of the UNSC when it used its considerable 'unipolar' power to get the UNSC to go beyond its legitimate role and interfere in a 'judicial' decision by granting immunity to American troops from the International Criminal Court. Similarly, Russia prevented the UNSC from responding in Kosovo in 1999. Similar examples can be found for the other three permanent members.

Power, however, is not static. Having served as Singapore's ambassador to the UN in two different historical phases, I saw at first hand how multilateral diplomacy is conditioned by the international geopolitical order. In the mid-1980s, when the cold war was still on, the UNSC was paralyzed by the gridlock between the USA and USSR. Hence, UNGA was the main focus of attention. It performed creditably in condemning both the illegal Soviet invasion of Afghanistan and the illegal American invasion of Grenada. When I returned to the UN in 1998, UNGA was completely ignored and all the attention and focus was on the work of the UNSC.

Multilateral diplomacy is now going to face the biggest test of its ability to adapt to a new geopolitical order with the impending biggest shift of geopolitical power we have seen in several centuries. As indicated earlier, we are reaching the end of the era of Western domination of world history (but not, of course, the end of the West) and the return of Asian countries, especially China and India, to their natural position of providing the biggest economies of the world. There is no doubt that the world will have to make massive adjustments trends to adapt to the huge shifts in power. Multilateral diplomacy will have to do the same.

This will be an extremely complex and difficult exercise. In the current multilateral order, the language, concepts, and definitions of legitimate and illegitimate international behavior are primarily Western in origin. Indeed, today's international system of states, international organizations, and multinational corporations find its roots in the Peace of Westphalia, a treaty signed in 1648 between European rulers who sought to establish the territorial integrity of their states. Since the Treaty of Westphalia, there has not been an occasion when the international community adopted a different view from that of Westphalian state sovereignty and one of the greatest difficulties facing us today is a tension between individual state sovereignty and a need for global solutions to global problems. On the one hand, the United Nations is a collection of sovereign states, and its mission is, to some degree, to protect their sovereignty. On the other hand, global problems demand a united global strategy that may transcend individual states' sovereignty.

However, there have been minor but revolutionary changes. Consider, for example, the latest concept in international relations: the 'Responsibility to Protect' adopted by UNGA in 2005. In theory, this concept overrides national sovereignty. What the leaders agreed to in the outcome document was therefore a landmark decision for international law. The enormous importance of this decision has not quite sunk in yet but it will in time to come. This was the result of a Canadian initiative. Will such concepts be retained or rejected when the West no longer dominates the multilateral order?

One critical, underestimated problem here is that most Western policymakers and public intellectuals believe that the international behavior of most Western states has been 'responsible' and 'legitimate'. That is why American leaders can, with a straight face, call on China to emerge as a 'responsible stakeholder' in the international order. Yet, the West only provides less than 12% of the world population. A vast majority of the 88% of the world population who live outside of the West increasingly question the 'responsibility' and 'legitimacy' of the West as they are acutely aware of the duplicity and double standards prevalent in Western international behavior. The West must learn to listen to the voices of the majority of the world's population or else we may face sad consequences. The story of the invasion of Iraq shows what can go wrong when the West ignores global opinion.

This huge shift in global history could also provide multilateral diplomacy its biggest opportunity to demonstrate its new relevance. Its primary function, as indicated earlier, is to serve as the 'Parliament of Man'. Hence, instead of trying to delegitimize and derail UNGA, the Western powers, especially the US, should try to revive UNGA's early critical role in providing a forum for hearing the voices of the newly-active members of the global community. The strong speeches of India's Jawaharlal Nehru and Egypt's Gamel Abdel Nasser, Indonesia's Sukarno, and Cuba's Fidel Castro in the 1950s and 1960s provided the world an understanding of what the newly-independent nations aspired to immediately after Western decolonization.

Today, we are witnessing a similar reemergence of long-dormant civilizations and societies. New voices are emerging, by the billions. The world needs to find an arena to allow these voices to express themselves. Fortunately, we do not have to reinvent the wheel. UNGA already exists. However, in the complex new world order we have, UNGA must capture the complexity of this new world. In their introduction to this Handbook, Cooper, Heine, and Thakur highlight the new actors on the world stage. They quote appropriately Anne-Marie Slaughter, who says:

> We envision getting not just a new group of states around a table, but also building networks, coalitions and partnerships of states and non-state actors to tackle specific problems... To do that, our diplomats are going to need to have skills that are closer to community organizing than traditional reporting and analysis. New connecting technologies will be vital tools in this kind of diplomacy.[7]

Hitherto, most of these non-state actors have been powerful Western NGOs (like Amnesty International or Greenpeace) or inspired by Western ideas (like the Club of Democracies). This traditional Western domination in the world of non-state actors is also coming to an end. This is why the story of the Turkish flotilla that attempted to reach Gaza in May 2010 provided a powerful harbinger of the world that is coming. Similarly, the pictures of young Chinese students in Western capitals demonstrating against the Western demonstrators who were blocking the passage of the Olympics

---

[7] In an interview with David Rothpokf, 'It's 3 a.m. Do you know where Hillary Clinton is?', *Washington Post*, 27 August 2009.

torch showed that young people all over the world are becoming politically aroused. Given the huge demographic bulge of youth in the developing world, their voices must also be heard. The new UNGA must strive to become an accurate mirror of the views of 7 billion people on our planet.

The arrival of new non-state actors, however, does not mean that some of the previous traditional tensions have disappeared. The failure of the Copenhagen Conference in December 2009 provides a wonderful case study of what can go wrong in contemporary multilateral diplomacy. On the one hand, virtually all the NGOs in Copenhagen, both from the developing and developed countries, argued in favor of stronger global action against global warming. Their voices were best captured by the United Nations Intergovernmental Panel on Climate Change (IPCC), which, unlike Western NGOs, had a global collection of representatives. Yet, all their moral force failed against the traditional dynamic of negotiations among government representatives.

Obama's hands were tied when he arrived in Copenhagen because the US Congress refused to pass any legislation that would restrict American greenhouse gas emissions. If the then-largest emitter in the world would not cooperate, it was obviously absurd to expect the two new emerging powers, China and India, to make any compromises. The Indian PM, Manmohan Singh, put it well when he said he could not deprive the Indian people of electricity: 'Our energy needs are bound to grow. We will be failing in the duty to our nation and to posterity if we do not look ahead and take steps for not just today and tomorrow but for future generations.'[8] More than 400 million Indians lack electricity and supply falls short of peak demand by more than 16%, according to the World Bank. At the end of the day, all the leaders, including Obama, Singh, Brazil's Luiz Lula da Silva, and China's Wen Jiabao, could not override their domestic national interests in favor of global interests.

The Copenhagen Conference also showed how a new geopolitical order was emerging. In the final meeting, the EU was not even represented in the room, showing what a geopolitical dwarf the EU had become. Apart from the US, China, and India were the key players. Despite their bilateral differences, China and India cooperated for a common cause. Brazil and South Africa also demonstrated the importance of newly-emerging economies. In short, a thorough case study of the Copenhagen Conference will draw out many lessons on the complexities of contemporary multilateral diplomacy. This conference also showed how urgently new thinking is needed if the world is going to succeed in global cooperation.

Fortunately, some failures of multilateral diplomacy at the global level are being compensated by successes at the regional level. In most regions of the world, regional cooperation is growing rather than receding. Apart from the well-known success stories of the EU and ASEAN, all regions see the value of working together. In most regions of the world (with the exception of South Asia which is bedeviled by India–Pakistan differences), intra-regional trade is growing. Intra-regional trade in East Asia, for example, accounted for only about 9% of trade in the whole region in 1990. By 2010 it had grown to over 50%, a spectacular increase by any measure.

---

[8] 'Nuclear energy essential for India: Manmohan Singh', *Thaidian News*, 24 March 2008.

The volume of intra-regional trade in Africa has increased by almost 20% in the first decade of the twenty-first century and a similar story is true in Central and South America. However, even more, important than the economic benefits, the general decline of wars globally can also be attributed to greater regional cooperation.

Having participated in several meetings between ASEAN and EU officials, I have become acutely aware that the culture and mores of regional multilateral diplomacy vary significantly from region to region. In Europe, there is a strong legalistic emphasis with most of the time taken up by long arguments over the draft document. Success is measured by the quality of the written document. In East Asia, most of the focus is on building trust and understanding among the participants. The document is a secondary product. The more important result is the unspoken trust that has developed. I am deliberately exaggerating the differences to draw out the distinctions. But my experience with ASEAN and EU also taught me that new generations of multilateral diplomats must learn to develop deeper cultural sensitivities.

Solutions

Looking ahead at the future of multilateral diplomacy, it is clear that the world's leading policymakers, including key world leaders, face an acute dilemma in dealing with it. With the shrinking of the globe, the demand for multilateral diplomacy is likely to increase by leaps and bounds. On the other hand, as already mentioned, the supply of multilateral diplomacy is beset with many inherent problems. To resolve this dilemma the world needs to take a step-by-step approach to ensure that the processes of multilateral diplomacy will be available and at hand when the world turns to them to resolve acute global and regional problems.

The first step is to change our mindset about world order. We need to acknowledge that we live literally, not metaphorically, in a global village. Hence, right now, our primary global contradiction is painfully obvious: the biggest challenges of governance are global in origin, but all the politics that respond to them are local. There are many wise leaders around the world, but there is not enough global leadership.

The first decade of the twenty-first century has only accelerated the emergence of such global challenges. The era began with 9/11 when a plot hatched by Osama bin Laden while living in Afghanistan brought down the Twin Towers in Manhattan. In 2003 SARS jumped simultaneously from a village in China to two cities on opposite sides of the world—Singapore and Toronto. Barely six years later, H1N1 haunted the globe. The speed and ferocity of the Lehman Brothers crisis brought the world to the brink of a meltdown.

The biggest challenge of all is progressing more slowly than the financial crisis. But climate change is the perfect example of just how ineffective our current leadership structures are. The solution to global warming is quite simple: we have to increase the economic price of greenhouse gas emissions equitably, with rich countries paying more and poorer nations paying less, but with all countries paying some price. Yet someone has to make the first move. America—whose population is only

5% of the world but consumes 25% of the world's gasoline—is the obvious candidate. If the price of a gallon of gasoline in the US were to be raised by one dollar (and that would still make an American gallon cheaper than a European or Singaporean gallon), the change in driving habits would dramatically cut emissions. And American leadership, by example, would likely change attitudes in other nations.

In many ways, the US is the wisest country in the world. It certainly remains the most successful, despite its recent travails. Yet in this land of wisdom and success, not one American politician would dare advocate a 'one dollar' solution to save the world. It would mean immediate political suicide. Herein lies the nub of the problem. Politicians are elected in local constituencies to take care of local concerns. Those who try to save the world will not last long.

This is why humanity needs a wake-up call. We can develop good domestic governance, from New Zealand to the Netherlands, Singapore, and Sweden. But good national leaders can only mitigate the shocks of global challenges, not solve them. Solutions have to be tackled through global organizations like the United Nations and the IMF, or global coalitions like the G20.

In theory, everyone agrees that we need to strengthen and open up these institutions. In practice, however, global organizations and coalitions are controlled by a few powerful national governments that put their interests ahead of the worlds. This is the ultimate global paradox. Great powers want to use their status to dominate global organizations—think of how the US and Europe still split the leadership of the World Bank and the IMF. But the more they control and distort the agenda of those institutions, the more they weaken them. And if these organizations are weak, solutions to global problems will simply not emerge.

The only way around this is to develop a strong, new international consensus, among citizens as well as governments, that the world needs more global governance (not global government).[9] Only then will the mightiest nations think of the greater good and allow institutions—from the G20 to the UN, from the IMF to the WTO—to be revitalized. Indeed, a cooperative solution should provide each stakeholder with a better outcome than a solution reached by individual stakeholders. Yes, these bodies are imperfect. But in the world of politics, it is easier to reform existing institutions than to create perfect new ones.

The second step needs to be taken by the world's greatest power. Ever since the strong leadership of Dag Hammarskjöld (1953–1961), the US has decided (and during the cold war, in complete agreement with the Soviet Union) that its national interest was best served by a weaker UN leadership and weak processes of multilateral diplomacy. Hence, all international organizations, treaties, and laws were seen by American policymakers as constraints on American power. This policy may have made sense if America could have guaranteed that it would remain in perpetuity as the world's sole superpower (although I would argue that it would not have made sense even then). However, with China about to overtake the US as the world's greatest economic power shortly, it is timely for the US to reconsider its old policies

---

[9] See Weiss and Thakur (2010).

of keeping multilateral institutions and processes weak. If America persists with these policies, there will be fewer constraints on China as it emerges as a great power.

Several beneficial practical consequences will emerge for multilateral diplomacy if the US decides to change its policy. First, the performance of international organizations would improve if the best possible candidates are chosen to run them rather than the weakest acceptable candidates. A UN, for example, with secretary-general of the caliber of a Kofi Annan rather than a Kurt Waldheim would be a more effective organization. A secretary-general with a strong moral voice would be perceived by the world as a secular Pope who could provide both moral and political leadership in bringing the world together to find strong collective solutions to the rapidly increasing 'global commons' problems we are facing. For this to happen, however, the P5, who wields the power to veto any candidate for the post, will need to overcome their desire to have more of a secretary than a general leading the UN bureaucracy. Indeed, even Kofi Annan was reported to have said that the 'S' and 'G' in his title stood for 'scapegoat'—a reference to the tendency of Western powers to blame the UN or its agencies for their own failures, making the UN the biggest convenient scapegoat.

Second, international organizations should be given the resources they need to meet growing global challenges in many areas. For example, the IAEA Commission of Eminent Persons, led by former President Ernesto Zedillo, recommended that the IAEA recruit and retain more nuclear-weapons inspectors in response to growing threats of non-proliferation. The US should go beyond lifting the Bush Administration's zero-growth budget policies toward international organizations to work with other developed partners to galvanize the necessary support for these organizations, all the while holding them accountable in terms of performance and efficient use of resources.

Third, the improved abilities, resources, and morale of international organizations would in turn increase their standing and prestige globally. The Western media, for example, would start looking to them for solutions to problems rather than portraying them as the problem. A reversal of the Western policy of delegitimizing international organizations would significantly improve their ability to perform better, which in turn would make multilateral diplomacy more attractive for capable young foreign service professionals. I can say this with great conviction because, as a young foreign service officer, I was actually discouraged from going into multilateral diplomacy. A senior Singaporean minister told me: 'Kishore, your job there is only to go to the UN and weep for the world. Don't expect to achieve anything concrete in the UN.' Equally, we should promote a balance between recruiting experts in areas such as finance or the global environment into the multilateral area, as well as encourage the brightest foreign service officers to take up global multilateral challenges.

My own life experience has taught me that the most successful organizations are those able to recruit the best and the brightest, whether the organization is Harvard or McKinsey, Bain or Goldman Sachs. Over the years, with the steady demoralization of most international organizations, fewer and fewer countries send their best diplomats to multilateral diplomacy. Instead, countries have sent their best diplomats to bilateral diplomacy. This has been a major strategic error as multilateral diplomacy has become more important for the world than bilateral diplomacy. Therefore, the branding and image of multilateral diplomacy must change in our brand-consumed world if it is to succeed in its mission.

It is vital to emphasize that different international organizations face different problems. The IMF and World Bank have been relatively well funded since they are profit-making institutions clearly controlled by the West. However, because they are perceived to be serving Western rather than global interests, their prestige, and standing, especially in Asia, diminished significantly after the Asian financial crisis. For the IMF and World Bank to remain relevant in the twenty-first century, the West must give up its controlling share of both organizations and allow their heads to be selected on merit rather than be the exclusive preserve of the US and Europe.

In short, multilateral diplomacy can be revived and strengthened with some clear practical steps including those mentioned in this chapter. However, these practical steps can only be taken after a new political consensus has emerged in key capitals, both in the established powers and in the newly-emerging powers, that the processes of multilateral diplomacy need to be strengthened, rather than weakened. The creation of this new political consensus will in turn require a concerted effort involving both key state and non-state actors.

Reference

Weiss TG, Thakur R (2010) Global governance and the UN: an unfinished journey. Indiana University Press, Bloomington

Can Humanity Make U-turns?

Abstract The coronavirus pandemic has underlined the importance of supporting multilateral organizations like the World Health Organisation, rather than progressively weakening them.

Humanity is supposed to be the most intelligent species on planet Earth. This species has just received, through Covid-19, one of its biggest shocks since World War II.

Thousands are dying daily, not through war or famine (the usual causes) but through a new disease caused by a novel Coronavirus that has effectively left humanity defenseless. No cure or vaccine is immediately available.

The rapid spread of Covid-19 also confirms that all of humanity now lives in the same boat, a boat akin to the ill-fated Diamond Princess that was stuck off Japan.

The big question that humanity now faces is a simple one: Is it intelligent enough to learn the big lessons from Covid-19 and, if necessary, make massive U-turns from current policies? In theory, we can. In practice, I fear that we will fail.

This essay will discuss one concrete example: multilateralism. Multilateralism sounds boring. To explain it simply, let's return to the boat analogy. If we 7.5 billion people are now stuck together on a virus-infected cruise ship, does it make sense to clean and scrub only our personal cabins while ignoring the corridors and air wells outside, through which the virus travels?

The answer is clearly no. Yet, this is what we have been doing. In the developed world, we have been protecting our own countries while neglecting the global routes through which the virus travels. Since we are now in the same boat, humanity has to take care of the global boat as a whole.

Fortunately, after 1945, the West took the lead in setting up a family of global governance institutions, centered on the United Nations, like the World Health Organization (WHO), to improve global governance. However, in recent decades, the West has been systematically weakening global multilateral institutions, including the WHO.

Originally published in The Straits Times, Apr 9, 2020

K. Mahbubani, *The Asian 21st Century*, China and Globalization,
https://doi.org/10.1007/978-981-16-6811-1_44

The essay will discuss the WHO, to illustrate the folly of undermining multilateral institutions. Its primary objective "is the attainment by all people of the highest possible level of health". A noble goal.

Yet, the real value of the WHO kicks in when health crises break out. It provides the only effective forum for states to cooperate against global health challenges. Hence, it played a leading role in the eradication of smallpox, the near-eradication of polio, and the development of an Ebola vaccine. For the most intelligent species on planet Earth, it's a no-brainer to strengthen, not weaken, the WHO.

Sadly, Western countries contrive to deny that they have been weakening multilateral institutions, including the WHO. This denial is very dangerous for the West. If it continues denying that it has weakened institutions like the WHO, it cannot make a U-turn and begin rejuvenating and strengthening them. Hence, the first step that the West needs to take is to engage in deep self-reflection on what it has done to organizations like the WHO.

The West has weakened the WHO in three ways; I have documented them in great detail in *The Great Convergence*, a book I wrote that was published in 2013.

First, the West starved the WHO of reliable long-term mandatory funding. This used to account for 62% of its budget in 1970–1971. In 2017, it collapsed to 18%. Why is this significant? The WHO can recruit long-term health inspectors and scientists only from mandatory funding, not voluntary contributions that vary from year to year.

The second way was to focus on biomedicine, with its focus on individual behavior, instead of social medicine. But understanding individual behavior is not enough to counter epidemics like Covid-19 that spread faster if we don't take care of social conditions.

The third way was to dilute the role of the WHO and favor institutions like the World Bank, which is controlled by the West. The World Bank's lending on health went from roughly half of the WHO budget in 1984 to more than 2–1/2 times bigger by 1996.

Giving more money to the World Bank should appear unobjectionable. However, as Professor Kelley Lee, professor of global health governance at Simon Fraser University, has documented in her book on the WHO, "for the WHO, it has meant a bypassing of its role as the lead UN health agency".

In a health emergency, like Covid-19, the WHO can help us. The World Bank cannot. As Prof Lee says, during the severe acute respiratory syndrome crisis of 2002–2003, the "WHO's worldwide mobilization of scientists to identify and genetically sequence the infectious agent was especially impressive".

So, given the critical importance of the WHO in fighting pandemics, why did the West starve it of mandatory long-term funding?

The ironic truth is that this was not even the result of a careful and comprehensive evaluation of the long-term strategic interests of the West. Instead, the policy was driven by "bean counters" who only wanted to save money.

They were also driven by short-term selfish interest—by making the WHO dependent on voluntary contributions from the West, the Western countries could get the

WHO to focus on areas of interest to the West, which makes up only 12% of the world's population.

Yet, in undermining the ability of the WHO to improve conditions in the remaining 88%, the West was essentially shooting itself in the foot as its own destiny, especially in health, is tied directly to the well-being of the rest, as demonstrated by Covid-19. We are all in the same boat.

Can the West make a U-turn? Yes, it can. In some ways it has. One of the most eloquent spokesmen in favor of multilateralism is President Emmanuel Macron of France.

He has said: "In the current state of the world, there is nothing more effective than multilateralism. Why? Because all our challenges are global, such as terrorism, migration, global warming, and regulation of the digital sector. All these issues can only be addressed globally, and multilaterally. Each time we consent to circumvent multilateralism, we hand victory to the law of the strongest." If he gave the same speech today, he would have mentioned Covid-19 first.

Words matter. Deeds matter more. To demonstrate its commitment to strengthening multilateralism, the West can reverse the ratio of mandatory versus voluntary funding of the WHO. Mandatory funding must go back to 70% or more because voluntary funding goes up and down and the WHO cannot rely on that to build long-term scientific capabilities.

When I served as Singapore's Ambassador to the UN, I saw how ferociously some ambassadors of Western countries fought to contribute less (on the basis of a UN formula where rich countries pay more in absolute terms and poor countries pay less). They would fight to save one or two million dollars. How much has the global economy lost as a result of Covid-19? We have lost trillions of dollars.

Trillions versus millions! Very little money is needed to strengthen the WHO. For example, the European Union countries contributed USD 150 million to the WHO in fiscal year 2018. This amount is just 0.09% of the budget of the European Commission, or one-tenth of 1%.

This makes the tragedy of Covid-19 even sadder. It would literally take "peanuts" to save and strengthen the WHO.

So where does all this leave us on the issue of multilateralism?

In the short run, we can only despair. Turning around entrenched habits in the West cannot be done overnight. In the long run, we can be confident that a new global consensus will emerge that all of us now live together in a small interdependent boat, like the passengers of the ill-fated Diamond Princess cruise ship did.

On such a global boat, it makes no sense to clean only our cabins when the boat is infected. The only way we can protect our own cabin is by coming together to take care of the boat as a whole.

Over time, we can only hope that the wiser voices of the West will be heeded and a more enlightened policy of supporting multilateral institutions, like the WHO, will prevail. After all, enlightened self-interest, if nothing else, dictates that it must adopt a multilateral stance toward global challenges.

As friends of the West, we should work with and encourage them to speak out more. We should tell them that the fate of the human species depends on our ability to make essential U-turns and work together to strengthen, not weaken, institutions of good governance, like the WHO.

This will be a key litmus test to assess whether humanity is truly the most intelligent species on planet Earth.

Appendix
Introduction to Kishore Mahbubani's Collections

A.1 The New Asian Hemisphere: The Irresistible Shift of Global Power to the East (New York: Public Affairs, 2008)

Kishore Mahbubani published this book in 2008, a year when pessimism and unpredictability clouded the world after the global financial crisis. Apart from the high cost of the rescue packages and the severe recession, the crisis also damaged confidence in Western capitalism as an ideal model. In the meantime, following the decades of impressive growth recorded by Asian countries, discourses on the "rise of Asia" gained new momentum as vigorous debates about the shifting of power away from Europe and the United States and towards Asia began. In this intellectually sophisticated and thought-provoking book, Mahbubani sets this discussion in a global and historical context and makes a thorough re-examination of the mechanisms and trajectories that have led to the rise and fall of different societies and cultures. His central argument proposes that it is clear that the rise of Asia has brought more "goodness" into the world, and the West should welcome the transformations. Backed by the findings of the British historian Angus Maddison, who refuted claims of the inherent superiority of Western civilizations and notes that from the year 1 to the year 1820, the two largest economies of the world were China and India. In this sense, the impressive achievements China and India have made in recent years are not "the end" but rather "the return" of history. Mahbubani perceived this shifting balance of power as unstoppable despite mixed signals from Western powers. However, growing "Western (in particular the United States) incompetence" in handling global challenges, and the extraordinary geopolitical competence from Asian nations, especially China, make the latter the natural option to take charge of unfulfilled responsibilities. Responding to the pervaded anxiety in the Western societies about their loss of world domination, Mahbubani comforts readers that relations between the East and the West are essentially synergetic rather than confrontational, and the two hemispheres could very well form a partnership beneficial to human development. While an Asian revival is thanks to an education in prudence and pragmatism from the West,

K. Mahbubani, *The Asian 21st Century*, China and Globalization,
https://doi.org/10.1007/978-981-16-6811-1

the West should also work to better understand and change its mindset and celebrate Asia's "march to modernity".

The first theme is that the re-rise of Asia is not because of rediscovering "some hidden or forgotten strength of Asian civilizations", but precisely because, after two centuries of slow and painful trial and error, they finally borrowed the best of the Western experience. "The seven pillars of Western wisdom", are namely free-market economics, science and technology, meritocracy, pragmatism, the culture of peace, the rule of law, and Western education. These seven pillars are the foundations of modernization in the West over the past two centuries and have been successfully applied in Asian societies. Mahbubani extensively elaborated on how Asian countries integrated these elements in their development. What distinguishes this book from other writings on the "Asian miracle" is that Mahbubani further explores the mechanisms that these seven pillars influenced to restructure societies and people's conceptions about the world. For example, he sees the essence of free-market economics as the freedom for every individual to sell labor or invest capital is a critical driver of economic growth. The functioning and progress of the economy are no longer dependent upon good top-down decisions in a hierarchical manner, but the capacity of individuals to make their own choices. Similarly, science and technology challenged the traditional religious mindset, which lacks a belief in human progress and emphasizes obedience to authority. Mahbubani's accounts of the impressive Asian gains in each of these seven areas show that the most important role of "Western enlightenment" is in the revolutionary liberation of the human spirit for ordinary individuals, who stopped believing that they were naturally inferior. Their brainpower and creativity (which had been suppressed for centuries under the hierarchical rule), along with hard work, are the most powerful resources driving Asia's growth. He adds that if the rest of the world were to implement these seven pillars, other countries could also join Asia in rapid development.

The second theme is that in contrast with Asia, Western societies, which were admittedly the most powerful civilization in the world, have become trapped in their arrogance and stubborn resistance to change. Mahbubani suggests that the West has two paradoxical sides: the "philosophical" West has indeed made enormous contributions to humanity, including equality and dignity of the individuals, leading to extraordinary advances in human knowledge and improvements of life. However, the "material West" is a distorted reflection of its own ideals. Firstly, in the "material West," short-term self-interests often trump the values they uphold—brutal military invasions of the Middle East that are in the name of peace and order; blaming newly-industrialized nations for global warming while intentionally ignoring historically cumulative emissions and wasteful lifestyles; and insistence on the promotion of democracy while only allowing pro-American rulers to be put in positions of power. The West holds the automatic assumption that the rest of the world is responsible for generating the problems while struggling to develop and deliver solutions. They also seldom look inward for the domestic problems that are being mismanaged.

Another paradox is that the undemocratic world order after World War II, was in fact sustained by the most democratic nation-states in the West. Mahbubani reminds readers that the global rules that govern billions of people on the planet were created by a minority elite from Europe and the US. The missions of multilateral organizations were fulfilled only when the Western interests coincided with those of humankind. Such distortion, exercise, and reinforcement of power are reflected not only in international institutions but also extend into military, currency, banking, media, etc. Mahbubani argues that the West can no longer sustain the illusion that their post-WWII dominance and privilege can last forever. It would be naive to assume that Western ideological concepts from the nineteenth and twentieth centuries would continue to work unchanged in the twenty-first century. A better future for humanity requires democracy, not just for the governance of a single country, but the world as a whole. The West should learn to share power with a rising Asia; otherwise, Asia may establish its own system and rules. As the West has strayed from their role as the champion of democracy, rule of law and pragmatism, it is time for Asia to take up the reins and repair the flaws. The rise of the West transformed the world, but so will the rise of Asia.

A.2   The ASEAN Miracle: A Catalyst for Peace (Singapore: NUS Press, 2017)

This book is co-authored by two passionate and experienced experts on South-East Asia—Kishore Mahbubani and Jeffery Sng who attempt to tell the story of ASEAN, helping people learn about this achievement and understand the spirit behind it. Southeast Asia has the most diverse range of cultures in the world, which makes it difficult to understand and describe well. The Association of Southeast Asian Nations (ASEAN) is a living and breathing modern miracle. Mahbubani and Sng have identified three contributions this organization has made to improving the living conditions of a broad swath of humanity in this region. Firstly, it has brought peace and prosperity to a troubled region, generated inter-cultural harmony in the most diverse corner of the earth, and brought hope to many people. Second, in an era of growing economic pessimism, where many young people, especially in America and Europe, believe that their lives will get worse in the coming decades, Southeast Asia bubbles with optimism. Third, in an era of growing geopolitical pessimism, when many leading geopolitical thinkers predict rising competition and tension between great powers—especially between America and China—ASEAN has created an indispensable diplomatic platform that regularly brings all the great powers together.

The other pressing reason why the world needs to understand ASEAN is that its success stories can bring hope to many troubled regions and lighten the planet's problems. An obvious retort that the Middle East has long been a region of war while Southeast Asia has been a region of peace is one of those problems. It is no secret that the West is deeply pessimistic about the prospects for the Islamic world. Those looking for hope in the Islamic world, and for a narrative that can counter such dark views, should learn from Southeast Asia. There are more Muslims in Southeast Asia, as a percentage than any other region outside the Middle East. If the large Muslim population of Southeast Asia—almost as numerous as the entire population of the Arab world—can live in peace with their non-Muslim neighbors and also, continue to progress economically, then ASEAN provides hope that the world is not destined for a clash of civilizations because it has successfully brought durable peace to a region that has experienced great conflict in the past. A Nobel Peace Prize for ASEAN is long overdue.

This book consists of six chapters, following a thematic order. Chapter 1 begins by explaining how the extraordinary diversity of Southeast Asia came about, which was due to at least four major cultural waves that swept through the region: Indian, Chinese, Muslim, and Western. Having absorbed aspects of so many different and distinct civilizations, Southeast Asia became truly unique and it is now the most culturally diverse region on the planet. The expression "four waves" highlights this distinctiveness. What's more, three of them arrived relatively peacefully. Chapter 2 explains how peace emerged in an unpromising region of the world in most unpromising times, developing a resilient ecosystem of peace through ASEAN. No two ASEAN states have gone to war with each other since the organization's founding in 1967. There have been quarrels, even minor military skirmishes (as between Cambodia and Thailand), but wars like those in the Middle East and Balkans have not broken out in Southeast Asia. One key assumption of this book is that this ecosystem of peace can be replicated in other unpromising regions of the world. ASEAN can serve as a beacon of hope for the world. A better understanding of the ASEAN experience can lead to a more peaceful world.

Chapter 3 emphasizes that ASEAN still needs the support and cooperation of great powers for this happy scenario to continue. The previous chapter explained how ASEAN benefited from favorable geopolitical winds coming out of the Cold War. The strong strategic alliance between the US and China in the 1980s played a critical role in reinforcing the cohesion of the ASEAN states. Indeed, the 1980s were perhaps most critical in developing a strong sense of ASEAN identity among the five founding member states. Yet, if favorable geopolitical trends helped ASEAN build its identity, ASEAN must now prepare itself for unfavorable geopolitical winds. The most important strategic relationship is always that between the world's greatest power (today, the US) and the world's greatest emerging power (China). Both worked closely together to thwart the Soviet Union in the 1980s. This helped ASEAN. Today, even though there is a remarkable degree of cooperation between the US and China, there is also a rising degree of competition. If this competition gets out of hand, ASEAN could be split apart. This is why a key message of this chapter is that all the great powers, including America, China, India, Japan, and the EU, have a stake in keeping ASEAN together. No great power is benign. No appeal is being made here to benevolent instincts. Instead, this chapter appeals to the naked self-interest of each great power.

The current situation of the ten Southeast Asian member states of ASEAN is covered in Chap. 4 in a series of brief pen sketches. Each of the ten countries has a rich and complex history, and while the pen sketches cannot do justice to these complex identities, the authors hope that the reader will gain at least some insight into the ASEAN states, their current challenges, their geopolitical postures, and their relationship to the regional organization.

Chapter 5 attempts an assessment of ASEAN as a regional organization today, by looking at its strengths and weaknesses as well as the opportunities and threats it faces (the well-known SWOT analysis). Like a complex living organism, ASEAN can die due to either neglect or wilful efforts. The current leaders of ASEAN bear an enormous responsibility. They cannot allow the work of ASEAN's founding fathers to go to waste. They must see it as their responsibility to sustain ASEAN as a strong regional organization that can continue to serve as a beacon of hope for humanity. If the current leaders of ASEAN succeed in sustaining and strengthening the organization (and so the region), they will benefit the region's 625 million people. But the authors argue here that they will also benefit the remaining 6.7 billion citizens of planet Earth, who will have a second beacon of hope (besides the US) that they can look up to.

Finally, Chap. 6 looks at ASEAN's prospects. It also suggests some concrete steps ASEAN can take to strengthen itself. Fortunately, none of these steps will be very difficult. Clearly, ASEAN needs to strengthen its secretariat. In contrast to the budget of the EU Secretariat, which is USD 154 billion, the annual budget of the ASEAN Secretariat is USD 19 million. Since the combined ASEAN GDP rose from USD 95 billion in 1970 to USD 2.5 trillion in 2014, it would be penny wise and pound foolish to starve the ASEAN Secretariat of badly needed funds. Once the ASEAN leaders recognize what a treasure the association has become, they should see it to be in their national interests to provide more funding. One important outcome of a stronger ASEAN Secretariat and a better-performing ASEAN organization should be to build over time a greater sense of ownership of ASEAN among the people of the region. In the first 50 years of its existence, ASEAN was owned and managed by its governments. They have done a marvelous job, despite the many flaws and weaknesses of ASEAN. However, if they are to ensure the region's continuing growth and success, then ownership of ASEAN must pass from governments to the people. When it does, ASEAN may become the world's number one regional organization.

Historically speaking, Europe has been the most successful continent for the past four centuries, especially in economic and social development. Europeans can barely conceive of the possibility that they could learn important lessons from other parts of the world. One reason for this volume on ASEAN is to stimulate the hitherto closed European mind to explore the possibility of learning lessons from other regions. Similarly, the American intelligentsia could also learn lessons from this volume. The ongoing politics of pessimism in America and Europe is dangerous. While pessimism does not signify that we cannot produce positive transformational leaders. Right now, this may seem like a wild prospect. But if we remember the organization's 1967 starting point, ASEAN's achievements are nothing less than spectacular. Many contemporary observers shared this pessimistic view of Southeast Asia's prospects. Even if politics had not troubled the region in 1967, Southeast Asia would still have been an unsuitable ground for an exercise in regional cooperation, considering that it is so diverse in cultures and civilizations. No other region in the world can match its cultural, religious, linguistic, and ethnic diversity. If ASEAN can keep up its current momentum, there is no limit. The higher it soars, the brighter it will become as a beacon for humanity. When the five founders, namely Thanat Khoman, Narciso Ramos, Adam Malik, Abdul Razak, S. Rajaratnam—one Buddhist Thai, one Christian Filipino, two Muslims, and a lapsed Hindu—came together to sign the ASEAN declaration, they could not have come from more diverse cultural universes. Still, one cannot understand the Southeast Asian story just by looking at the past 50 years. There are deeper cultural roots that drive the character and identity of ASEAN. Meanwhile, the authors pointed out that ASEAN is imperfect, it never progresses in a linear fashion. It often moves like a crab: it takes two steps forward, one step backward, and one step sideways. Despite its many imperfections, it keeps moving forward. This is what makes ASEAN so extraordinary.

In conclusion, the strengths and weaknesses, as well as threats and opportunities, that ASEAN faces are easily identified, and clearly, the region faces serious challenges. However, the strengths are far more substantial than the weaknesses, and the opportunities outweigh the threats. If ASEAN can find the right leaders to drive it forward in the twenty-first century, the strengths it has developed can propel it forward at an even faster pace. The purpose of this book is to make more ASEAN policymakers and the populations of ASEAN countries aware that they have inherited a precious resource that they should not neglect or take for granted. ASEAN is a gift from outstanding founding fathers to the current generation of leaders, it should be learned and adopted by countries from other parts of the world as well as ASEAN member states, to maintain and to promote the peace and prosperity it has brought.

A.3   Has the West Lost It?: A Provocation (London: Allen Lane, 2018)

Has the West Lost It? is a provocation for the West written by Kishore Mahbubani, exploring its past achievements, approaching challenges, and possible suggestions for the future. In the early twenty-first century, history has turned a most significant corner, yet the West refuses to accept or adapt to this new historical trend. From the year 1 to 1820, the two largest economies were always those of China and India. It was only after this period that Europe took off, followed by America, which is why this could be seen as an aberration. Eventually, all such aberrations come to a natural end. The Western share of the global economy is shrinking, which is inevitable and unstoppable. As other societies have learned to emulate Western best practices, the incomes of many Western middle-class populations have also stagnated in recent decades. Mahbubani analyzes these questions, including their historical background, challenges, past strategies of the West and the Rest by sharing his professional insights to the readers, providing a unique perspective.

The thirteen chapters of this book systematically outline how the West became trapped in the current situation. In Chap. 1—"A New Order of Things"—Mahbubani tracks human history and the path of Western development. The West has so far been the engine driving global economic growth, while the Rest hitched their wagons to the train. Now, the Rest have become the engine and Western societies have had to ensure economic growth for their populations by hitching their wagons to the Rest.

In Chap. 2—"The Gift of Western Wisdom"—he focuses on the key contribution of the West. The biggest gift the West gave the Rest was the power of reason, 'to think (something) through, work it out in a logical manner'. This gradually seeped into Asian minds through the adoption of Western science and technology and the application of the scientific method to solving social problems. This spread of Western reasoning triggered three silent revolutions that explain the extraordinary success of many non-Western societies in recent decades. The first was political. The rebellions inspired by the West against all kinds of feudal systems that gained momentum in the second half of the twentieth century were hugely liberating for all Asian societies. The second was psychological: The Rest went from believing that they were helpless voyagers in a life determined by 'fate' to believe that they could take control of their lives and make them better. The third revolution was in governance. This major transformation can be seen most acutely in Asia. The current leaders, Xi Jinping, Narendra Modi and Jokowi share a common conviction that good governance will transform and uplift their societies. This recent experience in the form of beneficial public policies may also explain why the populations of China, India, and Indonesia are more optimistic than their counterparts in the West.

In Chap. 3—"Suicidal Western Wars"—Mahbubani concentrates on the field of governance, where he sees a paradox. He points out that Asians learned the virtues of rational governance from the West, but while Asian levels of trust in government are increasing, many Western populations are losing faith in government. For centuries, the West used its military and technological prowess to conquer and dominate the planet. But they either didn't notice or didn't care that the liberation of billions of non-Western minds coincided with another moment of Western triumphalism: the end of the Cold War. Partly as a result of imbibing Fukuyama's opiate, triumphalists in the West didn't notice that the end of the Cold War coincided with a more fundamental turn in human history—China entry into the WTO in 2001. The Tiananmen Square incident in June 1989 convinced the West that the Chinese communist regime was another corrupt regime about to collapse, while 9/11 distracted them from the fact that China was only getting stronger.

Chapter 4 discussed the blindness of the Western elite. Mahbubani has observed that most of the educated elite in the West are distrusted by the general population when they should be working to understand this new era and develop thoughtful and pragmatic policy responses that will help everyone prepare for changes the world is experiencing. Statistics also show that considerable global growth in the middle classes shows a decline in human suffering and an increase in overall happiness, yet people are not celebrating. The ignorance of the extraordinary progress mankind has made may be due to the addiction people have to 'negative news' and this trend has been aggravated by the global supremacy of Western media, which dominates the world with its prevailing pessimism. Western media seems to only cover dysfunctional governments, leading to the impression that functional governance is rare or completely disappeared.

Chapter 5—"The Global Explosion of Travel"—re-emphasizes the historical turning point of the information revolution. Access to education and information propelled humanity towards the most promising era in human history and the necessity to realize it was happening and adjust policy approaches accordingly. In Chap. 6, the author tries to further explain the question: Why Hasn't the West Noticed? He claims that one keyword explains why the West lost its way at the end of the Cold War: hubris. Western were overjoyed after their great victory over the Soviet Union and they switched off all the signals that could have alerted them to other big changes. Fukuyama's essay *The End of History?* did a lot to damage the Western mindset. It provided the opium that put the West on autopilot just when it should have prepared for competition. They believed Western civilization had reached the ultimate level of human achievement and that other civilizations would have to struggle and work hard while they rested on their laurels.

Chapter 7 further elaborates on how the height of Western hubris coincided with the rise of the Rest, particularly in China and India. Chapter 8—"Strategic Errors"—continues the topic by illustrating how the West failed to notice the Asian Renaissance and ignored the real issues that were shaking up their societies. Blinded by hubris, the West made a series of strategic errors. First, it intervened in Islamic countries, underestimated Islam as a religion, and failed to address the root of the problem when it came to terrorism. Second, the West continued to humiliate an already dispossessed Russia. Third, it also continued with reckless intervention in the internal affairs of multiple countries. Chapter 9 provides suggestions for the West in "A New Strategy: Minimalist, Multilateral, and Machiavellian". Mahbubani states clearly that the time has come for the West to abandon many of its short-sighted and self-destructive policies and pursue a completely new strategy towards the rest of the world. He calls this new grand strategy the "3 M Strategy"—Minimalist, Multilateral and Machiavellian. The minimalist approach is a critical first step. The West should become more restrained. As Western power declines, it is perfectly natural for the Rest to ask for new terms of engagement, nor does the Rest need to be saved by the West or educated in governmental structures or the moral high ground. The second 'M' is multilateral. Every year each new crisis requires coordinated global action and the West needs to better understand the Rest, work with it and grow stronger and more effective global councils. Multilateral institutions and processes provide the best platform for hearing and understanding the views of the world. The third 'M' calls for the West to learn more from Machiavelli in a rapidly changing world and be more cunning in protecting its long-term interests.

Chapter 10—"The West on Autopilot: Europe and America Do Not Face the Same Challenges"—interprets this strategic cunning. It begins by talking about the difference in the main challenges that the US and Europe face. America's biggest challenge is China, while for Europe, it's the Islamic world. He points out that America has taken advantage of European strategic passivity to hijack European states and get them to support various American initiatives that are against long-term European interests. Europe is threatened by an aging population, weak leadership, and an explosion of Islamic demographics. While the Americans have destabilized Europe's geographical neighborhood, America itself failed to recognize that China

was becoming an economic, not a military challenger to its position. In Chapter 11—
"A More Dangerous World"—Mahbubani lists the reasons for calling for more
strategic cunning in the face of a naïve and ideological West. He proposes that the
world will become more unstable unless the West radically changes course, because
democracies are not designed to take on long-term challenges, but respond to immediate threats. He agrees with Western scholars on the many virtues of democratic
political systems, including saying 'democracy is the worst form of government,
except for everything else'. The West is wrong in believing that democracy is a necessary condition for economic success. The shortcomings of democracy are dominating
Western societies and failures to make strategic changes at the right time do lead to
disasters.

In Chap. 12—"A Better World"—he calls on Americans and Europeans to recognize that they have been aggressive and interventionist for over two centuries and now
it is in their strategic interests to be prudent and non-interventionist. He also suggests
that a less adversarial relationship between the West and the Rest will help to dispel
the clouds of pessimism that now envelop Western societies. In his view, Western
elites have failed to prepare their populations for the inevitable 'creative destruction'
that flowed from China's admission into the WTO in 2001, which caused them to
lose the trust of their populations. In conclusion, Chap. 13—"So—Has the West Lost
It?"—states that the crux of the problem facing the West is that neither the conser-
vatives nor the liberals, neither the right-wing nor the left-wing, understand that the
course of history changed at the start of the twenty-first century. Mahbubani believes
that the era of Western domination is coming to an end and that the West should
shift their gaze from domestic issues to larger global challenges. The world will face
a troubled future if the West doesn't shake its interventionist impulses, refuses to
recognize its new position, or decides to become isolationist and protectionist.

This book is intended as a gift to the West and shows how much the West has done
to elevate the human condition to a level higher than ever before. From Mahbubani's
perspective, it would be a great tragedy if the West were to be the world's primary
instigator of turbulence and uncertainty at the hour of humanity's greatest promise.
This outcome would perplex future historians to no end, wondering how the most
successful civilization in human history failed to take advantage of the greatest
opportunity ever presented to mankind.

A.4   Has China Won?: The Chinese Challenge to American Primacy (New York: Public Affairs, 2020)

Following the dismantling of the Communist Bloc in 1989 and the dissolution of
the Soviet Union in 1991, the past three decades have been dominated by a concept
known as "The End of History" particularly in Western societies. Not only did American policymakers refuse to recognize the different trajectories in which "history"
was moving, but they also insisted on framing the current rivalry with China as a

return to the Cold War with the Soviet Union. The audiences in the West may buy into the image of China as another revisionist and expansionist superpower, while America and its allies remain the vanguard of democracy, free market, and rule-based international order. The more China is demonized, the more firmly Americans believe they could eventually win. Mahbubani argues that the world has drastically changed in critical ways, which few Americans have realized or admitted. He opens this book with a warning that it is a fatal mistake for America to rashly stir up conflicts with China especially since they failed to first develop a comprehensive, global strategy to deal with China. However, Mahbubani is not trying to give a simple "yes or no" answer to the title. The question "Has China won? " encompasses multiple complex dynamics that exist in the twenty-first century's greatest geopolitical contest: Why and in what ways is America losing? Why is China one of the most important, but often misunderstood major powers? What are the blind spots for Chinese policy-makers? How should the rest of the world respond to the changing international order and balance of power? Is full-scale rivalry between America and China avoidable?

One of the book's central themes is that America is suffering from deep strategic and structural flaws, and lacks a capable leader to help it navigate away from the delusion that America will remain number one forever. America is now on the opposite side of what the master strategist George Kennan said—making the country capable of coping with problems both internal and on the international stage. Contrary to Americans' imaginations, America is behaving more like the Soviet Union or China's Qing Dynasty, burdened by overzealous ideological confrontations, inflexible institutions, and decision-making process, increasing inequalities, and intolerance of different development models. On the other hand, China is a more rational, pragmatic, adaptable, and self-strengthening competitor. Kennan also proposed a patient containment of the Soviet Union, and the need to maintain America's spiritual vitality to hold its own among the major ideological currents of the time. Mahbubani elaborated on the launching of the trade war with China and the estranging of international institutions and contended that even though the post-WWII liberal international order was built on Western values, America under the Trump administration has been walking away from them. Yet Trump is not the only one responsible for the decline of American power and prestige. America faces severe structural challenges in the political, economic, and cultural dimensions predating Trump's uncoordinated and unpredictable actions.

It is important to stress that, for decades, America has been taking advantage of the US dollar hegemony. The US dollar has been well-protected by the global financial system, and America can fund its deficits and excess expenditures by simply printing more money. The very idea that the US dollar serves as the global reserve currency is a sign of the trust in the government behind it—the belief held by the world that the American government is capable of making informed and rational decisions for global economic interests. However, that trust has been eroded as America systematically weaponized such privilege to sanction foreign firms and countries (e.g., transactions with Iran). Imperiled by unilateral American foreign policies, countries worldwide have stronger incentives to reduce their dependency on the US dollar. This is where China has an opportunity to build a global payment infrastructure and create alternative currencies backed by its booming economy and technological advancements. Mahbubani comments that "no sensible strategist would risk these enormous benefits for the paltry benefits of punishing one relatively small country, like Iran. Yet, this is exactly what America has been doing." America's most sacred institution—democracy—ironically has blocked rational and coherent decisions that are beneficial for the long-term national interests. A powerful, moneyed yet short-sighted elite have manipulated the major aspects of liberal democracy like the public election of representatives and the division of power. As a result, they left a country that failed to preserve its primacy in the international system and improve the well-being of its citizens. A crucial issue is that America has been hijacked by a bloated military-industrial complex that lobbies the politicians in Washington. They exaggerate foreign threats to persuade decision-making bodies to increase defense budgets and get involved in costly, painful, and unnecessary conflicts overseas. Meanwhile, the power and resources distributed to the State Department and professional diplomats have declined. It is also shocking that in a country with the most well-funded and active strategic think tank, as Mahbubani sharply criticized, is seeing an unstoppable trend towards a 'groupthink' mentality.

Despite the problems with America, this does not mean China has not made strategic mistakes. The following essential part of the book is Mahbubani's practical suggestions on how China should move ahead. Interestingly, he also warns China about pursuing short-term gains and displays of arrogance. It is unwise for government officials (particularly those at local level) to use government procurement, technology transfers, and non-tariff barriers as tools. There are prevailing accusations that China has taken advantage of its developing country status while Chinese firms are permitted to operate in other countries in ways that foreign firms are not permitted to in China. These practices have alienated the American (and European) business community, who were supposed to be the strongest advocates of good bilateral relations. China could be smarter about engaging with the Western businesses and rekindle enthusiasm for investment and trade with China. This would also serve as a valuable political buffer to prevent a dramatic breakdown of US-China relations as well as a bridge that brings both sides back to constructive dialogues.

The other key message Mahbubani sends is that the rest of the world, especially the West, has deeply misunderstood China and enjoys lecturing it to be "more like us" regardless of the different realities and historical legacies. Many Western scholars and commentators resist recognizing that the CCP has done very well because of their "residual abhorrence of communism and authoritarian rule" and make the mistake of equating the Chinese Communist Party with the Communist Party of the Soviet Union. They tend only to pick out and exaggerate particular deficiencies in the system while overlooking the overall picture of economic and social progress that China has achieved. They like to portray its fragility and vulnerability, but lack more careful observations of the resilience and flexibility that has allowed China to constantly fix its flaws. A crucial misconception is that the CCP depends solely on political repression to consolidate its rule. Instead, its legitimacy and mass support comes from the CCP's ability to deliver political stability and economic prosperity, which the Chinese people lacked in the past. Mahbubani adds that if America ever wanted to promote a "moral" agenda in their dealings with China, they should stay out of the country's internal affairs, which will only cause it to descend into chaos. While addressing the question of "Is China Expansionist?", Mahbubani clarifies that historically China has not been an aggressive country interested in conquering or occupying overseas or distant territories. Unlike America, for two-thousand years China has been reluctant to use military options which drain resources. What America and the Five Eye Club have labeled Chinese expansionism is more accurately explained by the intent to maintain stable and peaceful relationships with neighboring states; and China's obsession with securing its borders is due to the painful "Century of Humiliation" of subjugation and invasion. America and other Western countries tend to frame those "normal" activities as "abnormal" when they are done by China. The systematic demonization, usually for profit and attractive headlines, could be dangerous as they hinder effective interaction and communications with China.

Through the points mentioned above, Mahbubani points out where America and China are currently situated. America is inevitably sliding into a number two position and must fundamentally rethink its own position and also the changing dynamics in other parts of the world (especially Asia). On the other hand, China would be put in the spotlight of international attention for almost every single issue but meanwhile, as one of the most misunderstood powers, China would also find itself in a very challenging environment. Despite the fact that both America and China intertwined deeply with each other and a complete decoupling is impossible, so far they still have a long way to go to figure out the most important bilateral relations in the world today. Resonated with his critiques about the mistakes both countries have made, the answers lie in the virtue of pragmatism, rational and calculations forward-looking strategies.

Index

© The Editor(s) (if applicable) and The Author(s) 2022
K. Mahbubani, *The Asian 21st Century*, China and Globalization,
https://doi.org/10.1007/978-981-16-6811-1